SUAVE

First published in the United States of America in 2001

by **UNIVERSE PUBLISHING**

A Division of Rizzoli International Publications, Inc.

300 Park Avenue South

New York, NY 10010

2001 2002 2003 2004 2005 2006 / 10 9 8 7 6 5 4 3 2 1

Printed in Hong Kong

SUAVE
THE LATIN MALE

UNIVERSE

CONTENTS

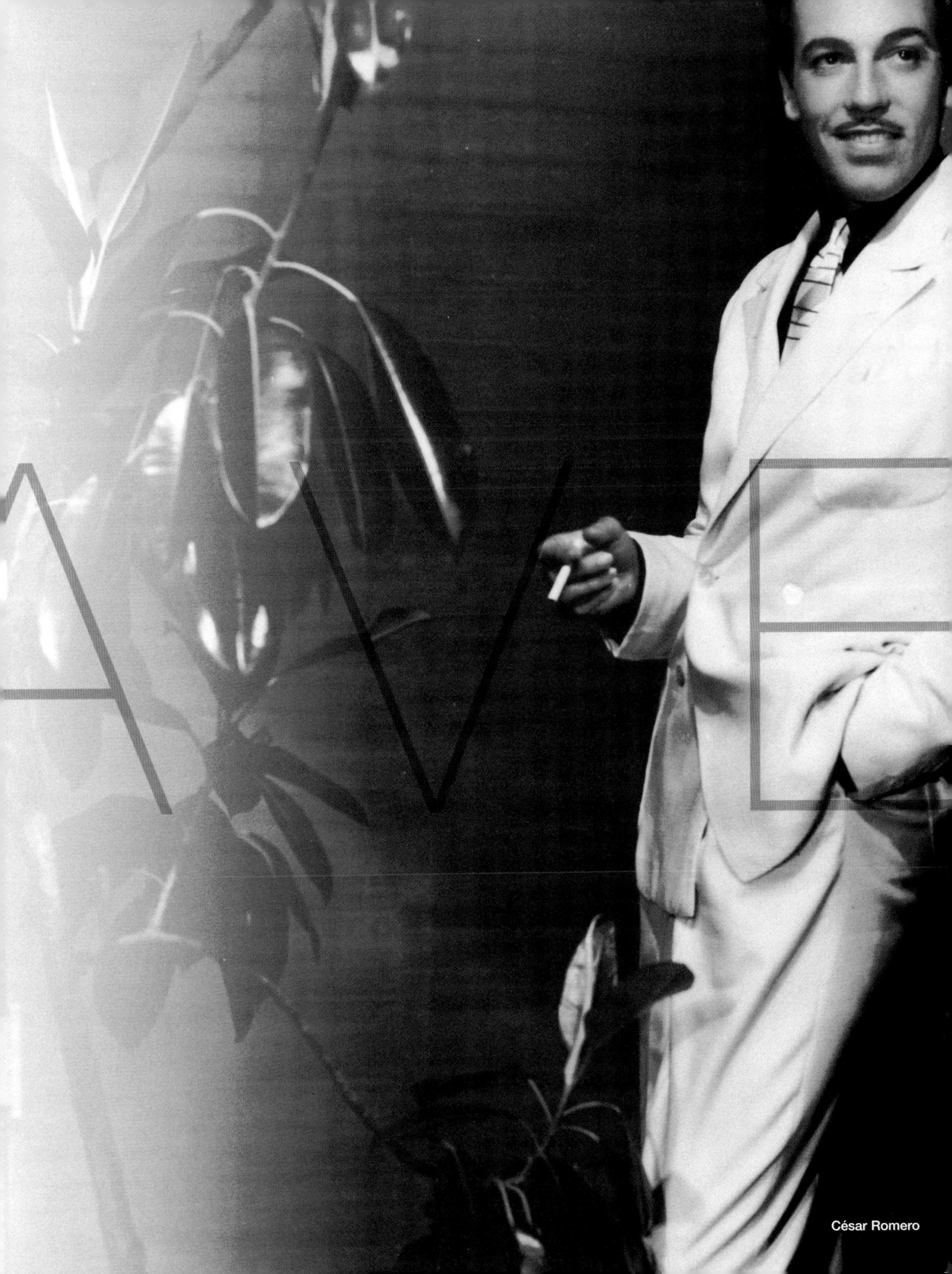

César Romero

Style isn't a scientific formula—one part fashion to two parts attitude—or even an aesthetic of taste and tailoring. Men's magazines will tell you style is what you wear and how you live. For Latin men it is so much more than that. It is our personal identity on display, our response to the world. It is how we feel about being alive.

From Andalusia to Zacatecas, in any language, culture or ethnicity, Latinos live out loud, and here in the United States, we break sound barriers. It doesn't matter if you're a *vato* from East L.A., a salsa sensation from *Nueva* York or a Miami *hombre de negocios*. Regardless of fashion trends or lifestyles, Latinos have changed men's style for everyone because Latin men first and foremost love being men. We love everything about it and it shows. It's the best side of machismo and courses through each of the generations and major styles represented here.

Latin style is in the renegade *pasión* and posture of men like actor Javier Bardem; revolutionary and '60s icon Ché Guevara; soccer great Pelé; and guitar maestro Carlos Santana, men who embody the *estilo rockero*.

It's at the heart of the playful sexiness and exhuberant style of *los jovenes* that make model Richard Lima, heartthrobs Freddie Prinze Jr., Cristian de la Fuente, and Nicholas Gonzalez, and pop stars Ritchie Valens, Cheyanne, and Howie Dorough, daring in both fashion and life.

Or look at the casual elegance and seductive body language of *galanes románticos*, from silent screen legends Rudolf Valentino and Ramon Navarro; leading up to *salsero* Marc Anthony; boxer Oscar de la Hoya; and leading men Antonio Banderas and Benjamin Bratt. These Latinos have set and maintained the gold standard for romance and sex appeal.

Just try to ignore the colorful plumage of peacocks like painter Salvador Dalí; rock *en español* singer Beto Cuevas; dancer Joaquín Cortéz; matador El Cordobéz; and original '60s Warhol superstar Holly Woodlawn. They take risks, create sensations

and stand out proudly.

And then there's *los poderosos*, Latinos who emanate authority and embody alpha-male chic from the eye contact out, power players like Nobel-winning novelist Gabriel García Marquéz; baseball great Sammy Sosa; mogul Emilio Estefan; activist César Chávez; and legendary artist Diego Rivera.

But it's not just artists, entertainers, sports stars and power brokers that create the *modas*. For generations Latinos have also helped define style from the streets. The Zoot suit is not only a twentieth-century icon, it defined a period in cultural history, just like the everyday wear of guys such as disco king Tony Orlando, poet Reinaldo Arenas, the artist Basquiat, and Oscar-winner Benicio del Toro defined their own look. That's street smart.

Living with gusto is what enables a man to walk in a room, no matter what he's wearing, and know he belongs. He knows not just how to carry himself, engineer a wardrobe, and buy the right flowers for his *novia* but also how to speak his mind, hold onto his dreams and sing a love song. It's a cliché but the rest really is just fashion. Latinos know this. That's why it's impossible to carry off anyone else's style. That's why we don't try. It's why the men in these pages are unique.

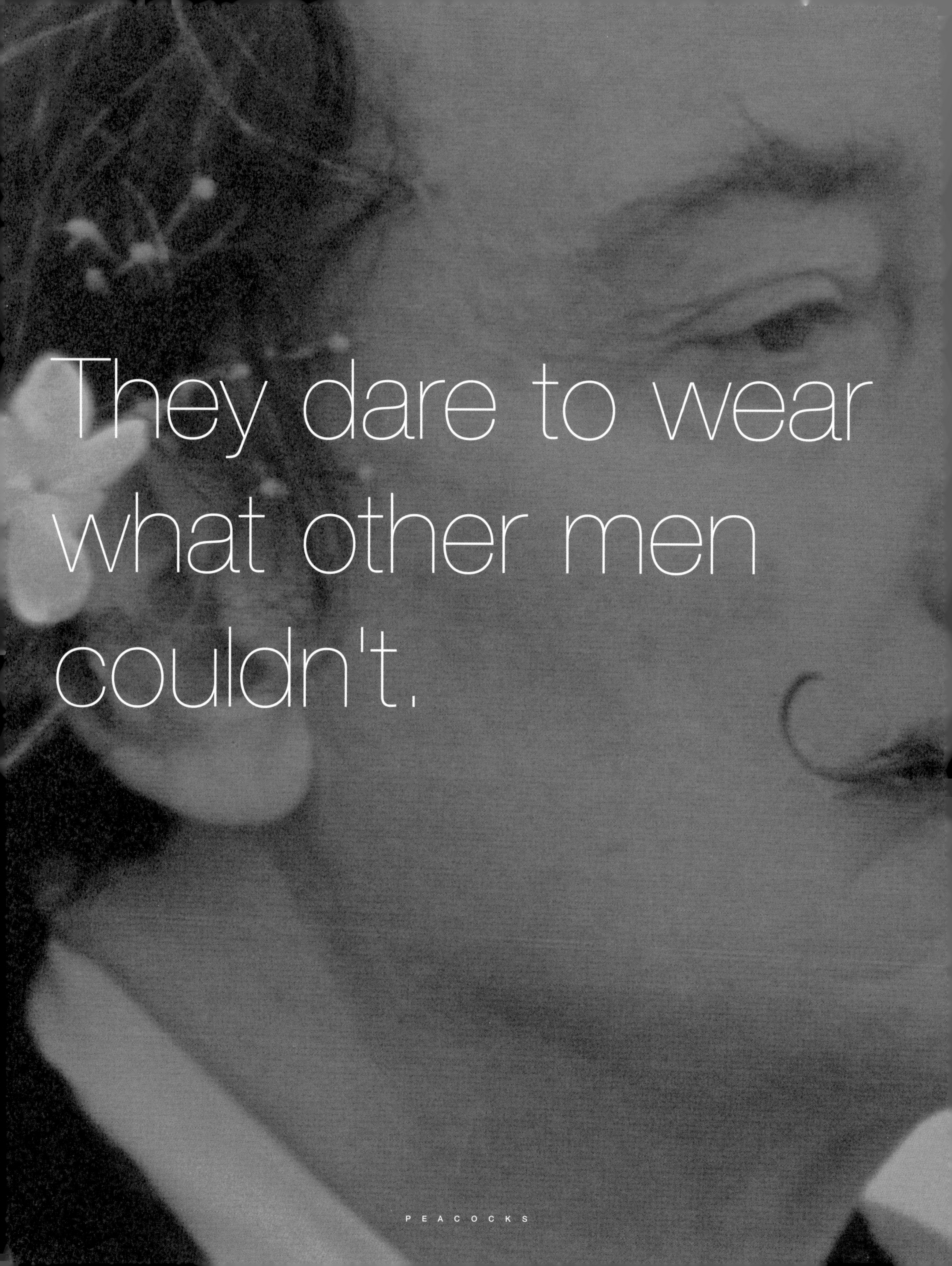

They dare to wear what other men couldn't.

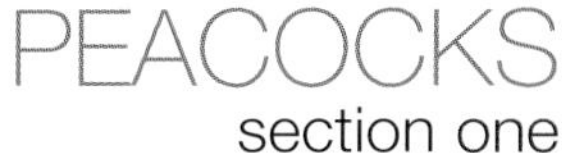

PEACOCKS
section one

Some men can't be ignored. They won't be. Rather than stride, they strut. Instead of expressing a personality, their clothes cultivate a persona. They are the peacocks of style and wherever they go, they command the spotlight.

From the Mayan empire to MTV, the peacocks are singular, one-man pageants of panache. They dare to wear what other men couldn't and, frankly, shouldn't. On most *hombres*, striking colors and cuts would look like a costume but on the peacock they are natural plumage. He would look out of place without them. Sure, *los pavos reales* are sometimes scoffed at as flamboyant show ponies but no one can deny they are the pioneers of style, as equally breathtaking in their failures as in their successes.

In the '30s and '40s, the Spanish surrealist painter Salvador Dalí was himself his greatest work of art. His fanciful wardrobe and surroundings, even his face with it's waxed moustache twirled like fine filigree, were larger than life. He affected the foulard, the Victorian walking stick, and the lush fabrics and tailoring of the dandy. Although he was completely out of fashion, Dalí was a paragon of peacock style.

In the fifties, when the legendary matador El Cordobéz entered the bullring, the air was seared with the feverish screams of his fans. Hollywood stars like mexicana Rita Hayworth and cultural titans like Ernest Hemingway joined the throngs cheering themselves hoarse. Forget the suit of lights. It was his own overwhelming star wattage that was so compelling, so unforgettable. Other matadors found glory in the bullring. With his royal bearing and virile grace, El Cordobéz brought glory with him.

In the sixties, peacock chic took acid. Holly Woodlawn was the beautiful love child of the decade that threw off the center of cultural gravity. The part-Puerto Rican Warhol superstar wore haute couture as if it were an old T-shirt, and wore trashy thrift store like runway originals. The genius of it is that Holly didn't "do" drag. Holly did Holly. In the process, she made the world a safer place to shine, donning sequins and beads, feathers and fishnets, not as some cheeseball alter-ego but as a conquering hero(ine).

Today's peacocks wield their signature styles just as powerfully, whether defying trends or setting them. Walter Mercado, the Liberace of astrology, is like an eastern European aristocrat or the odd superhero, one of the few men born to wear a cape. With his leather, colorful clinging shirts, and body that won't behave, Ricky Martin reminds women (and men) that style is a base element for sex appeal. Like a wild stallion, the flamenco sensation Joaquín Cortéz is all flowing mane and feral intensity. Rocker Beto Cuevas manages to be both glitzy and gutsy, carrying off snake-skin, vinyl, and ambitious facial hair as if it were just another day at the office.

What keeps these guys from the heap of poseurs and fashion casualties is that they absolutely don't care what's in or out (capes? *Quiana?*) as much as they care about what it feels like and how it looks. And, baby, it looks suave.

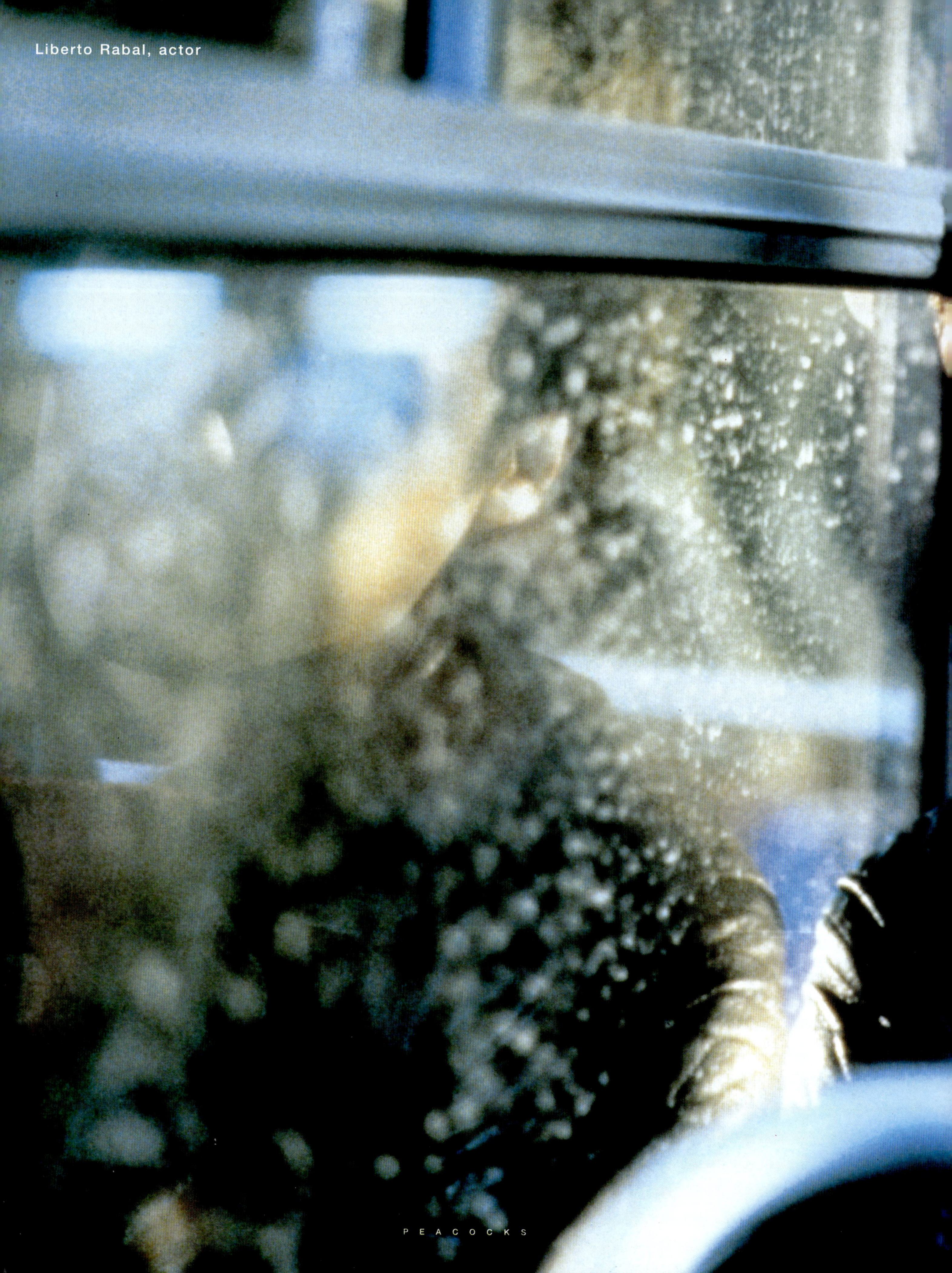
Liberto Rabal, actor

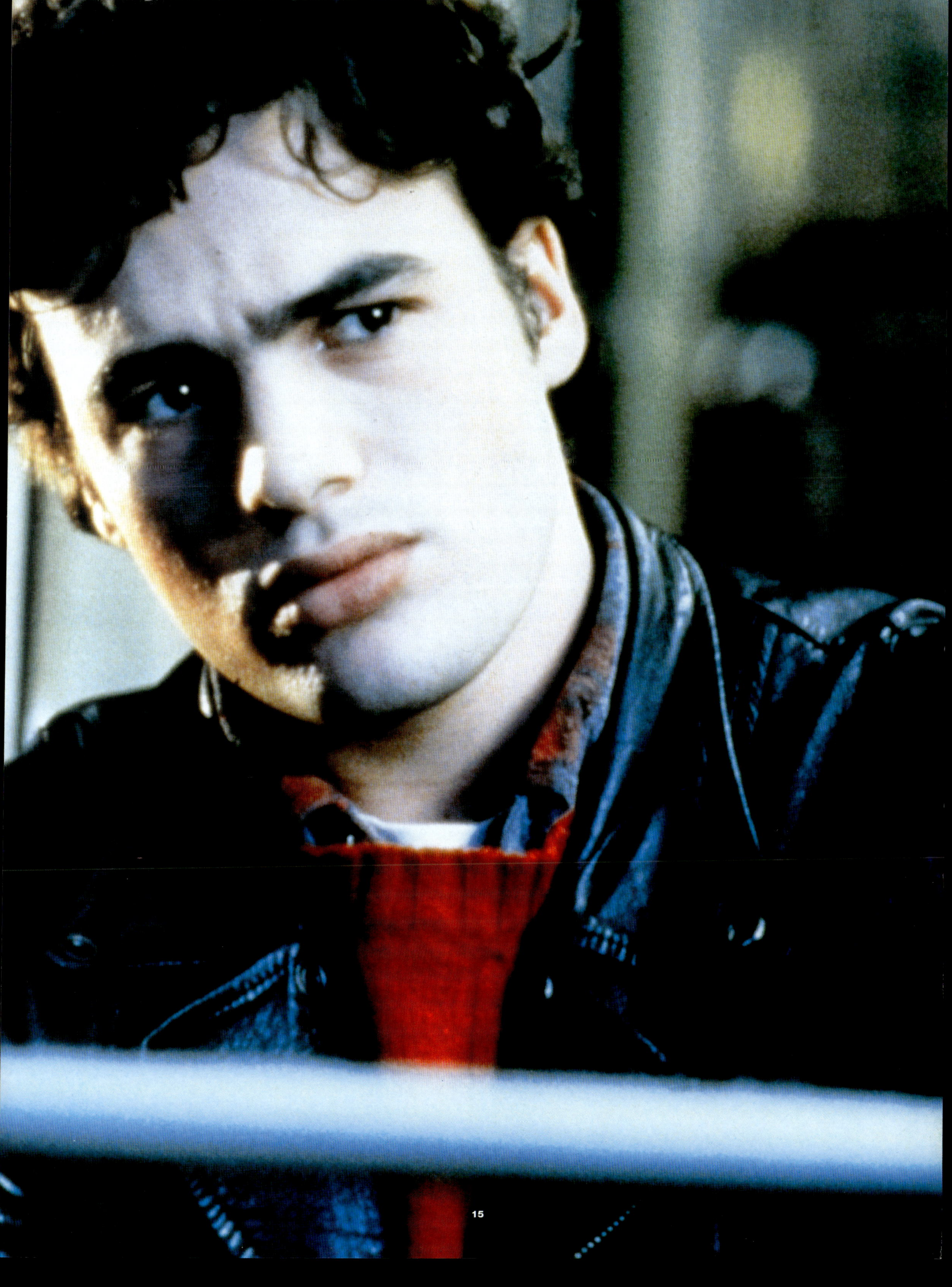

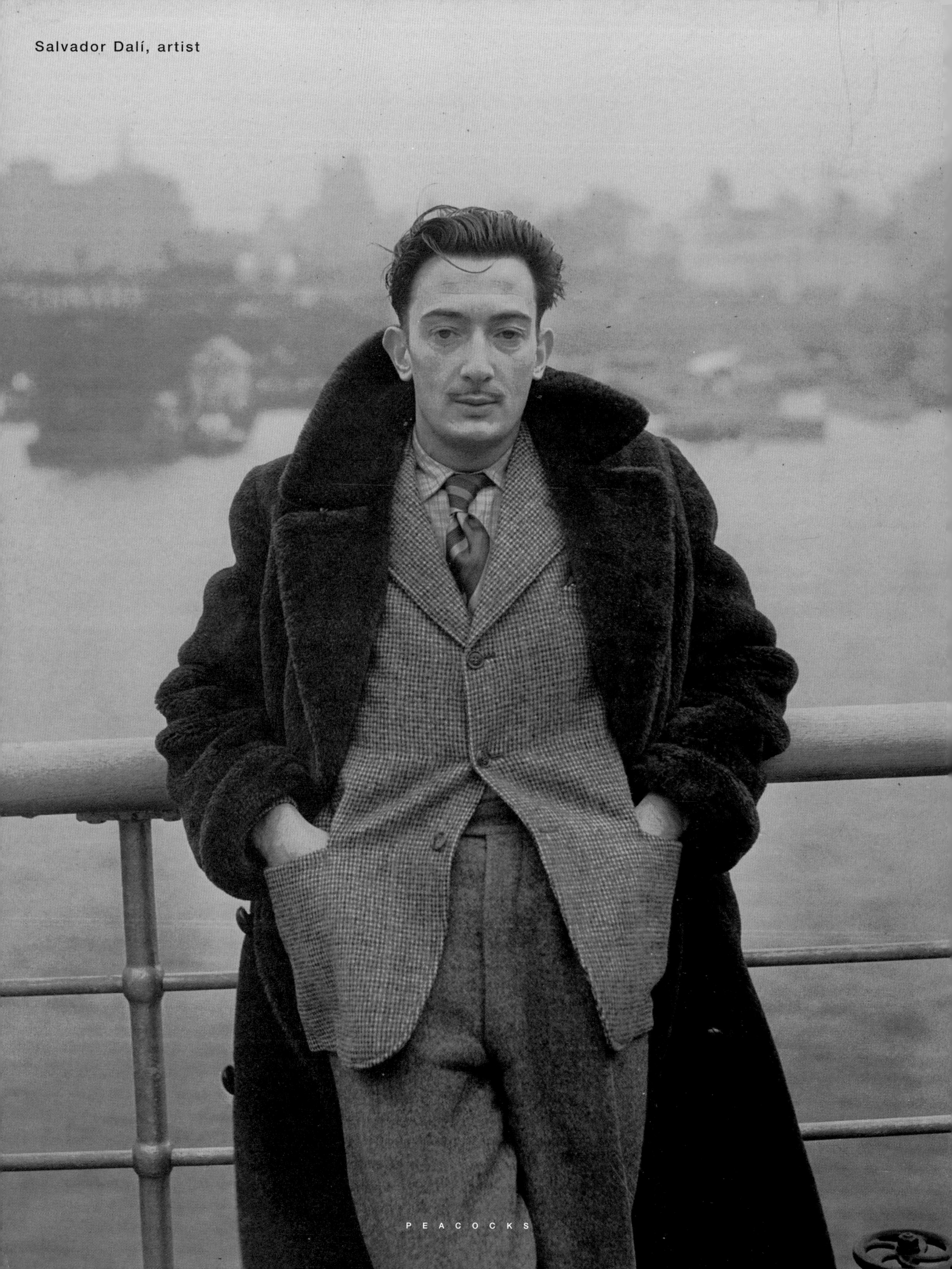

Salvador Dalí, artist

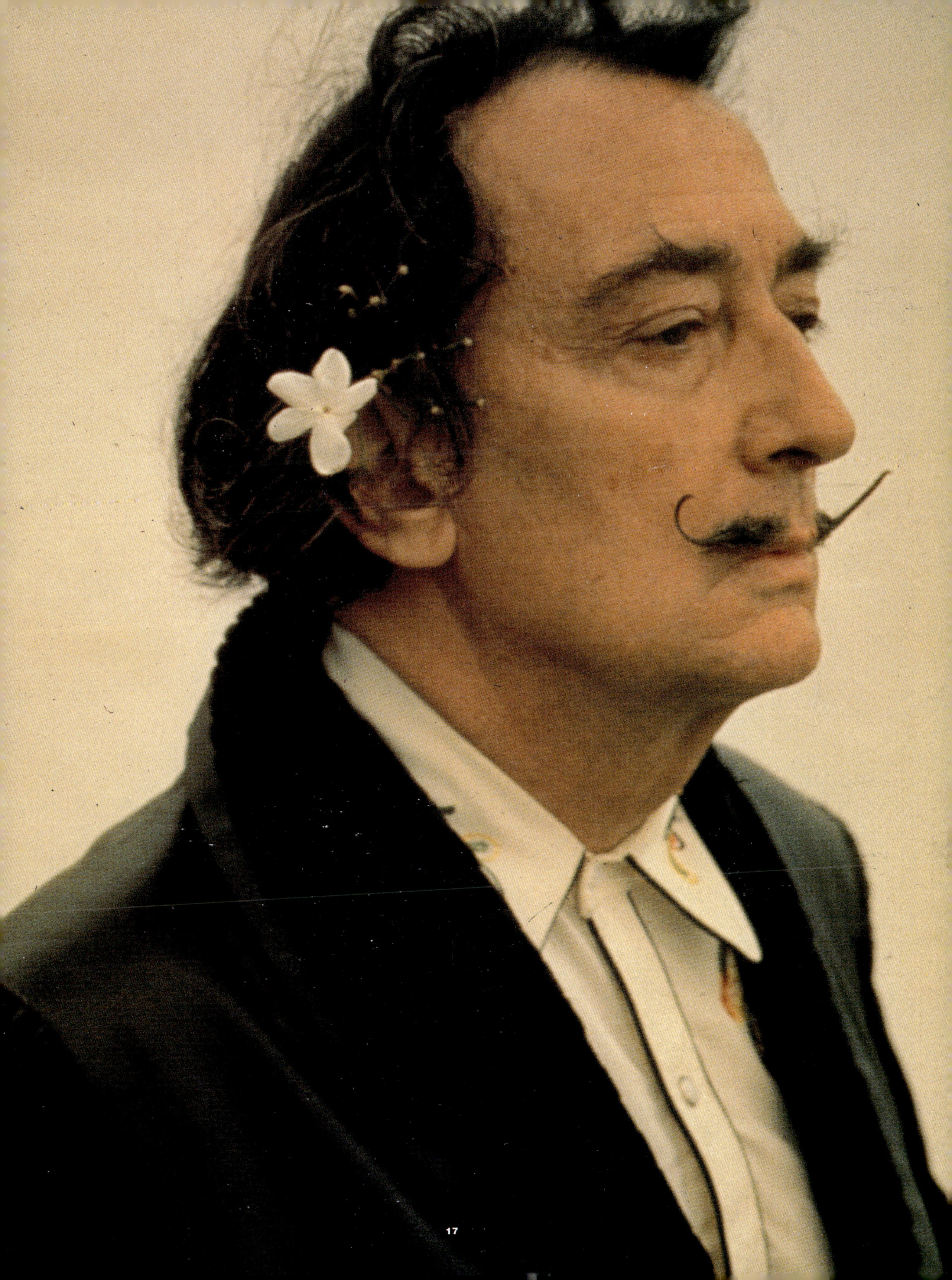

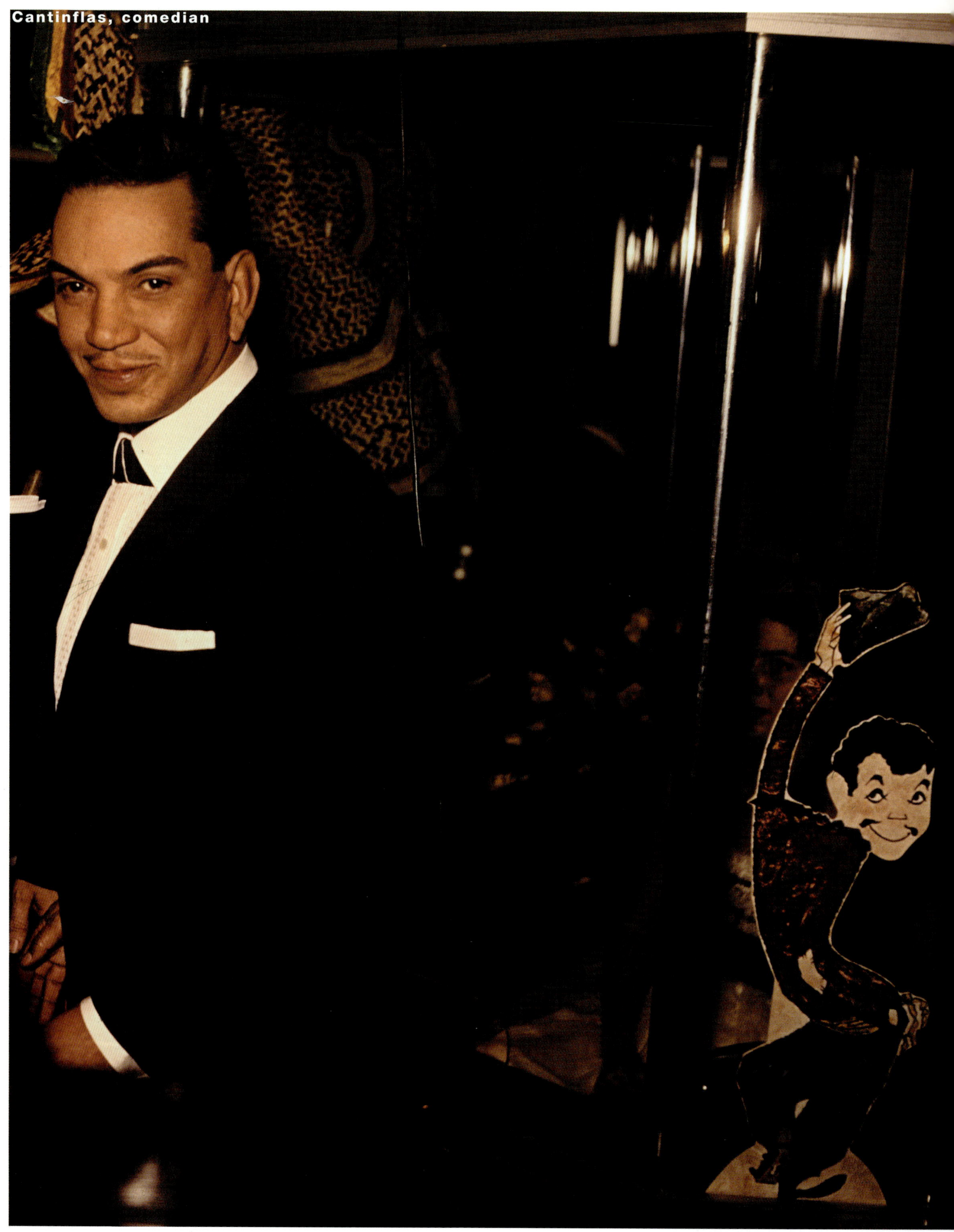

Cantinflas, comedian

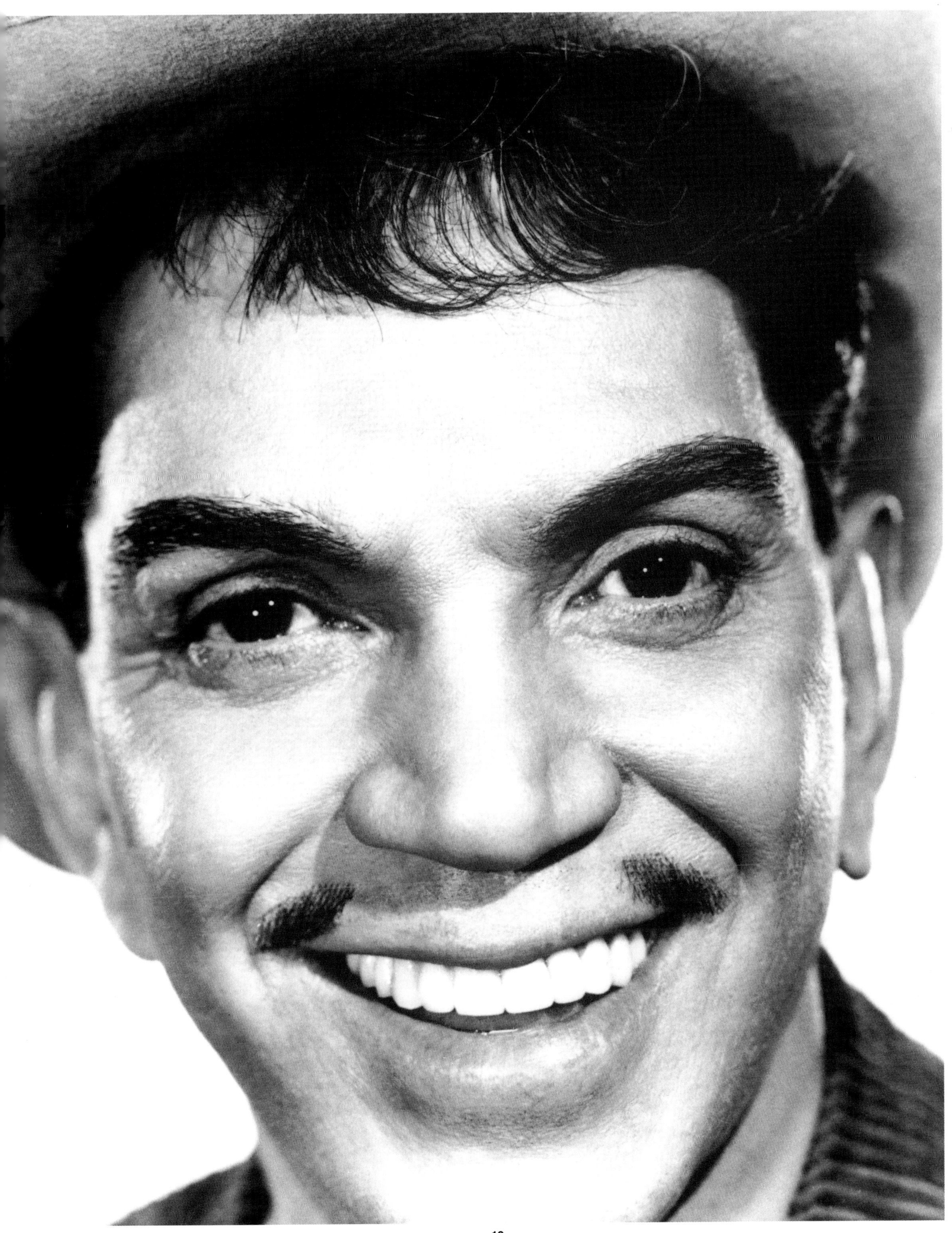

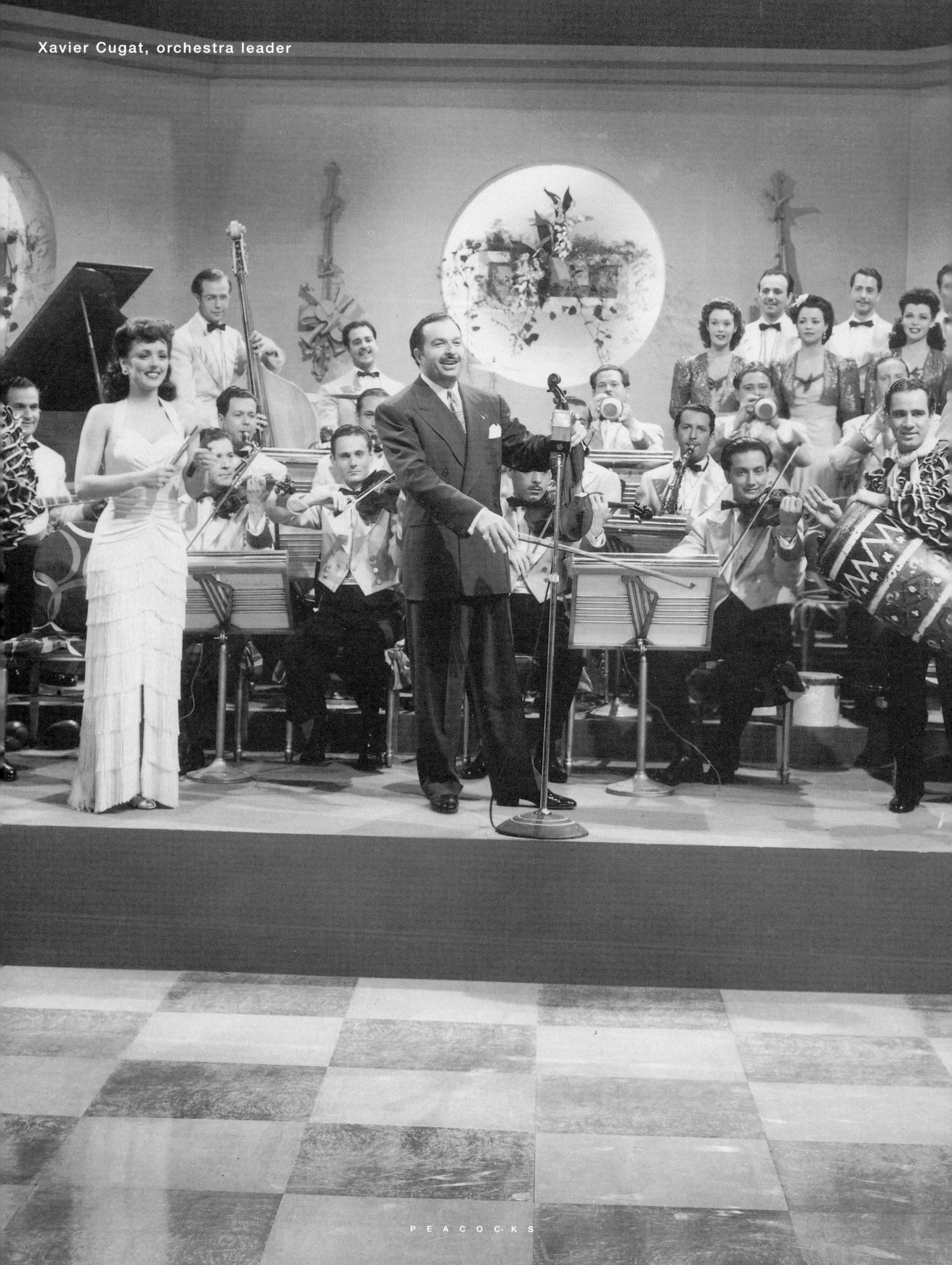

Xavier Cugat, orchestra leader

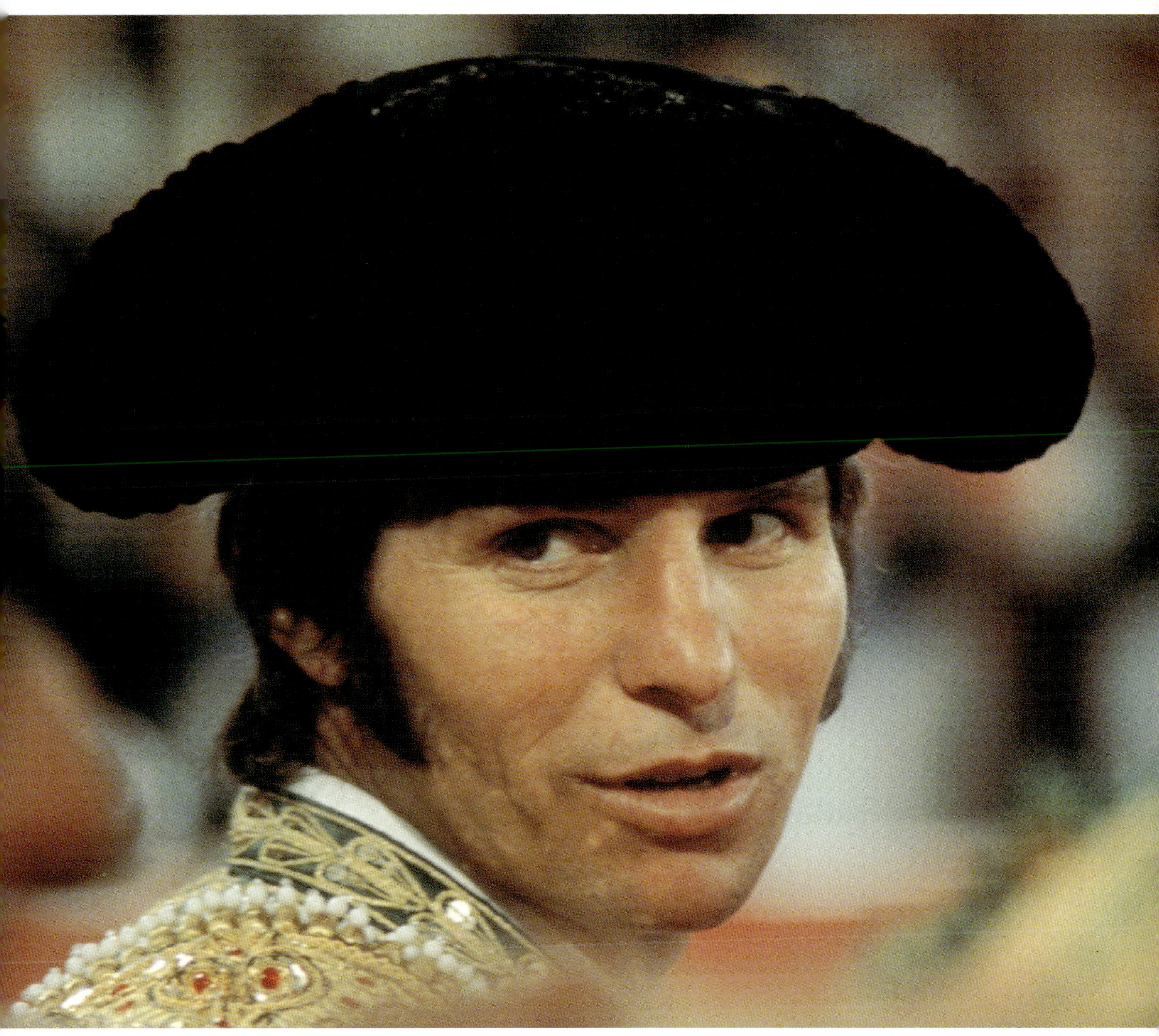

Sammy Davis Jr., entertainer

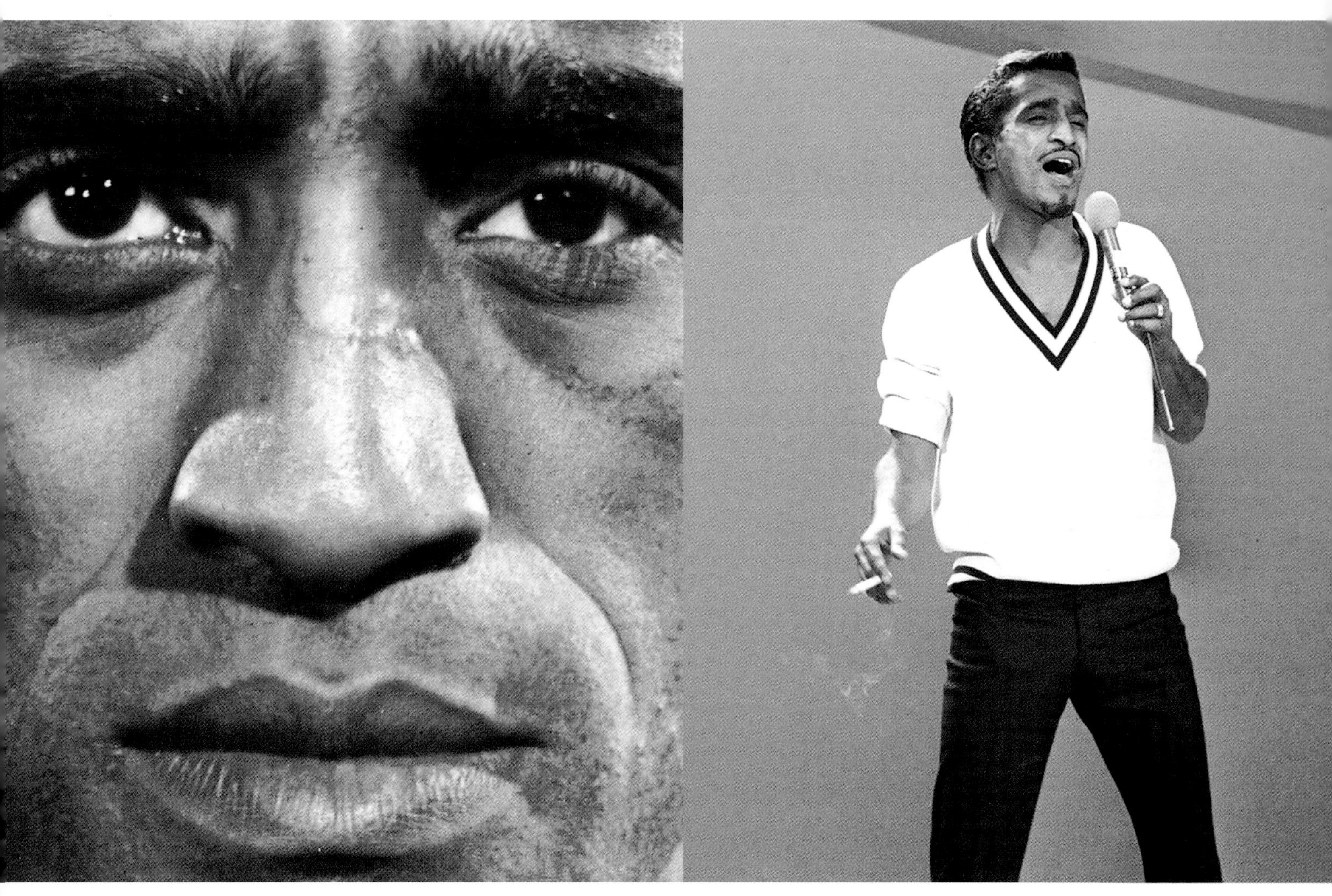

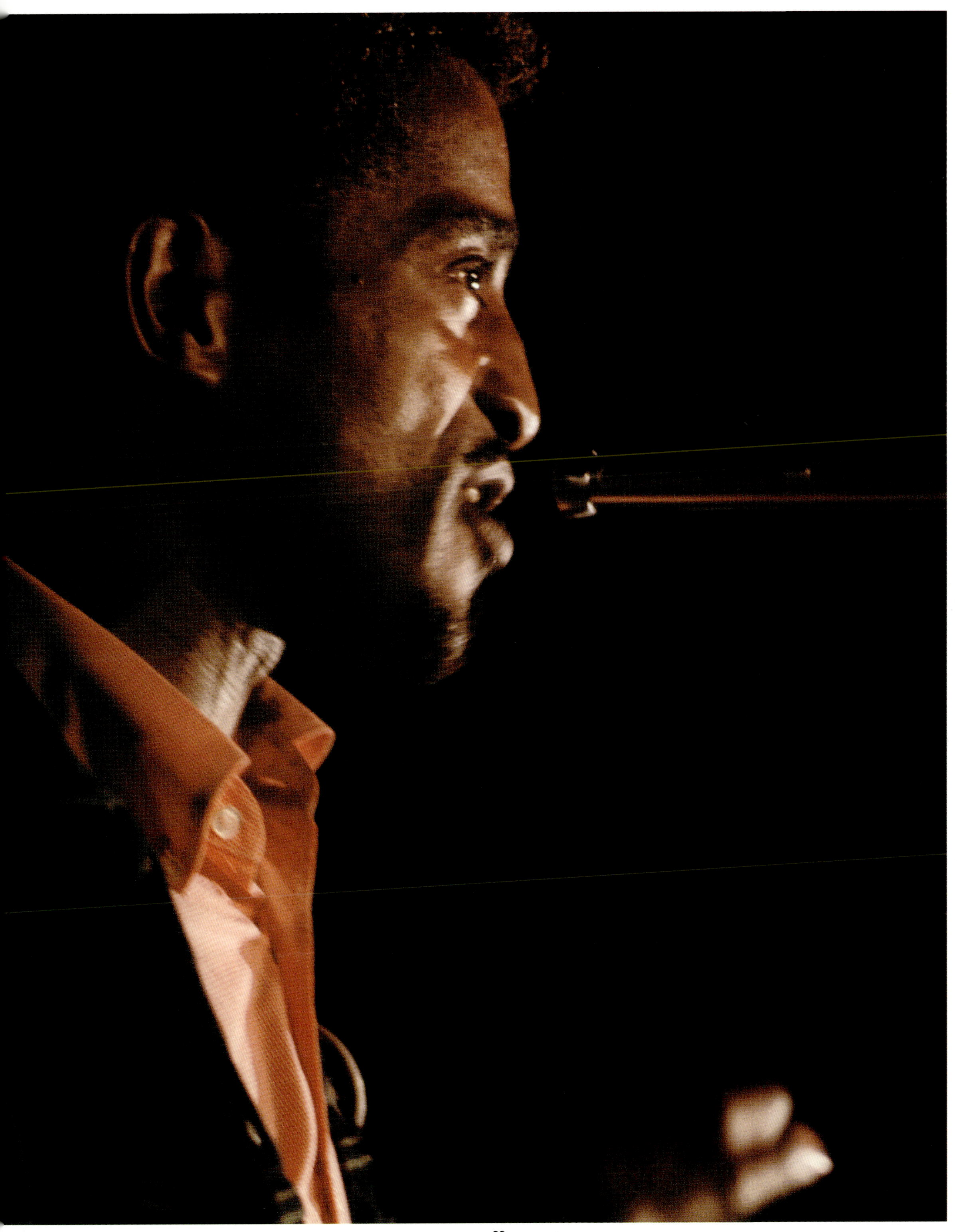

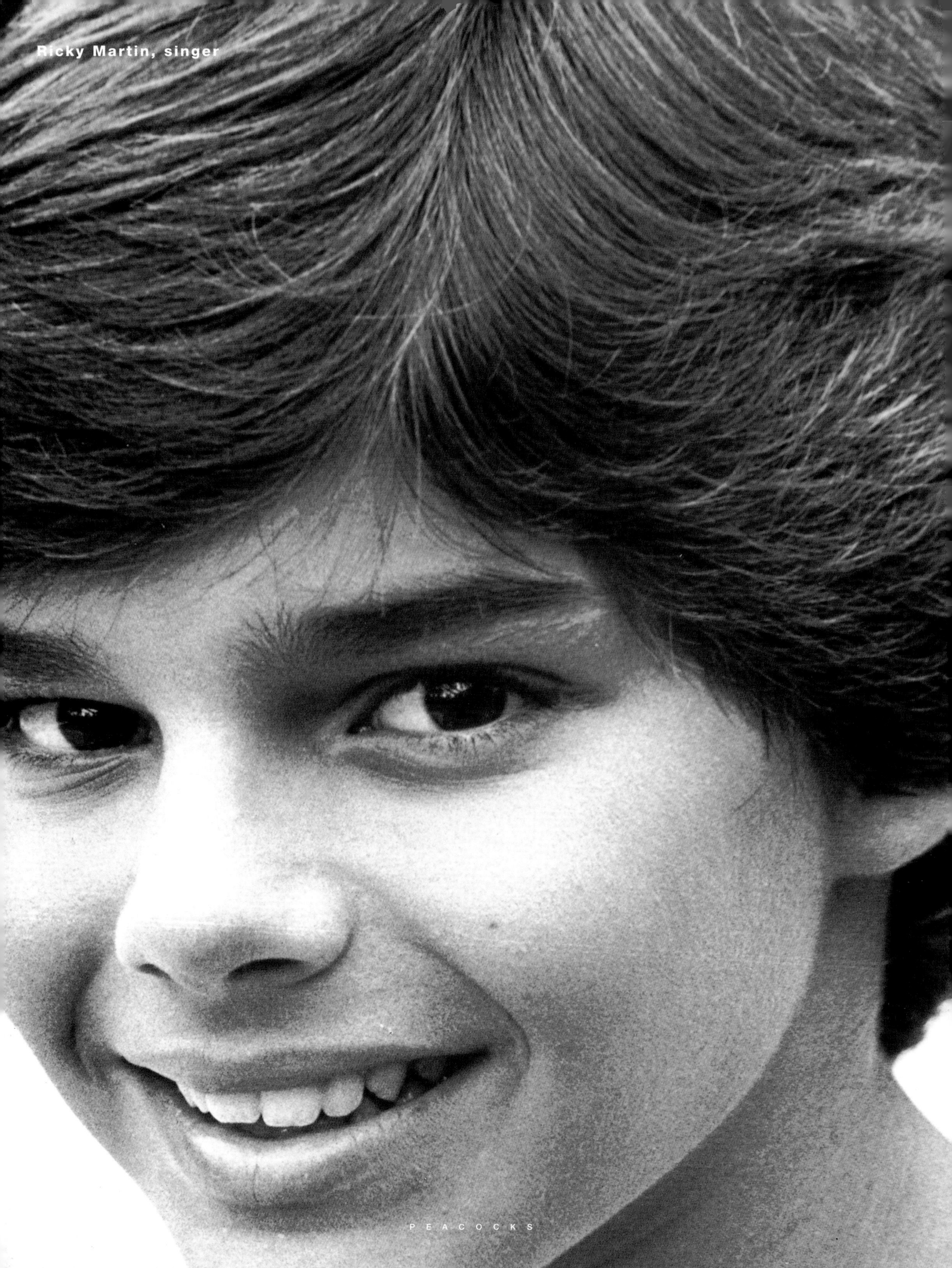
Ricky Martin, singer

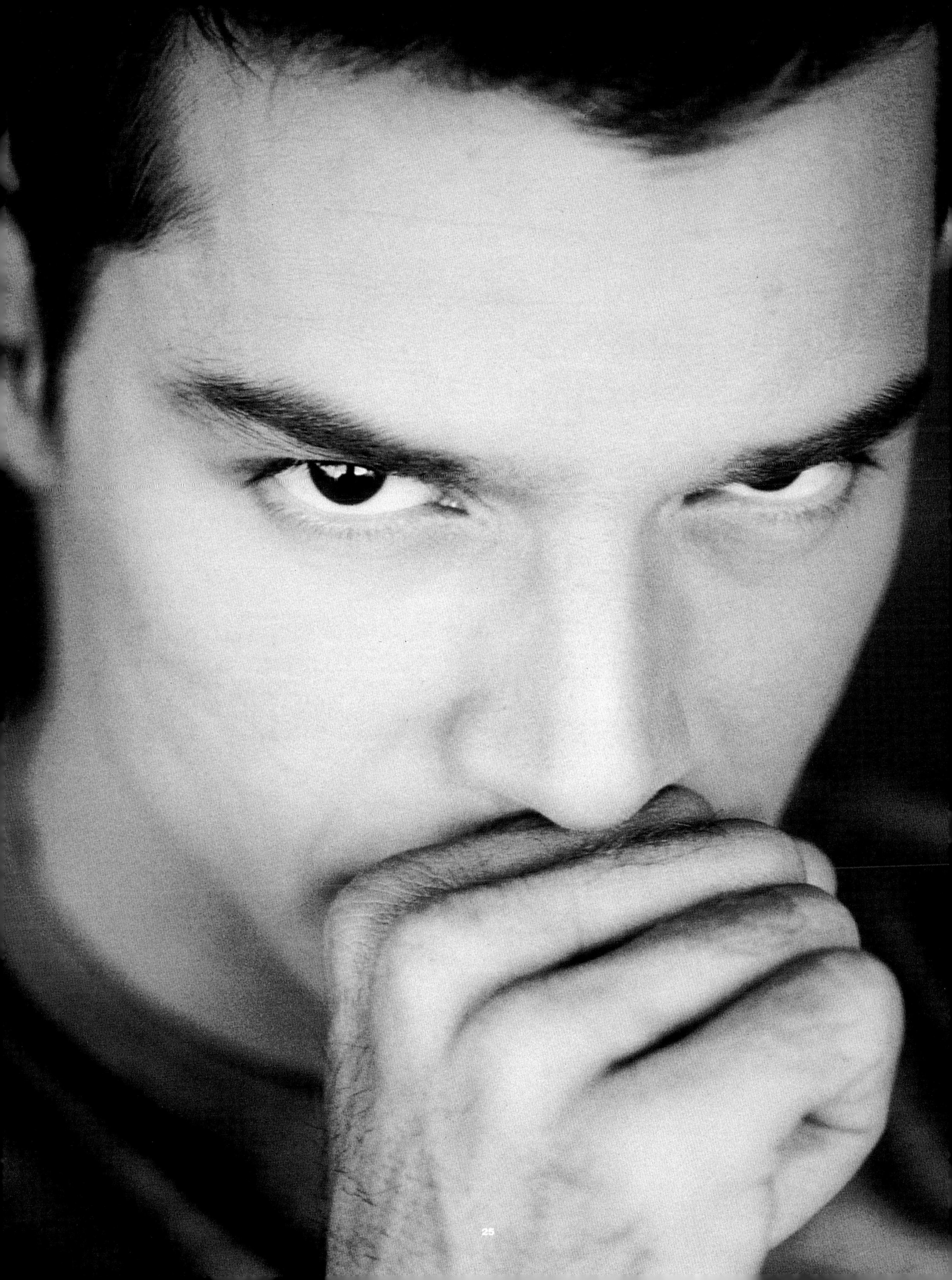

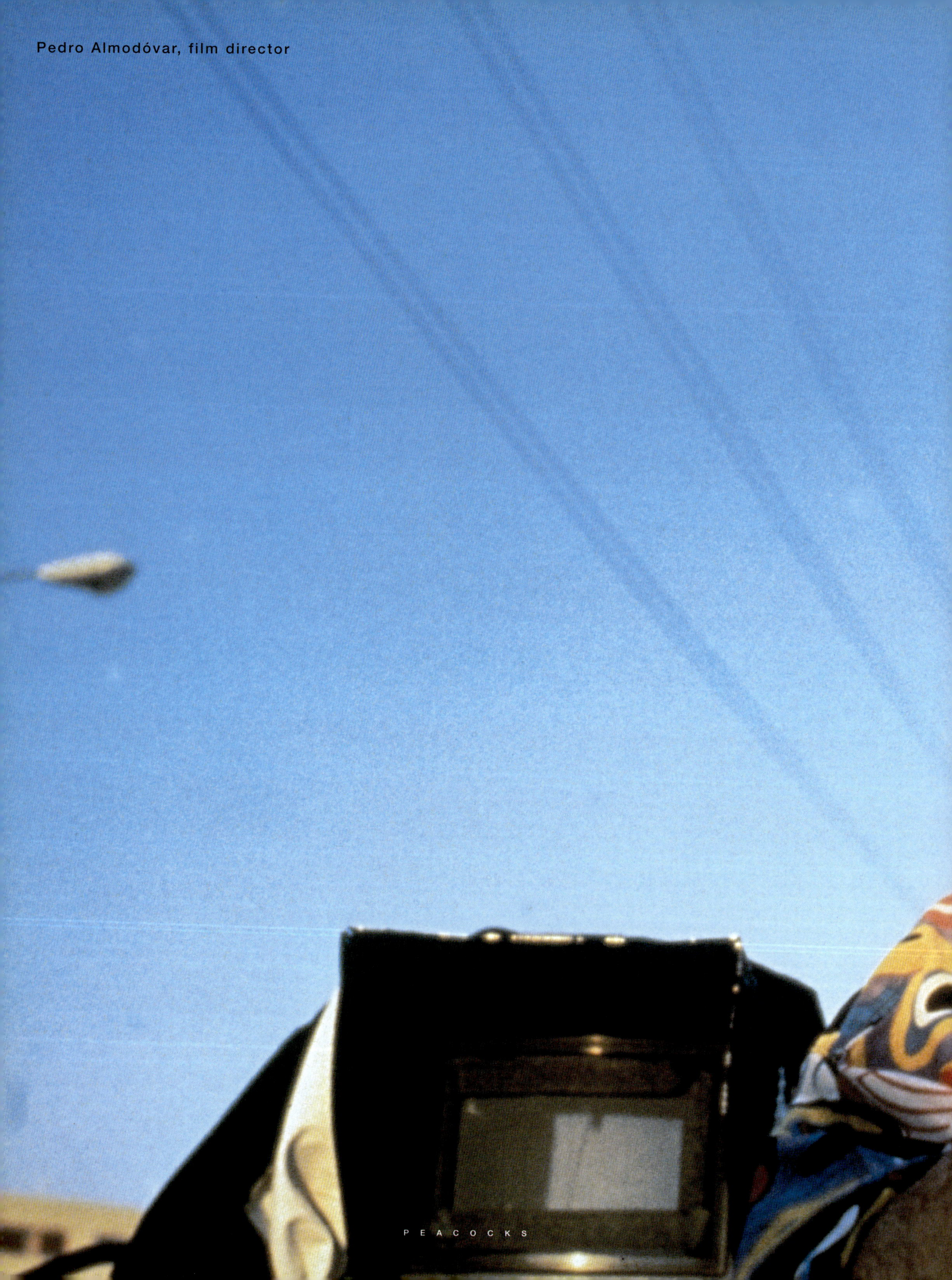

Pedro Almodóvar, film director

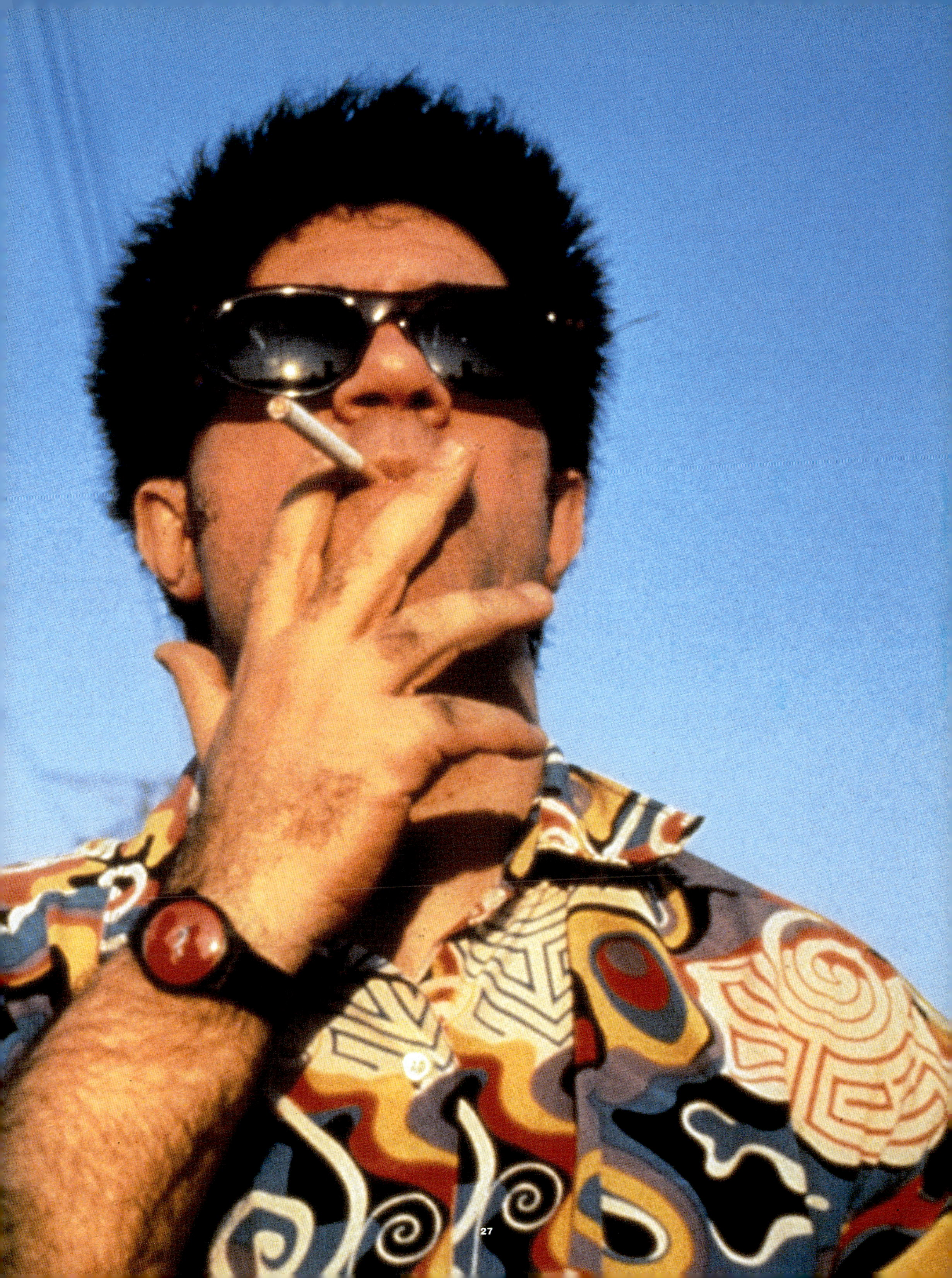

Joaquín Cortéz, dancer

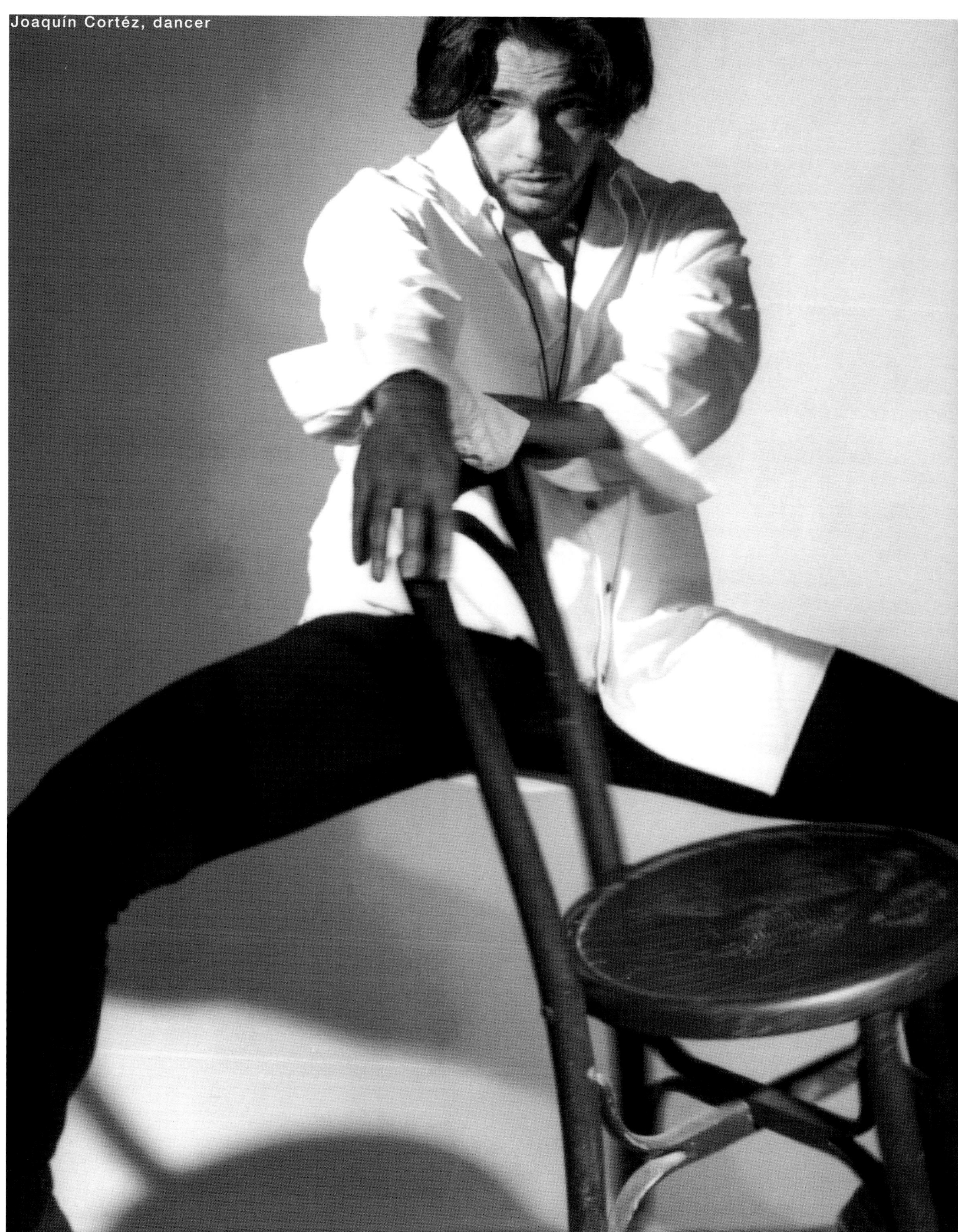

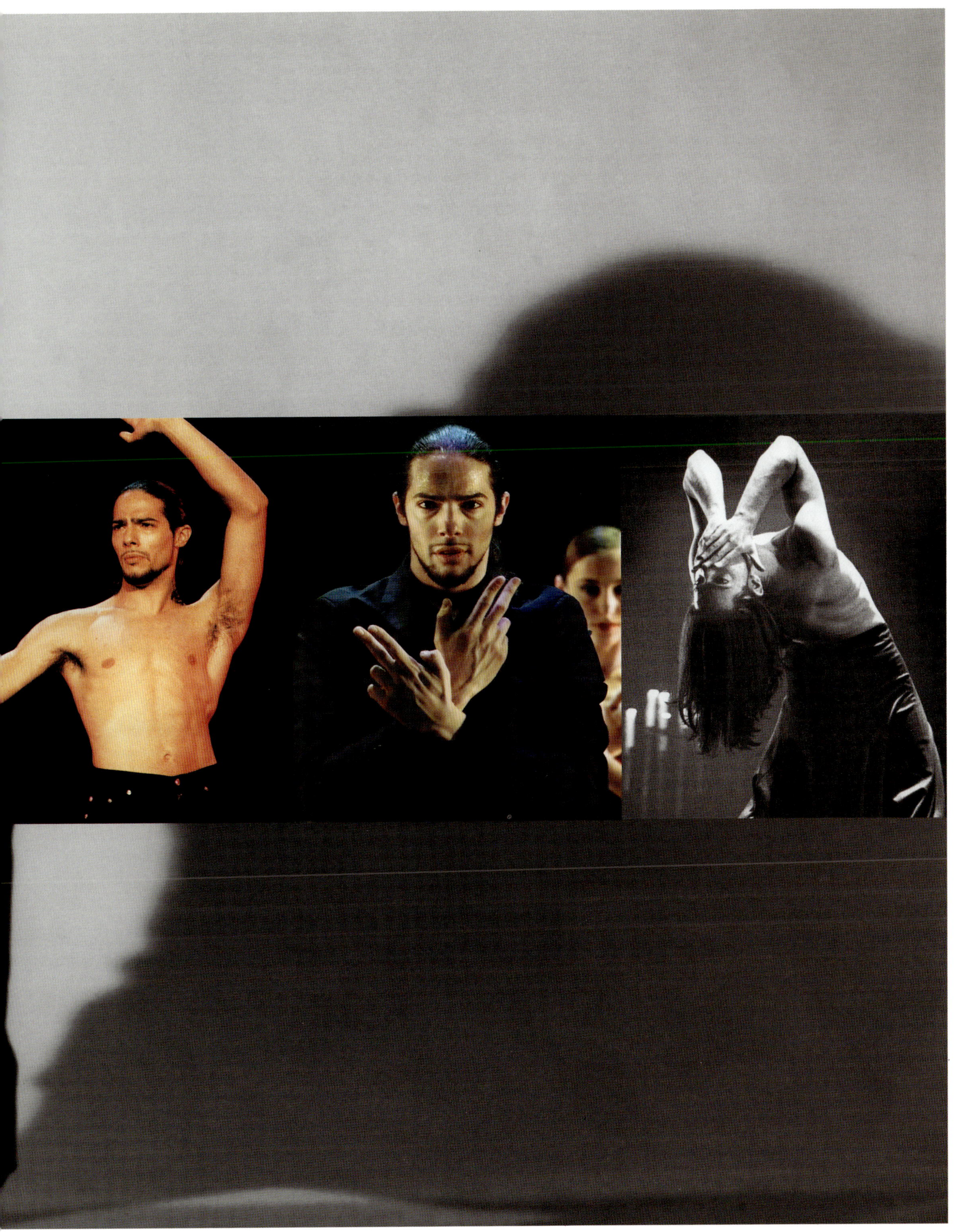

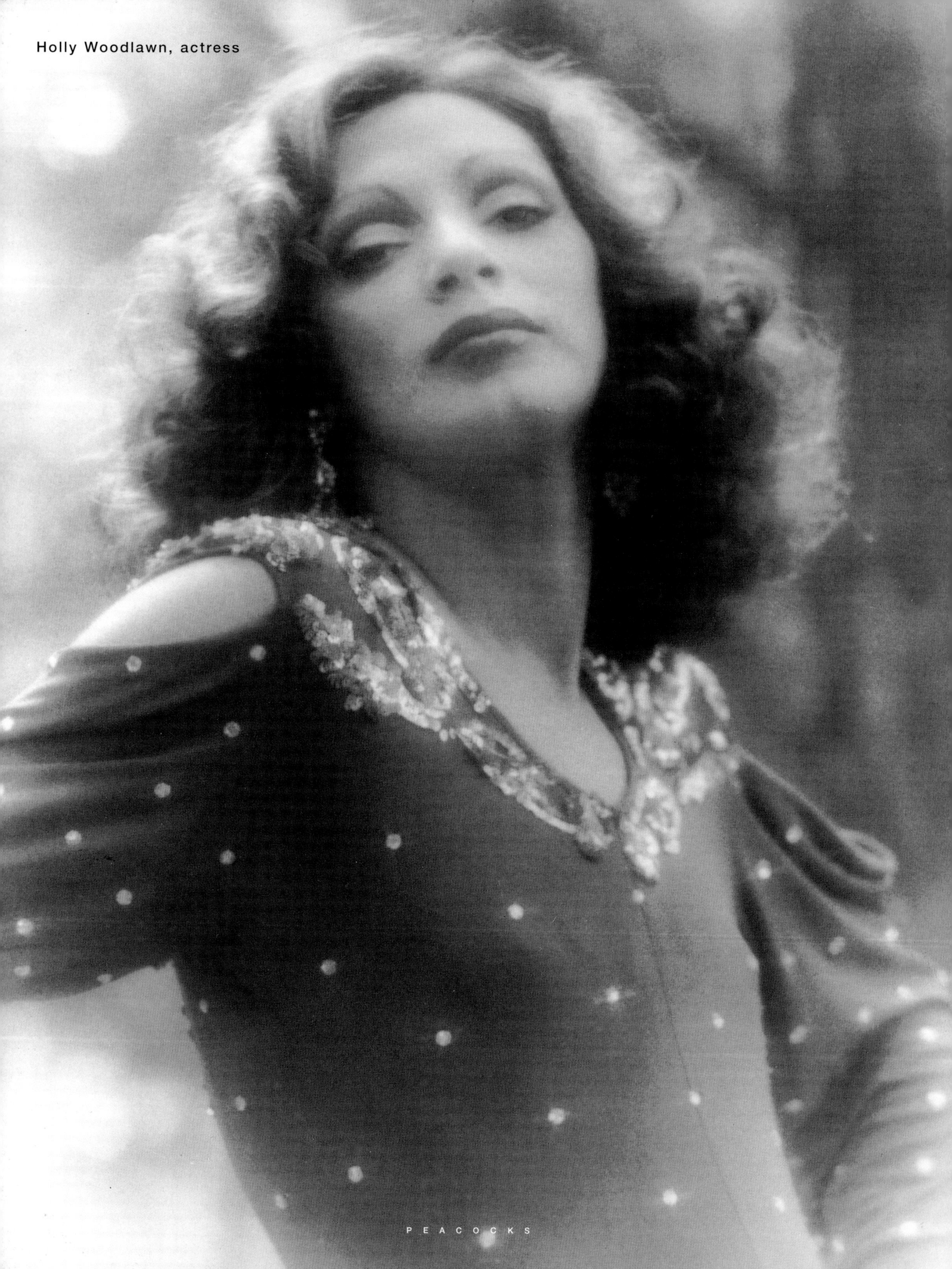

Holly Woodlawn, actress

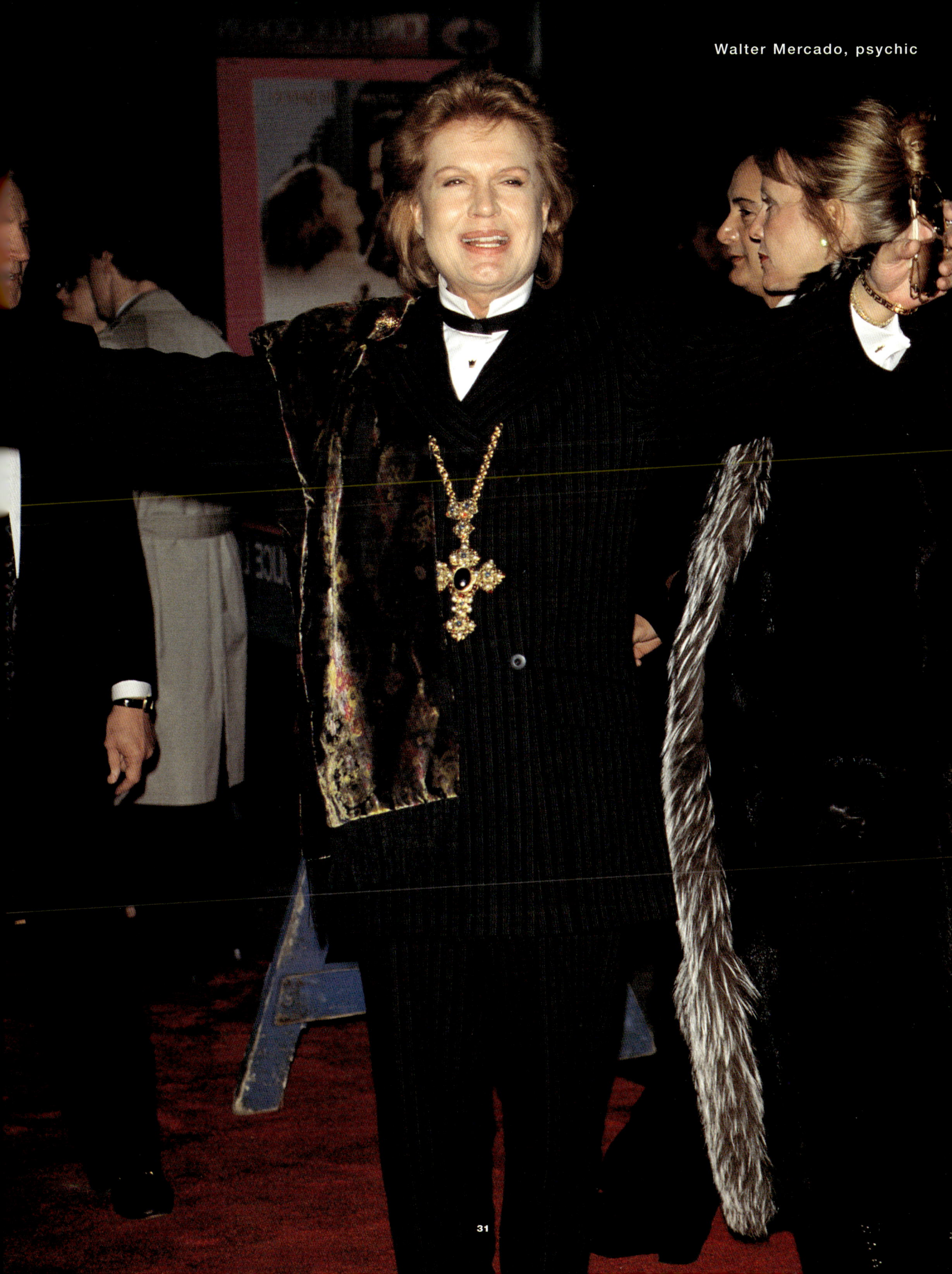

Walter Mercado, psychic

One part intelligence, two parts charm.

They're the all star cast of *Latin Teen Beat.* Think of Sean Cassidy's style gone Latino and you've got the picture. A flash of a flirty smile or the shake of a rhythmic hip from one of these *papi chulos* and we're reduced to giddy schoolgirls reminded of our obsessions during adolescence: a world of button-wearing frenzy and fan club memberships; a special moment in time when we passed notes and consulted Ouija boards at slumber parties to see if we were destined to marry our fantasy lovers.

Ritchie Valens was the quintessential Latino heartthrob. In the 1950s Valens sang rock-and-roll in Spanish while sporting a pompadour. He romantically dedicated songs to his *novia*, and captured our hearts as well. This chubby-faced Chicano grew up listening to traditional Mexican music on his mother's records and the local California rock-and-roll radio stations, making his music a hybrid affair. Valens's clothes, too, were a mix: he looked like the *mariachi*-next-door. Valens alternated '50s-era argyle sweaters and chinos with billowy purple satin shirts and silver-studded vests. Valens's style reflected his blended cultures—Mexico and America—fusion he pulled off easily. Because we've all seen the film, *La Bamba*, we know how the story ends: Valens will forever be a teenage idol.

Fast forward to 1985. A fab five burst onto the music scene. No, not the Beatles incarnate, but to a nation of Hispanic teenagers, even better—Menudo. Clad in parachute pants and shirts with lots of zippers, these young Latin singers triggered a mania and a marketing craze. Every teenage Hispanic girl had a Menudo t-shirt. While the band has been criticized as processed cheese of the 1980s, comparable to fleeting trends like acid-washed jeans and paisley shirts, Menudo helped launch the careers of Ricky Martin and Robi Rosa. Like the cyclical world of fashion, the current popularity of boy bands has put its current lineup, MDO, back in vogue.

The nineties brought us an athletic papi-Oscar "Golden Boy" De La Hoya. Oscar's early look was *puro* East LA He has since graduated to the GQ brigade. Beyond his eye-candy good looks, the former Olympian boxer has proved he's also a contender in the musical arena by earning a Grammy nomination for his self-titled debut album. De La Hoya's diverse talents continue to knock us out.

Our dish du jour is Cheyanne. This *telenovela* star-turned-singer has got the Latin lover act down. Although his sexy moves in the film, *Dance With Me*, had women of all nationalities wanting a turn on the dance floor with him, Cheyanne's smooth style has yet caught America's full attention. But that's all right, he can remain our little secret.

For Nicholas Gonzales, the secret was out the moment his 25-foot shirtless body was splashed across billboards around the United States advertising the television show, *Resurrection Blvd*. The Texas native's sculpted chest and dimpled smile has helped increase cable subscriptions and is responsible for sore necks [from high billboards] around the nation. Our unanimous response: Nicholas good. This Stanford-educated, brown sculpture of muscle combines one part intelligence with two parts charm, creating his own recipe for Latin chic.

These pretty boys excite us with their sexy eyes and muscular bodies, and yes, we like their bonbons too, but beyond their physical attributes lies substantial talent. Their magnetic styles and staying power prove there's more to them than just good DNA.

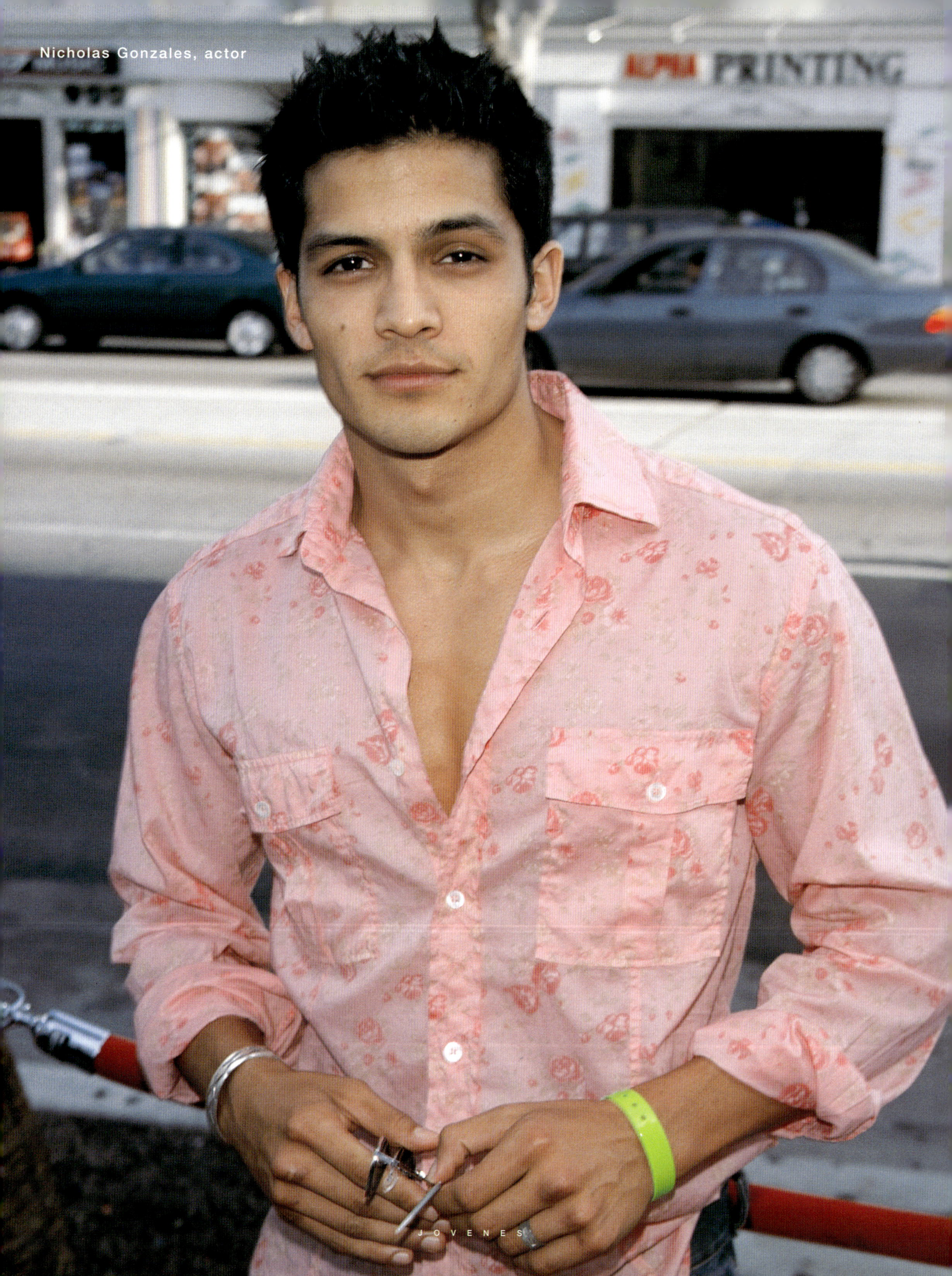

Nicholas Gonzales, actor

Charlie Sheen, actor

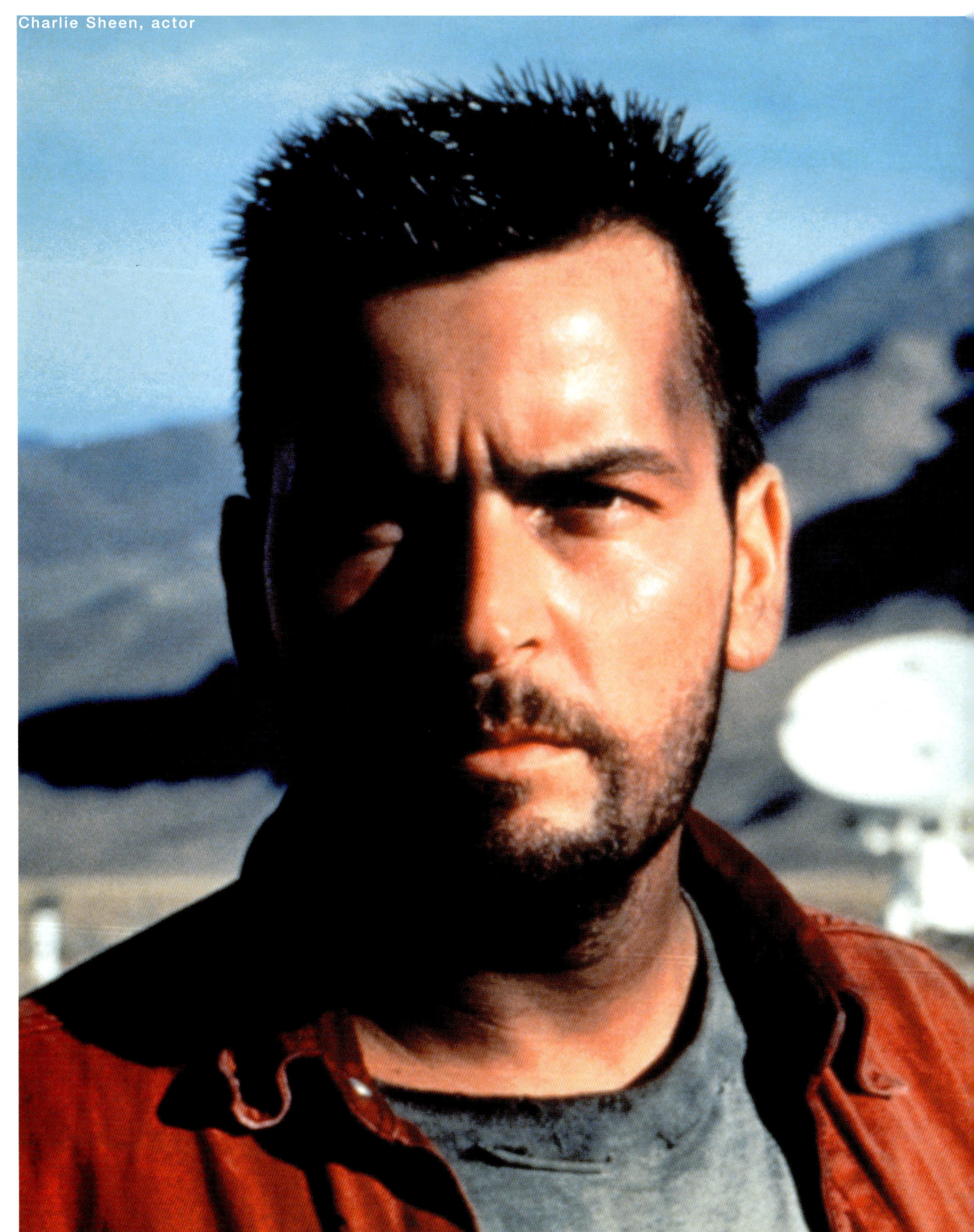

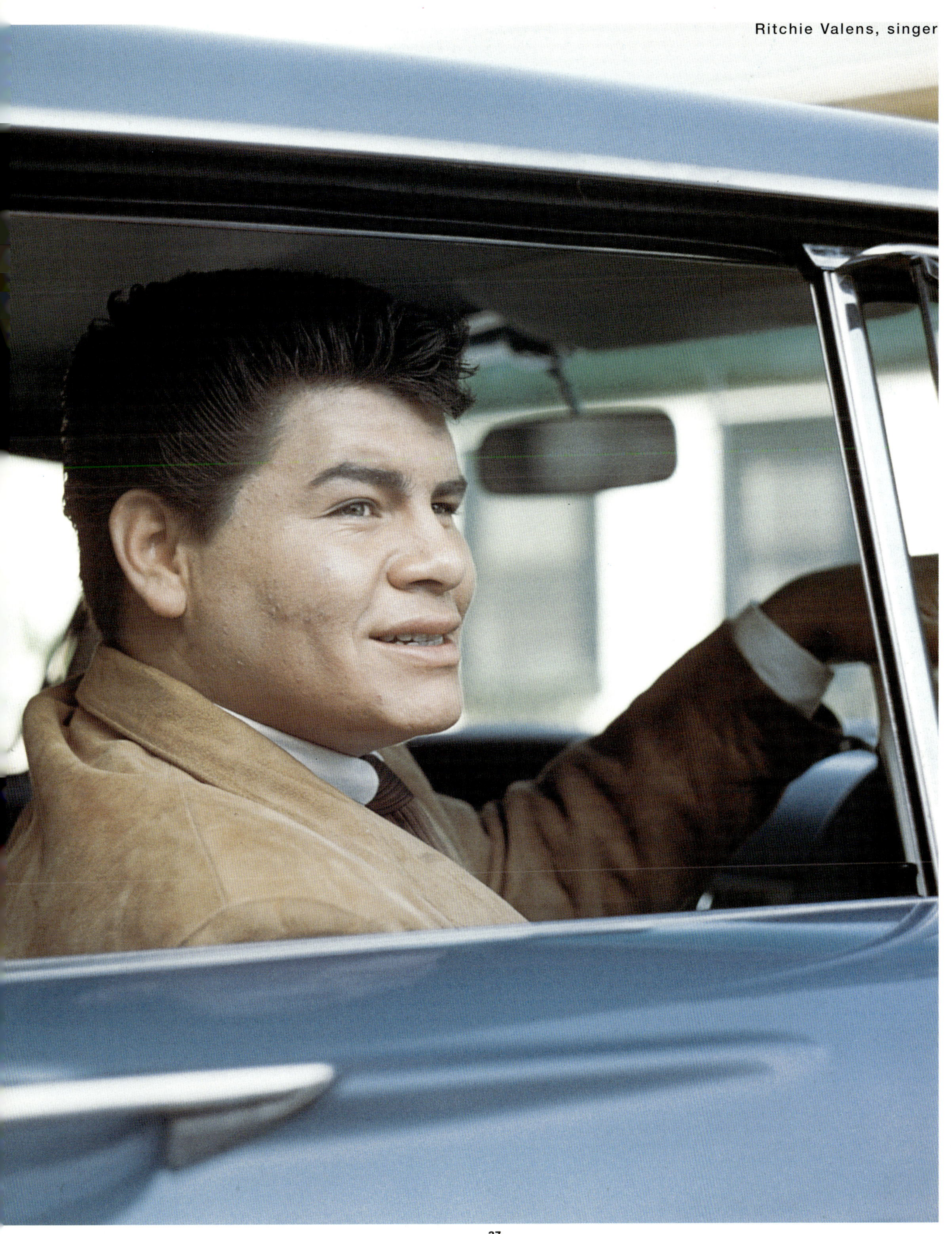
Ritchie Valens, singer

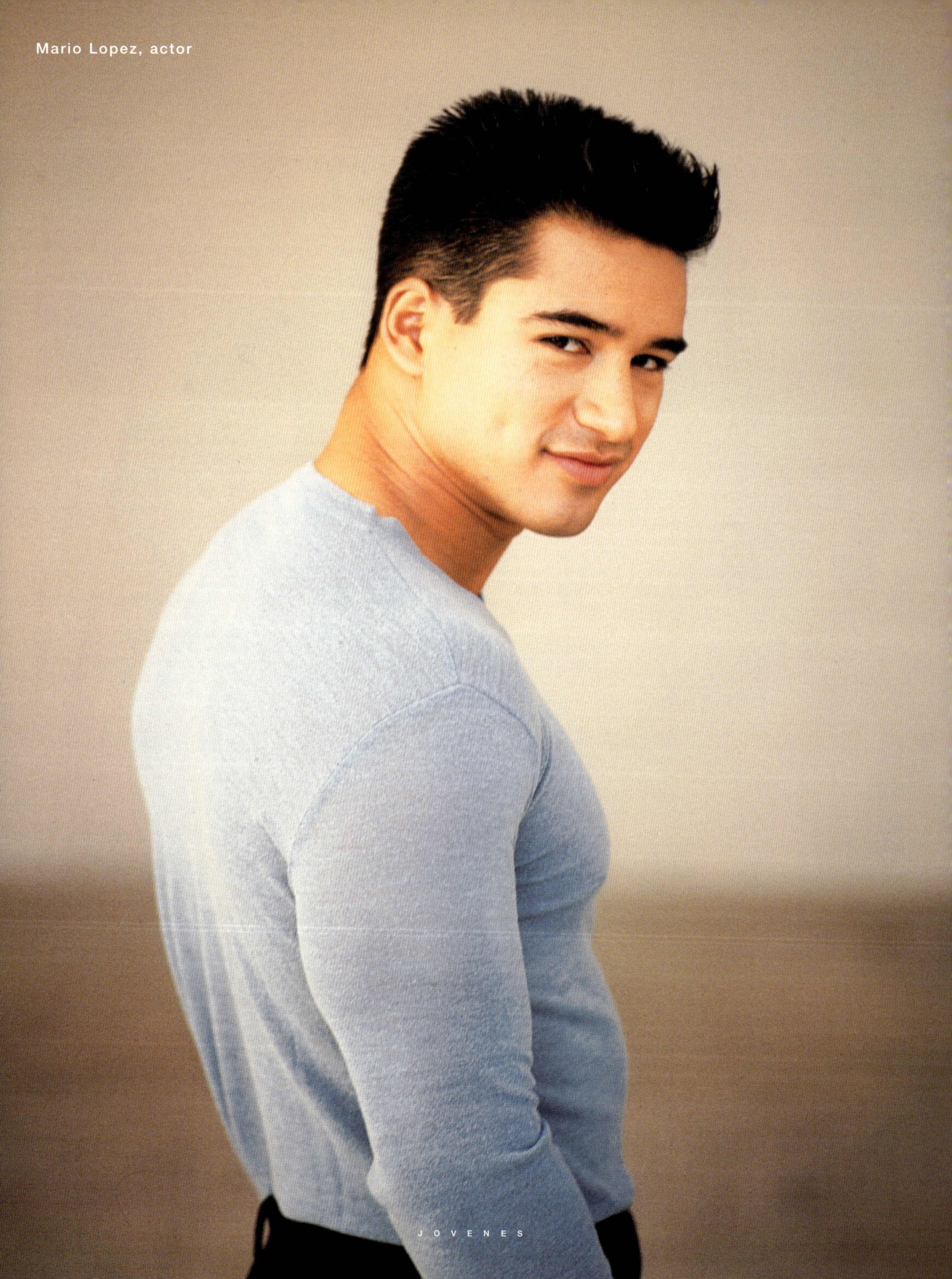

Mario Lopez, actor

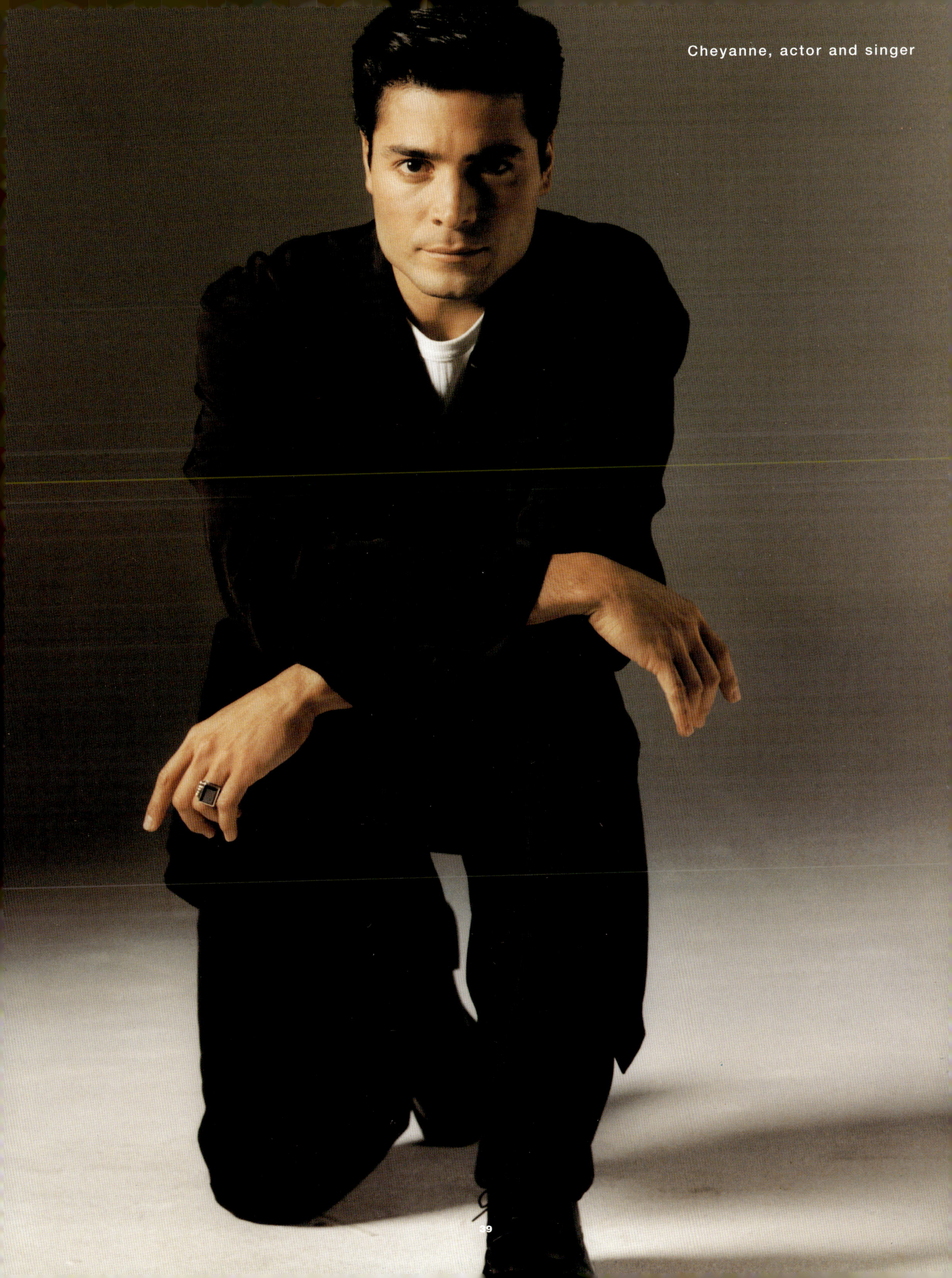

Cheyanne, actor and singer

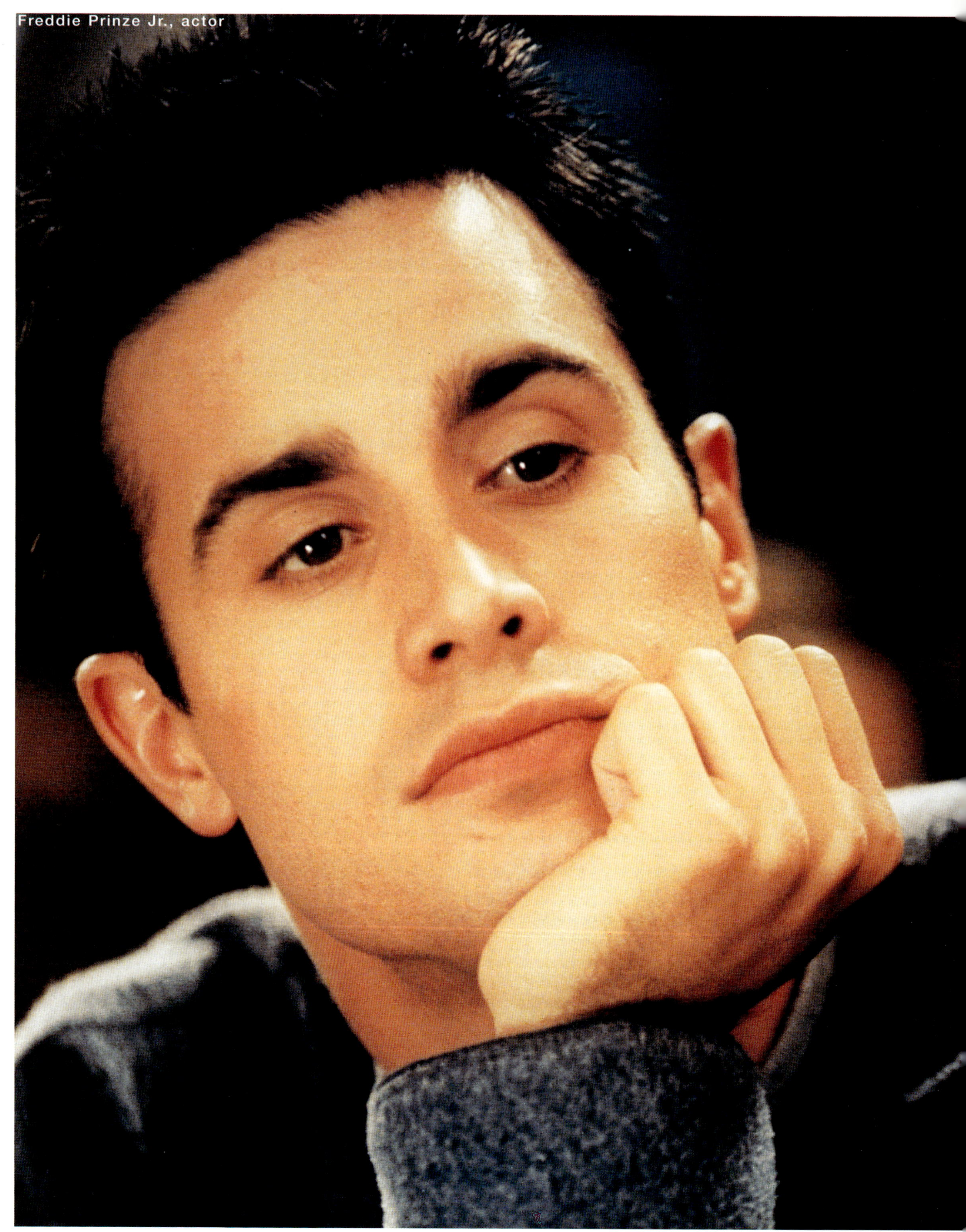
Freddie Prinze Jr., actor

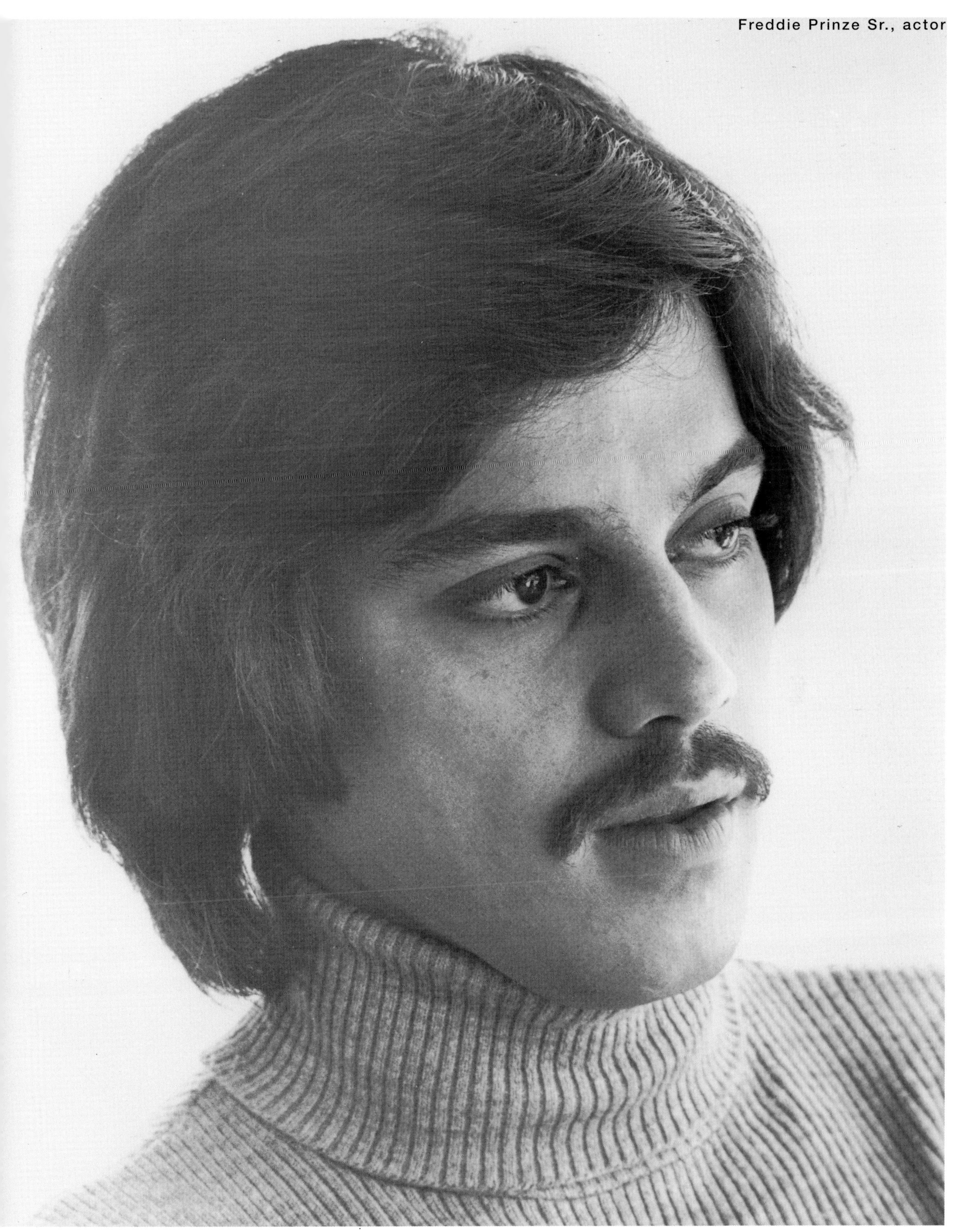

Freddie Prinze Sr., actor

Jon Seda, actor

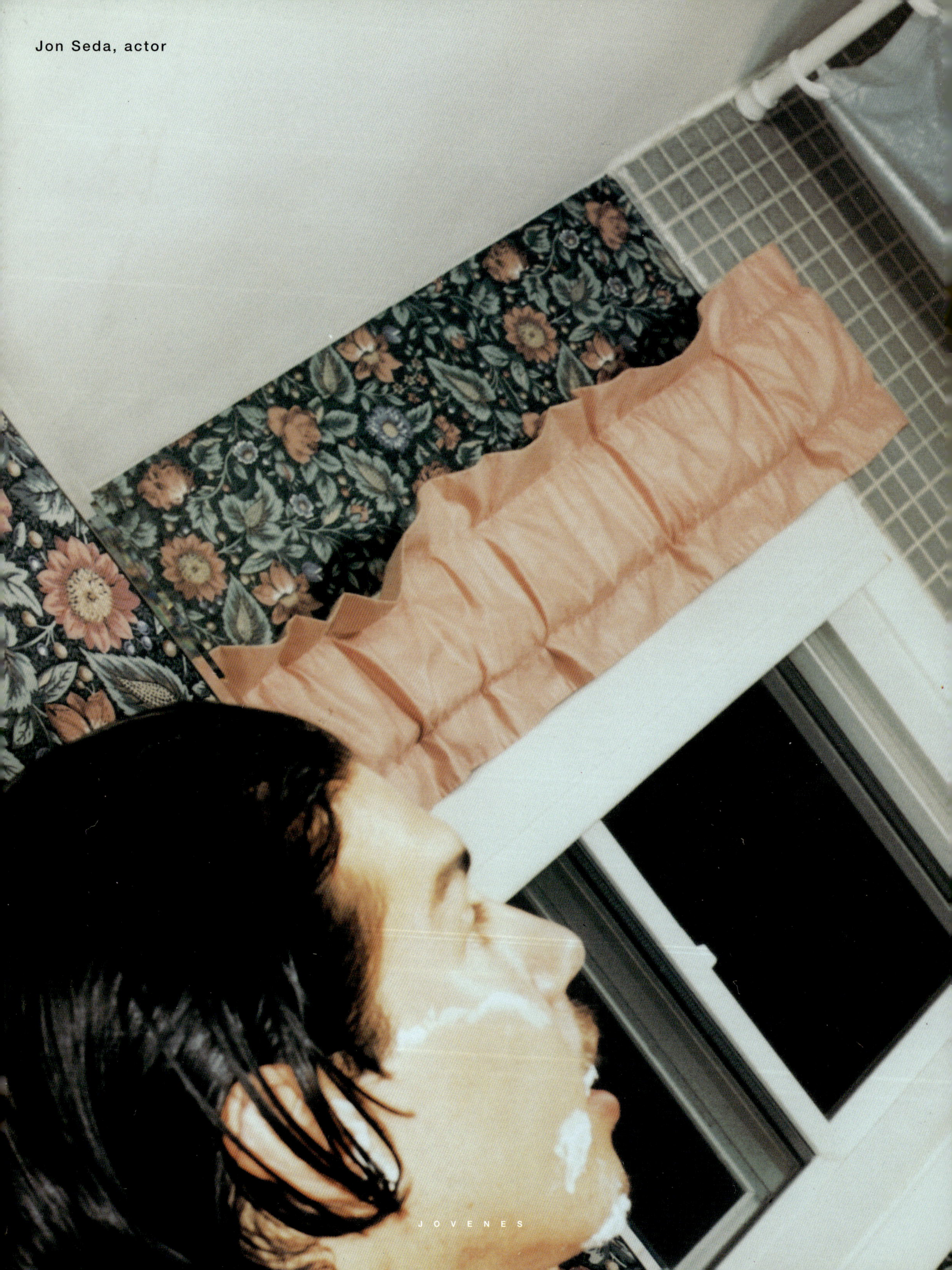

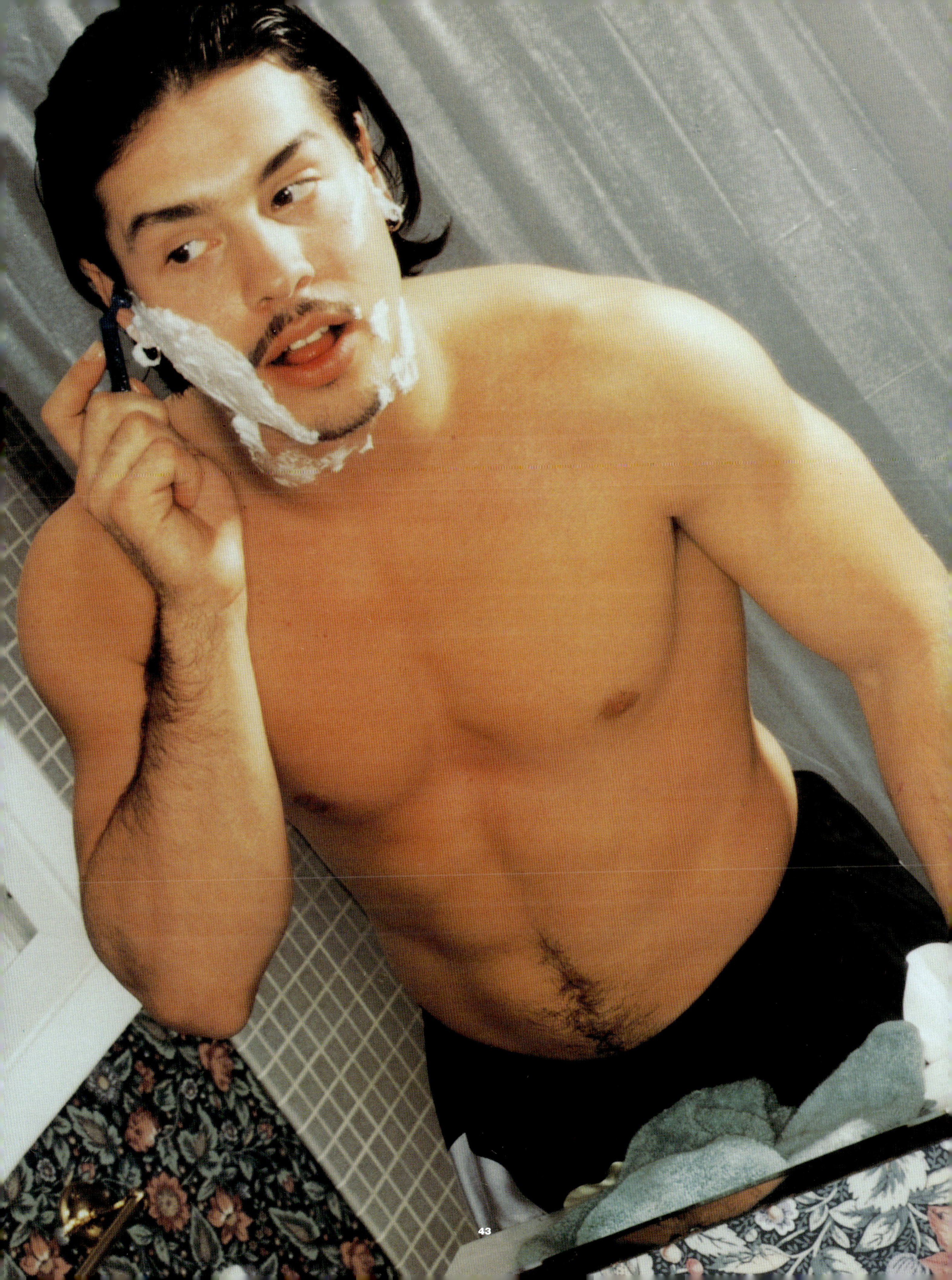

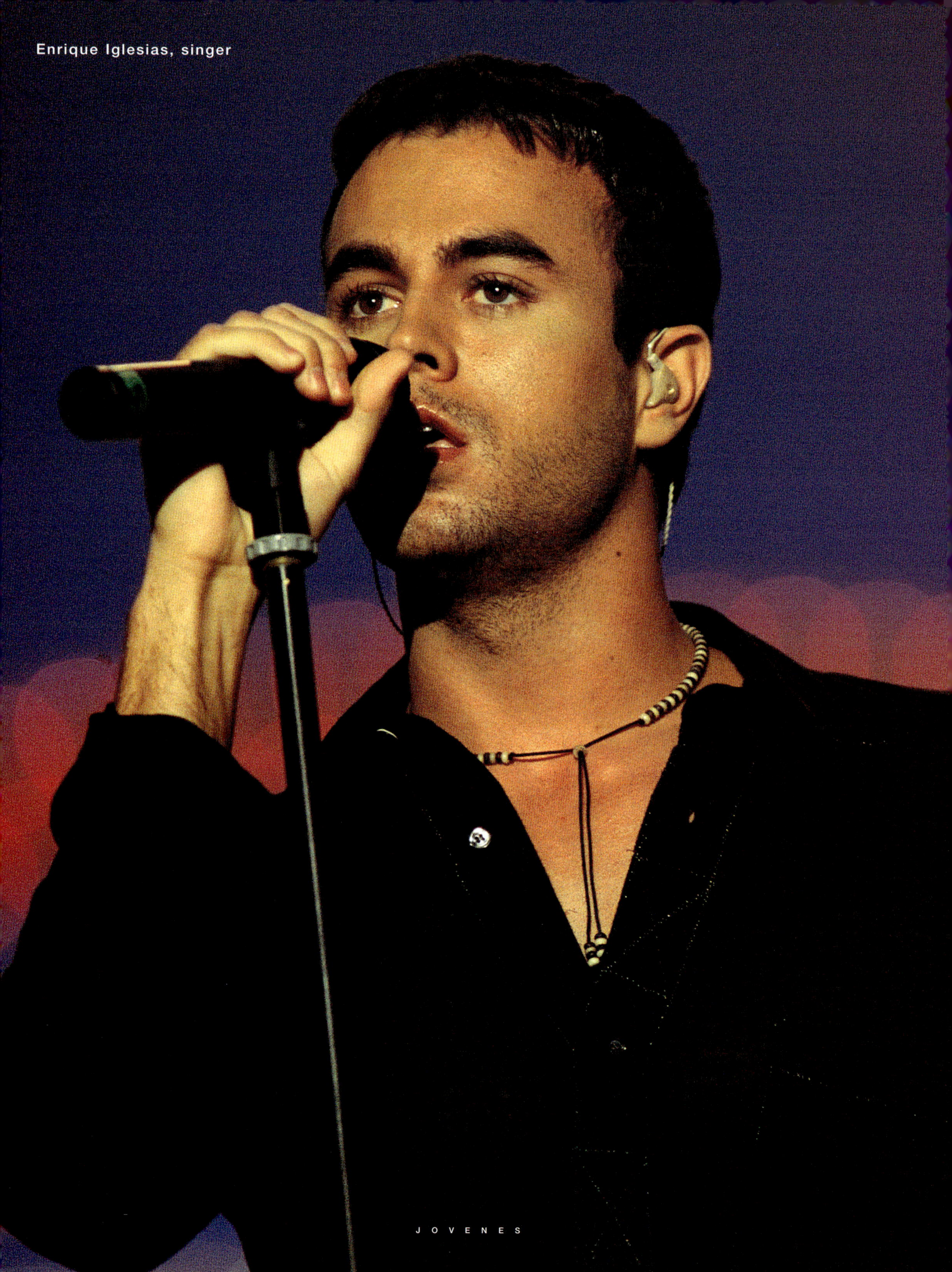
Enrique Iglesias, singer

Carlos Vives, singer

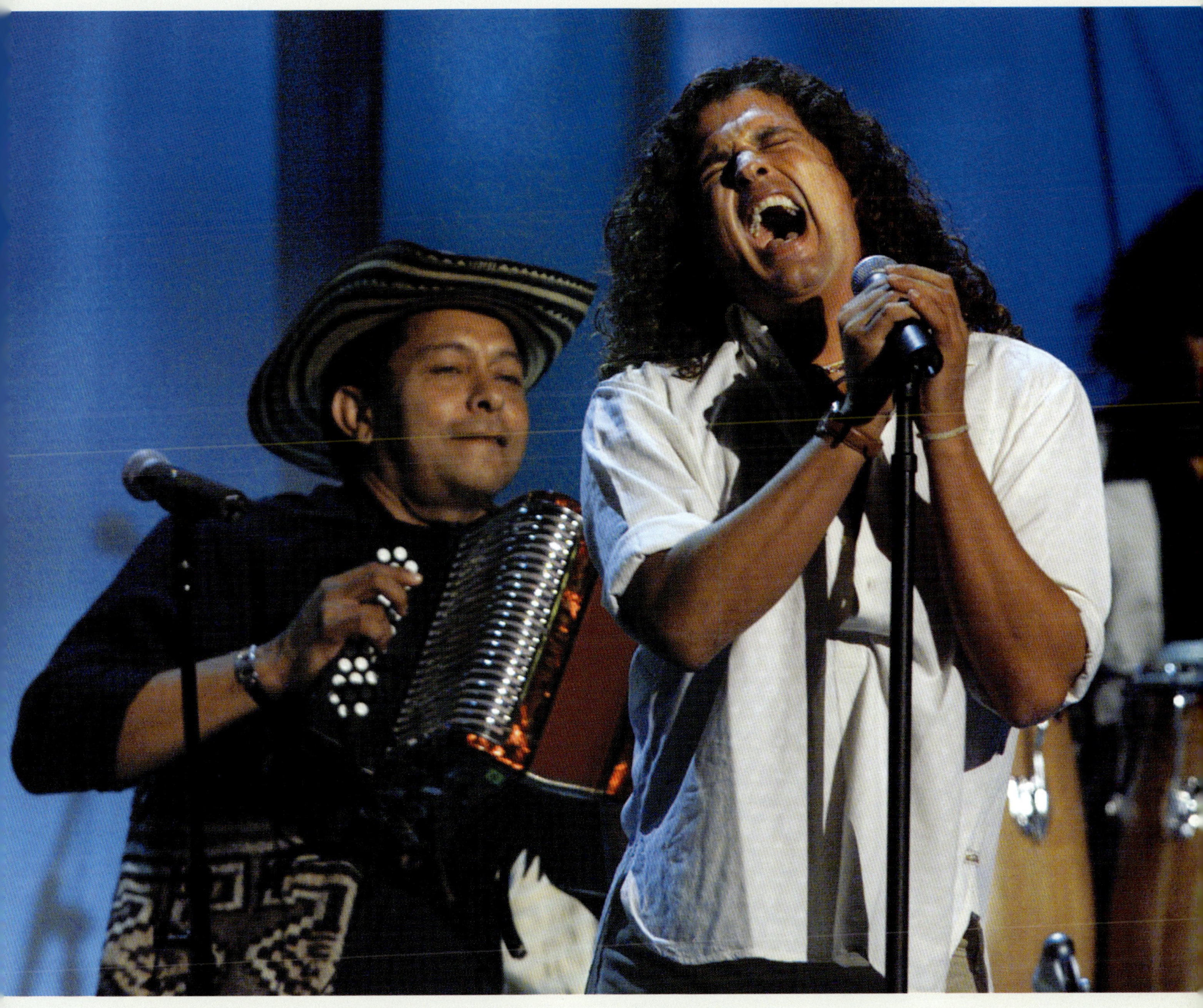

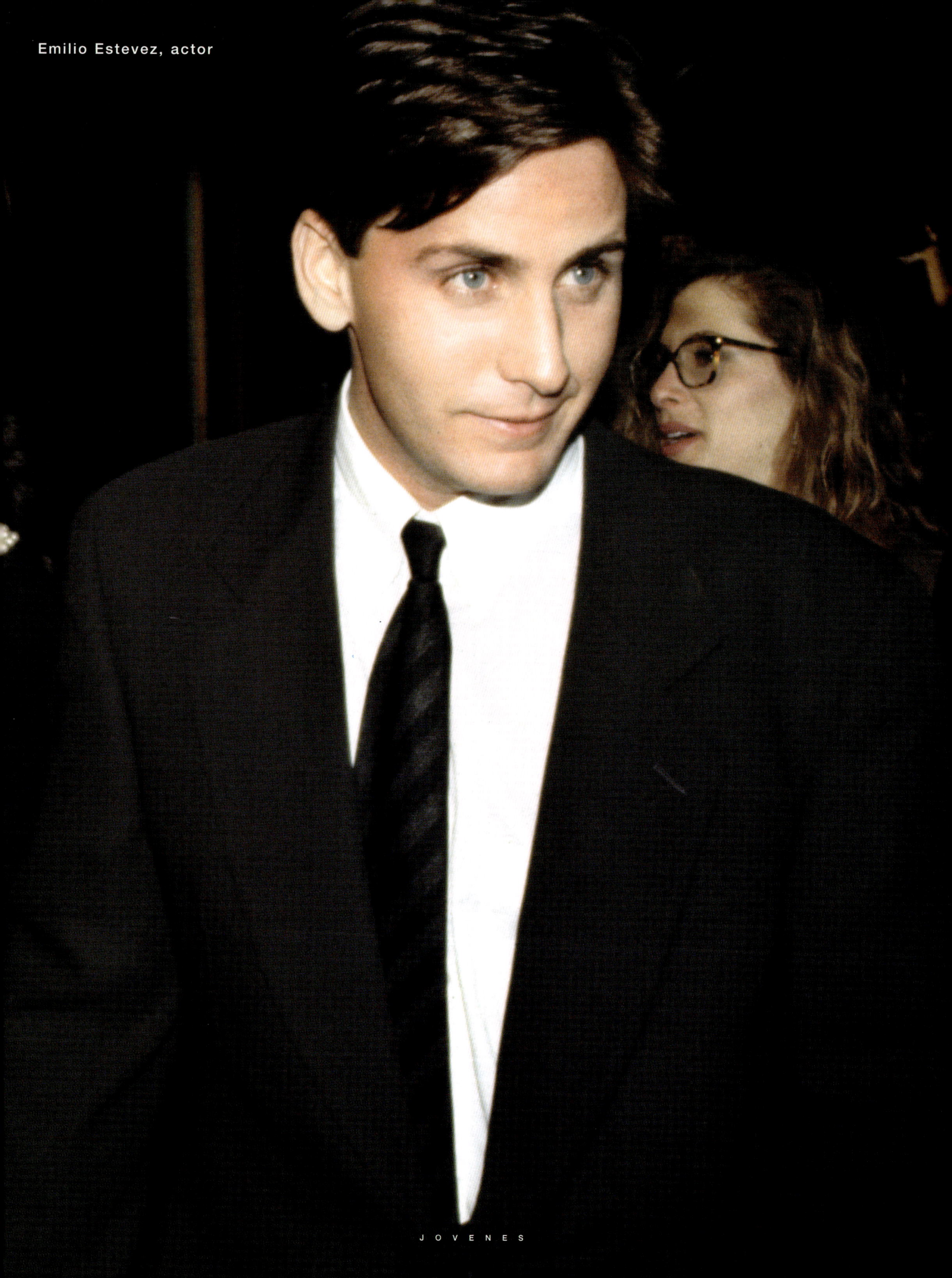

Emilio Estevez, actor

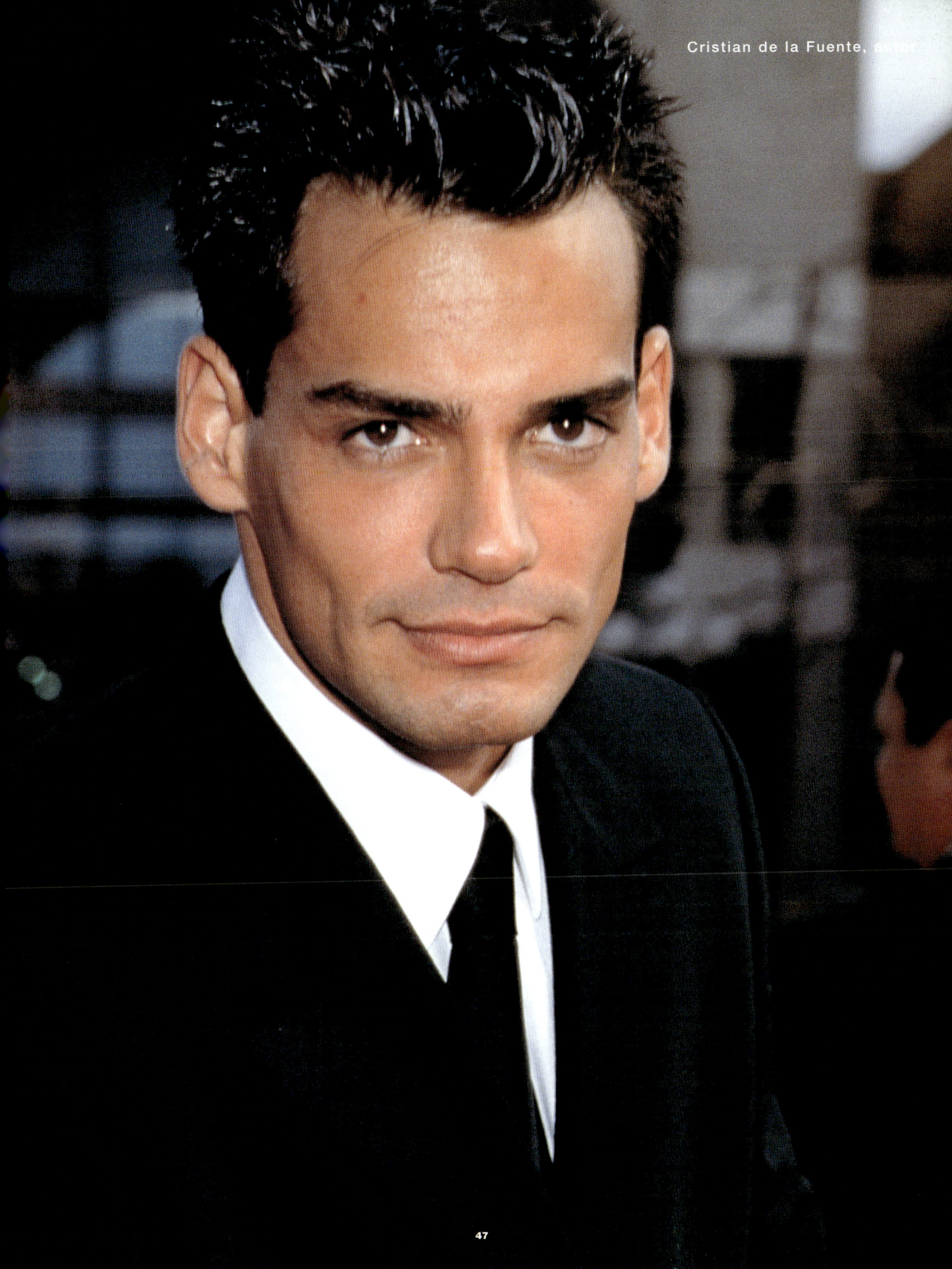

Cristian de la Fuente, actor

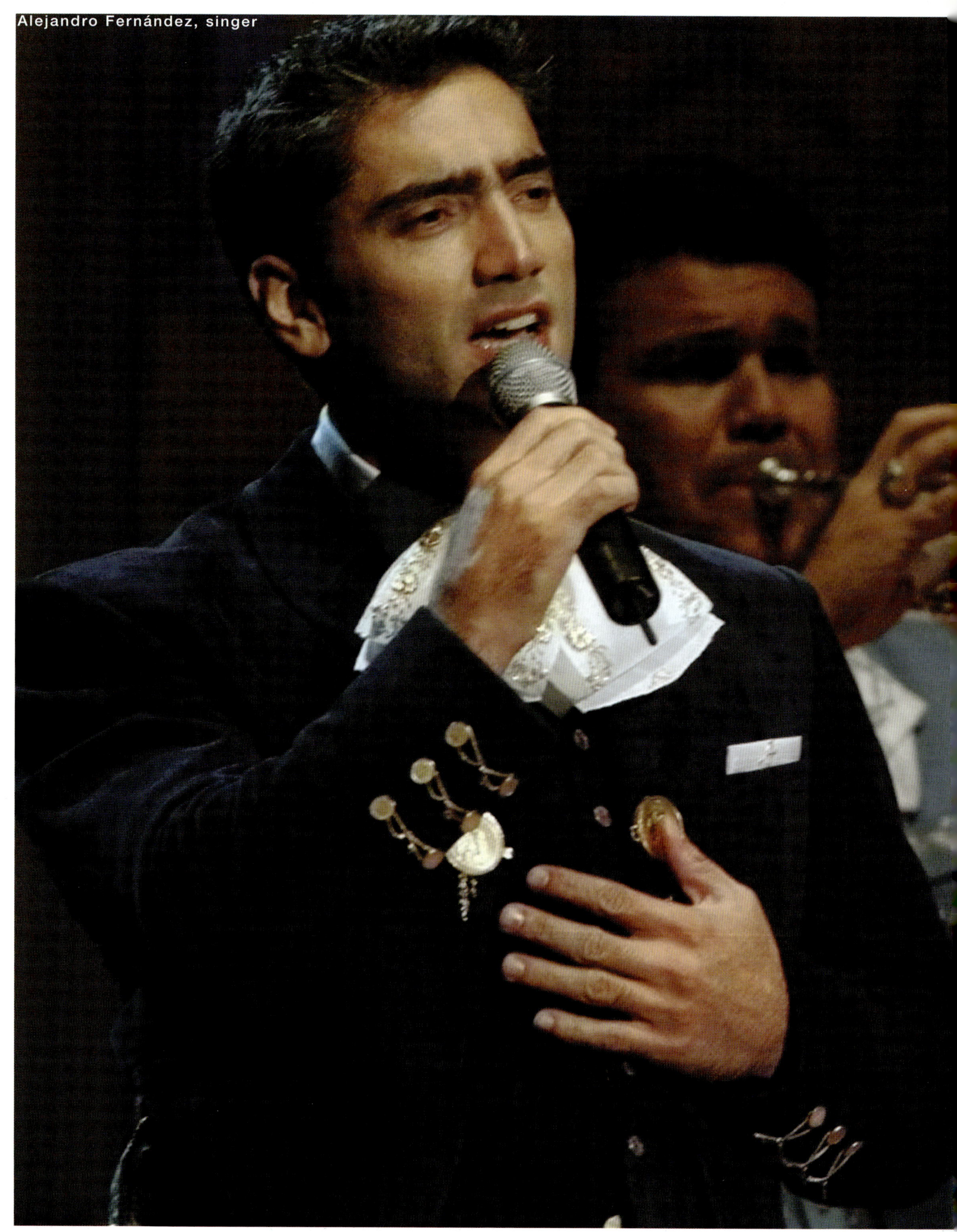
Alejandro Fernández, singer

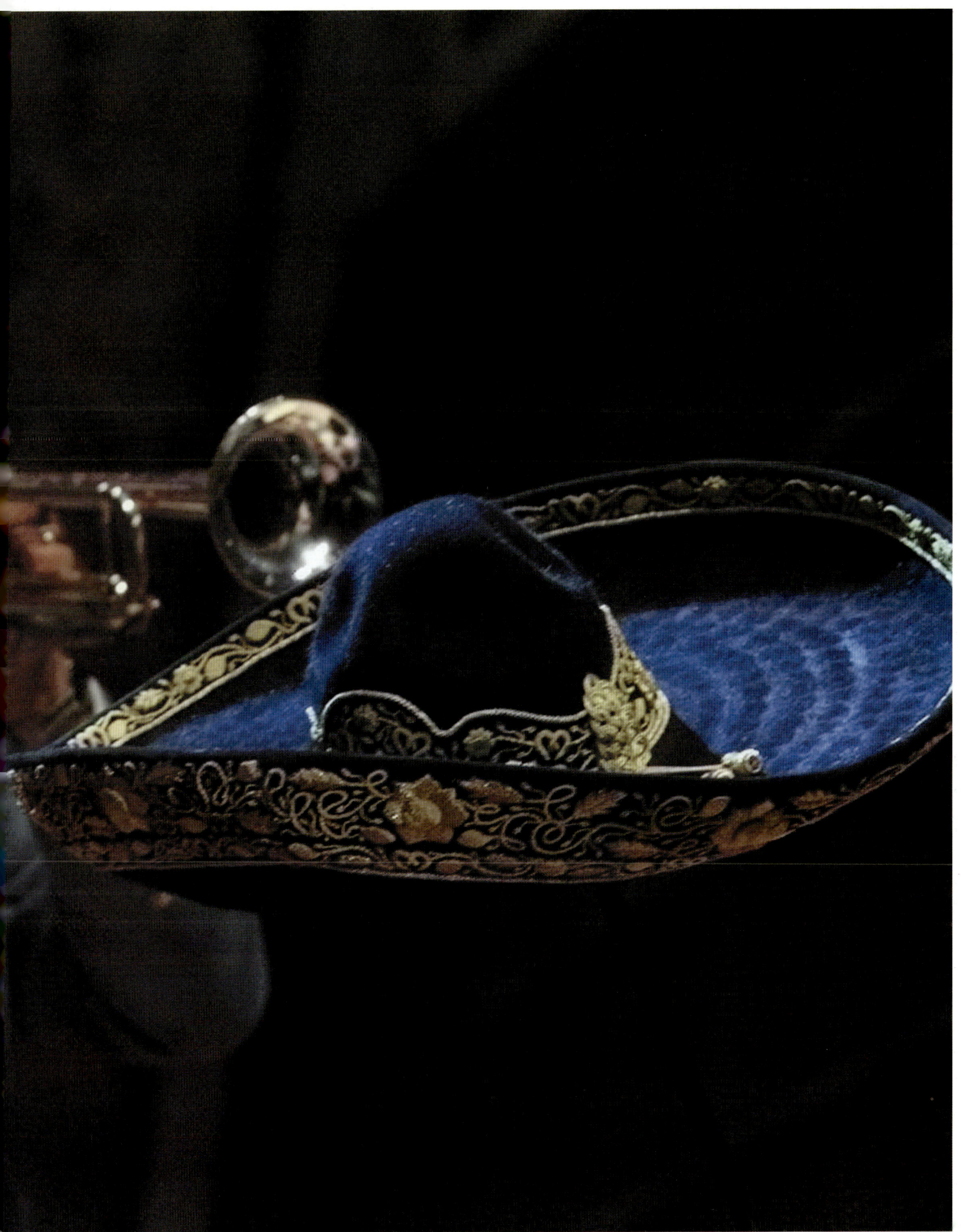

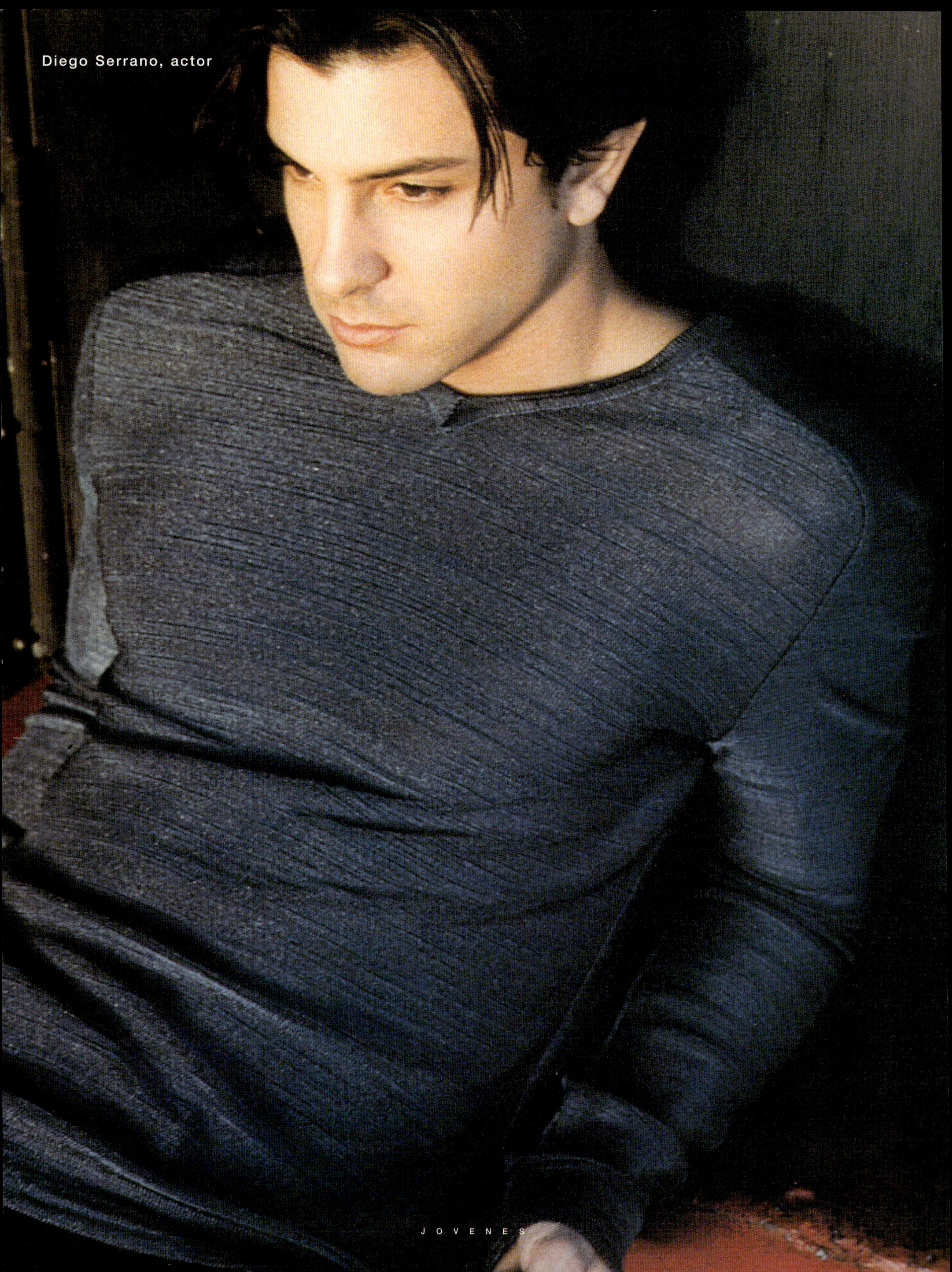

Diego Serrano, actor

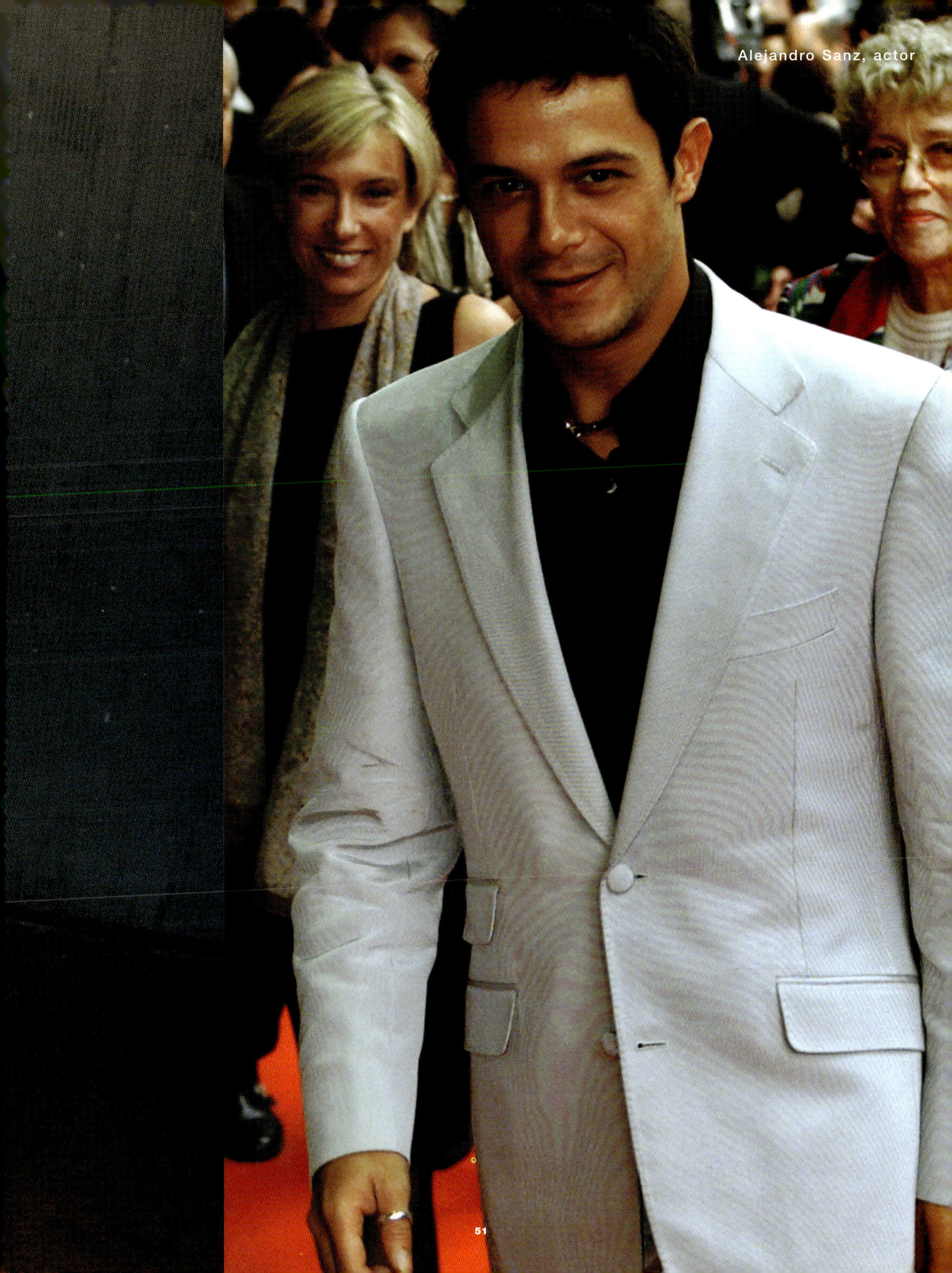

Alejandro Sanz, actor

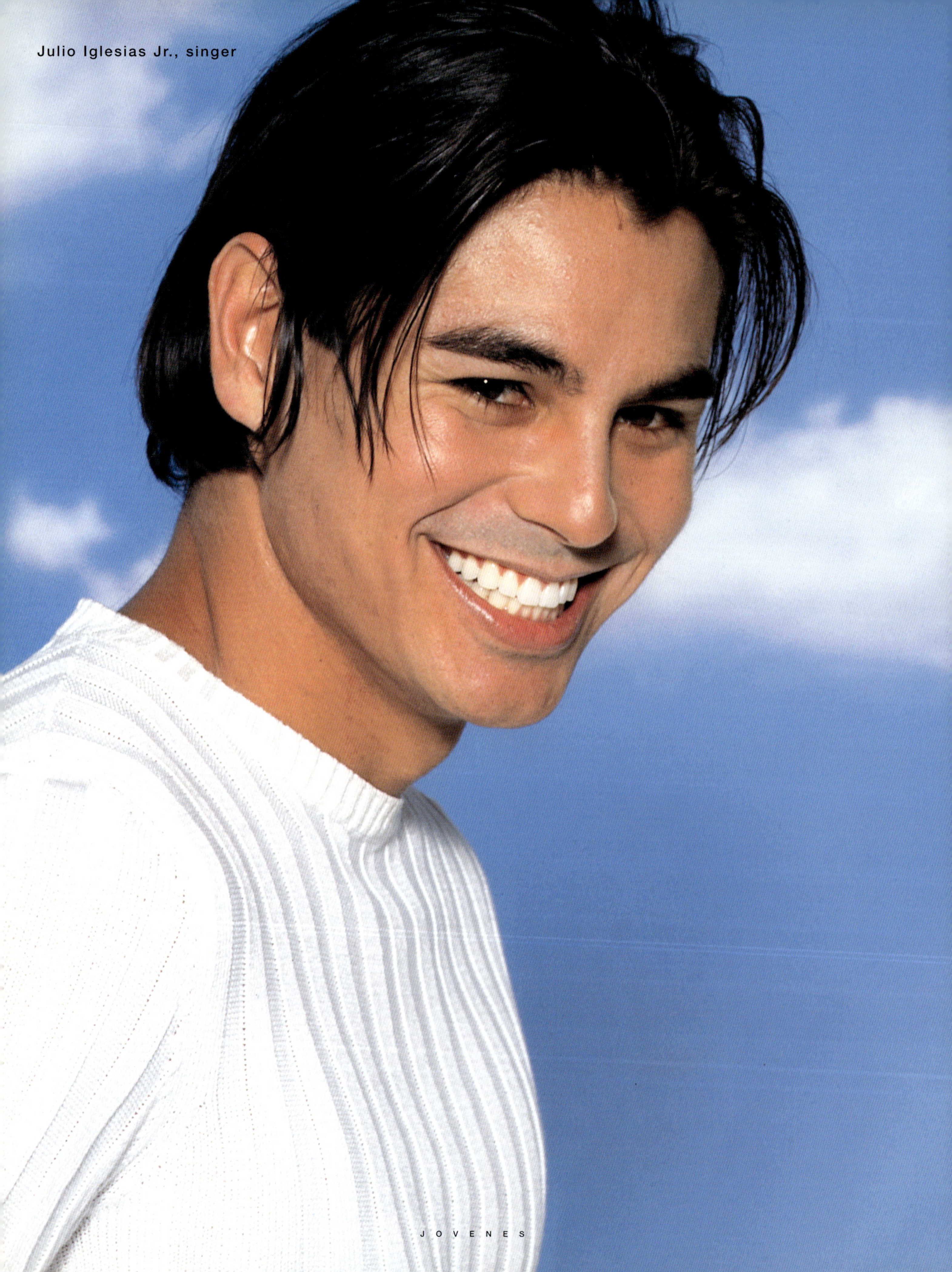

Julio Iglesias Jr., singer

La Ley, singers

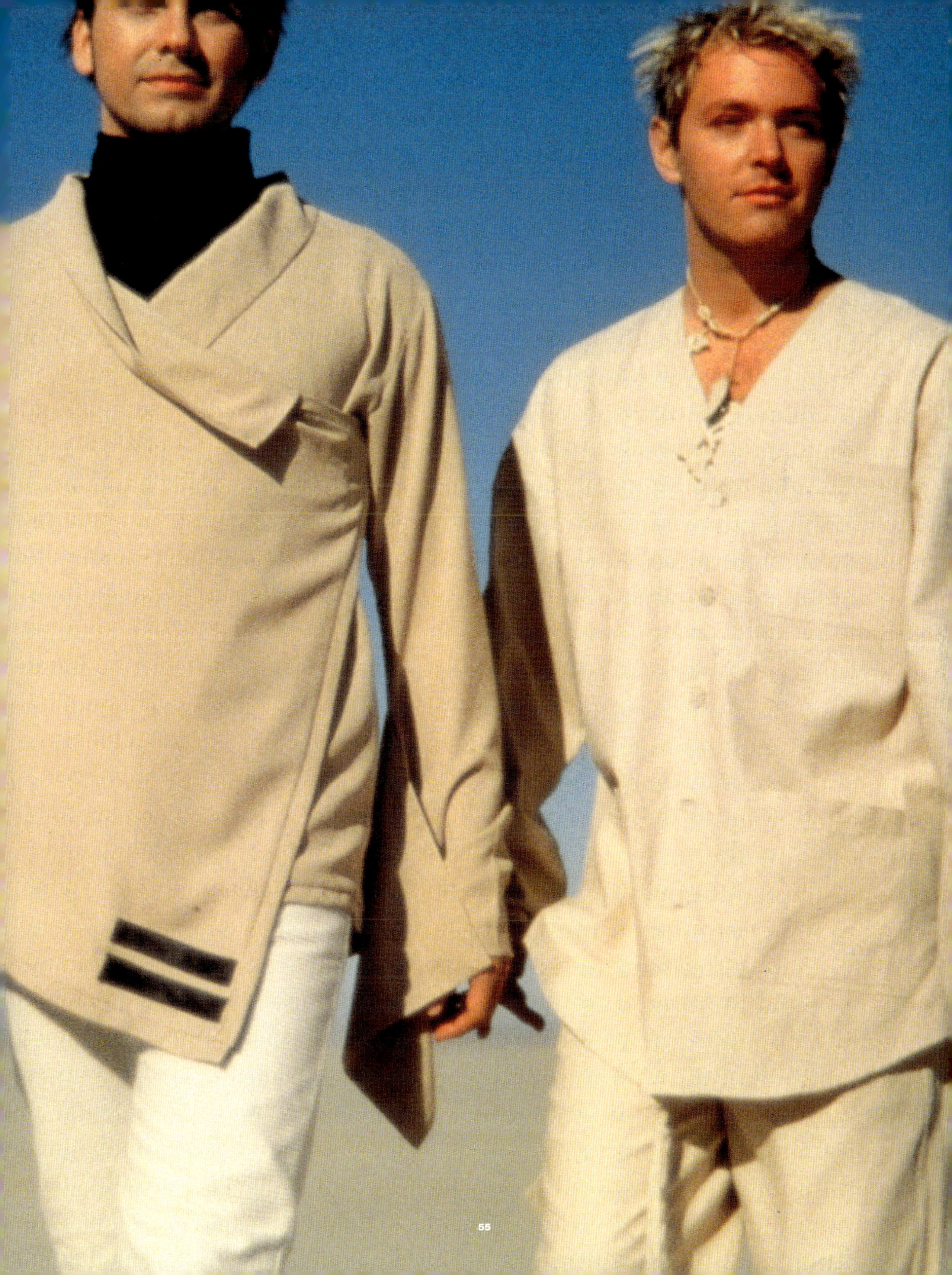

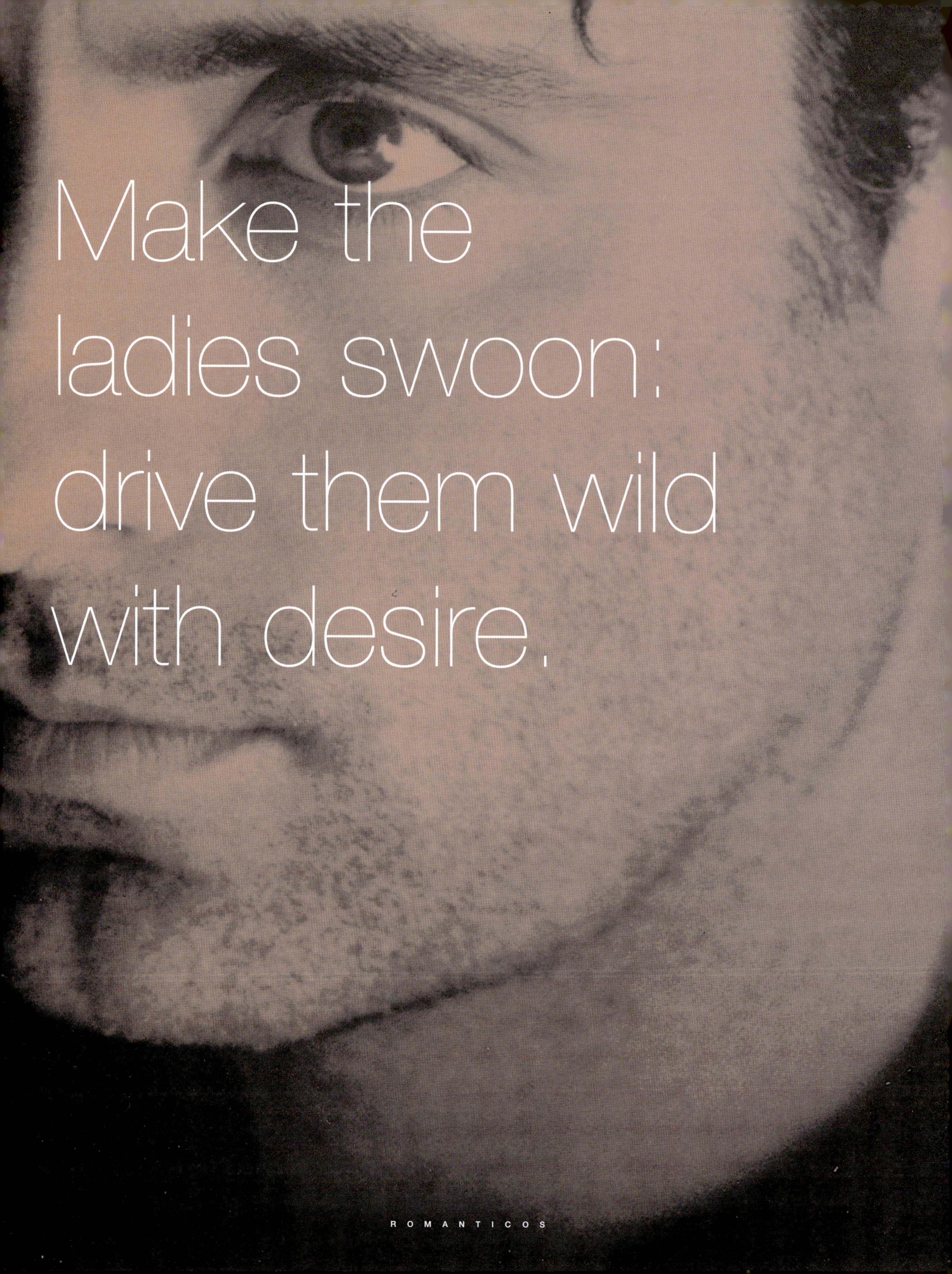

Make the ladies swoon: drive them wild with desire.

America is once again in the throes of a love affair with all things Latin, and it's primarily because of Ricky Martin's explosive performance at the 1999 Grammy Awards. But before him, it was Italian-born, silent-film star Rudolf Valentino who drove the ladies wild with desire. His on-screen magnetism obviously being wasted playing villains, he was recast as the dark, mysterious stranger in *The Four Horsemen of the Apocalypse* and became an instant success, to be forever immortalized as the original "Latin Lover." Looking to cash in on Valentino's success, Hollywood began casting Latin actors in other major roles, like Ramon Navarro, who starred in the 1925 version of *Ben-Hur*. Some non-Hispanic actors adopted Spanish monikers in an attempt to get more work, as was the case with Ricardo Cortez (a.k.a. Jacob Krantz), while there were some Latin actors who opted for Anglo names, like Gilbert Roland (most famous for his swashbuckler roles and as *The Cisco Kid*), but played upon the image of the dashing romantic gentleman. This love affair continued through the '40s, with such gallant figures as Fernando Lamas (father of '80s heartthrob, Lorenzo Lamas); César Romero (later known as The Joker on TV's *Batman*), and José Ferrer (not classically handsome, his appeal relied more in his commanding presence, rich, distinctive voice, and incomparable talent—he won the Academy Award for his portrayal of *Cyrano de Bergerac*).

Latin musicians, too, were lured by Hollywood. "The Songbird of Buenos Aires," Carlos Gardel, who is most famous in his own country as the inventor of the tango-song, proved to cut as romantic a figure on celluloid as he did on vinyl. More recently, his most recognizable hit, *El Día Que Me Quieras*, was given new life in the dance scene in *Scent of a Woman*. Spanish-born, Cuban bandleader Xavier Cugat ignited the screen in several 1940s MGM musicals with his electric performances, leading the way for '50s bandleaders Desí Arnáz, Tito Puente, and Perez Prado, who hit the Top 40 twice with exotic, jazzy instrumentals popularized in the cocktail clubs where society folk mingled in the late '50s and early '60s, emulating Havana's pre-Castro casino high life, a must-stop on the jet-set circuit.

Once World War II xenophobia set root, however, this would be the last fling America would have with any Latin culture on whole, although individual Latin artists would come and go from the public consciousness, and there were some who would sustain a career through several mediums. José Ferrer, César Romero, and Desí Arnáz branched out into television, while Ricardo Montalban gained greater fame later in life with his '70s TV portrayal of the ubiquitous and fastidiously dressed Mr. Roarke on *Fantasy Island*, and Cantinflas, the "Hispanic Charlie Chaplin," for his latter-day appearance in *Around the World in 80 Days*. Still, others passed under the radar unnoticed, like baseball legend Ted Williams, because their ancestry was ambiguous, or because it was less of a defining factor in their field, as with Dominican haute couture designer Oscar de la Renta or Spanish opera singer José Carreras.

Culling from this rich past, and benefiting from the cultural revolution of the late '60s and early '70s, new stars like hip comedian and heartthrob Freddie Prinze, crooner Julio Iglesias, gentleman-statesman-musician-actor Ruben Blades, and dedicated family man and earnest leading man Andy García started coming into their own in the '70s and '80s. And with the demographic composition of the United States shifting toward a larger Hispanic makeup in the '90s came more of a demand for representation, more of an audience for such universally appreciable and smoldering hot talents as the actors Antonio Banderas and Benjamin Bratt as well as musicians Maxwell and Marc Anthony (another singing-acting multiple threat). With this trend continuing, perhaps someday these ethnic distinctions won't even be made.

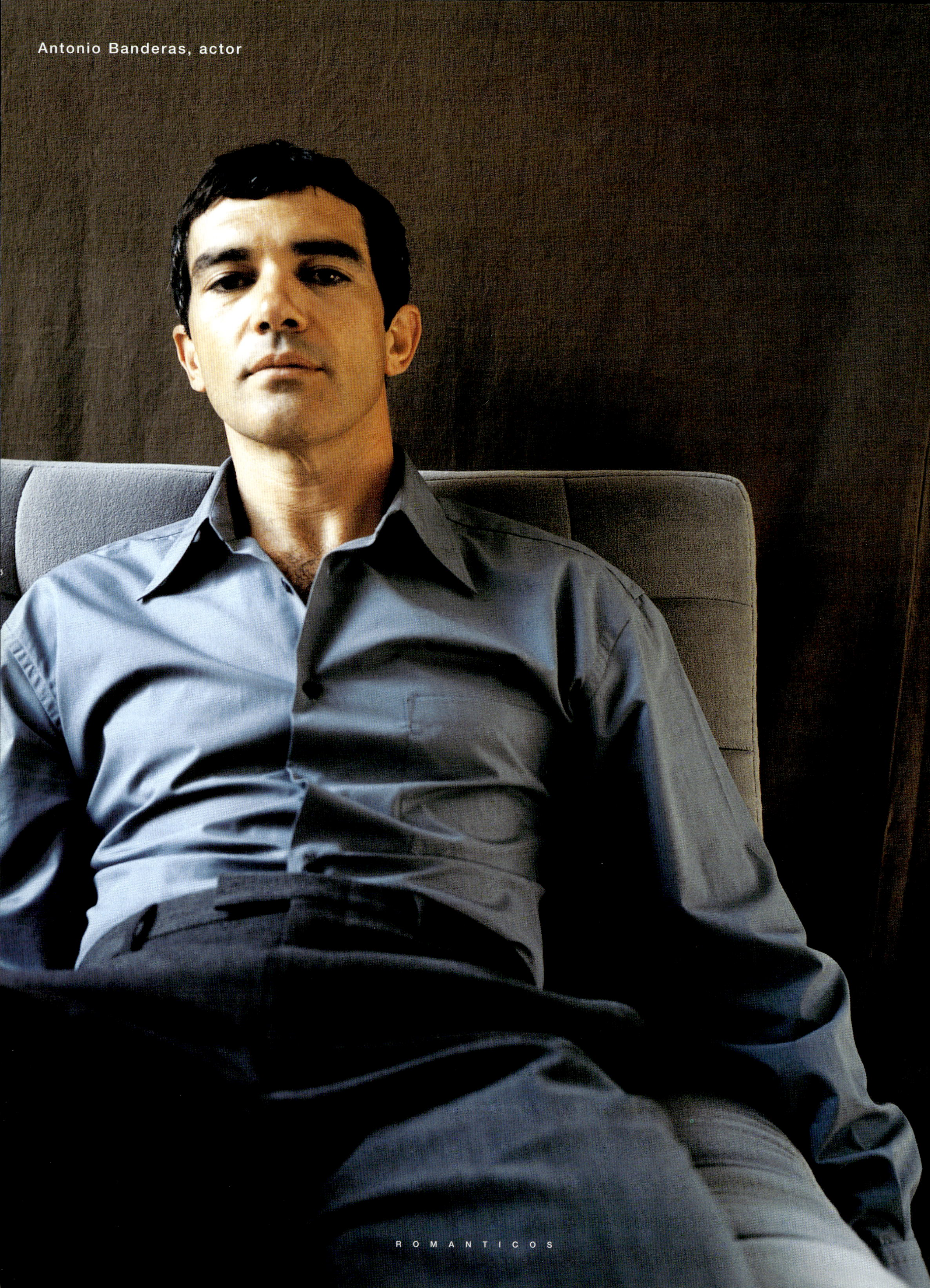

Antonio Banderas, actor

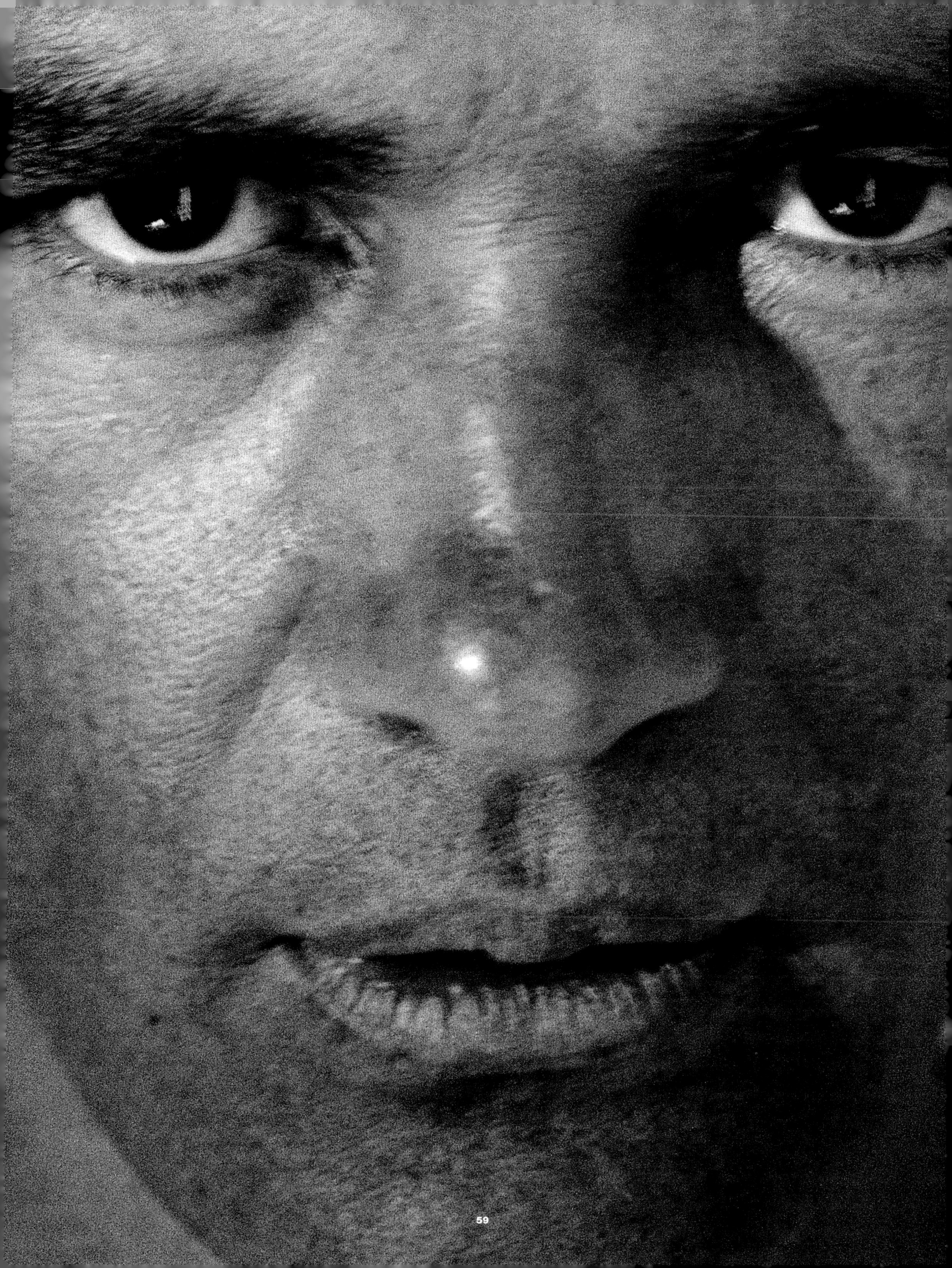

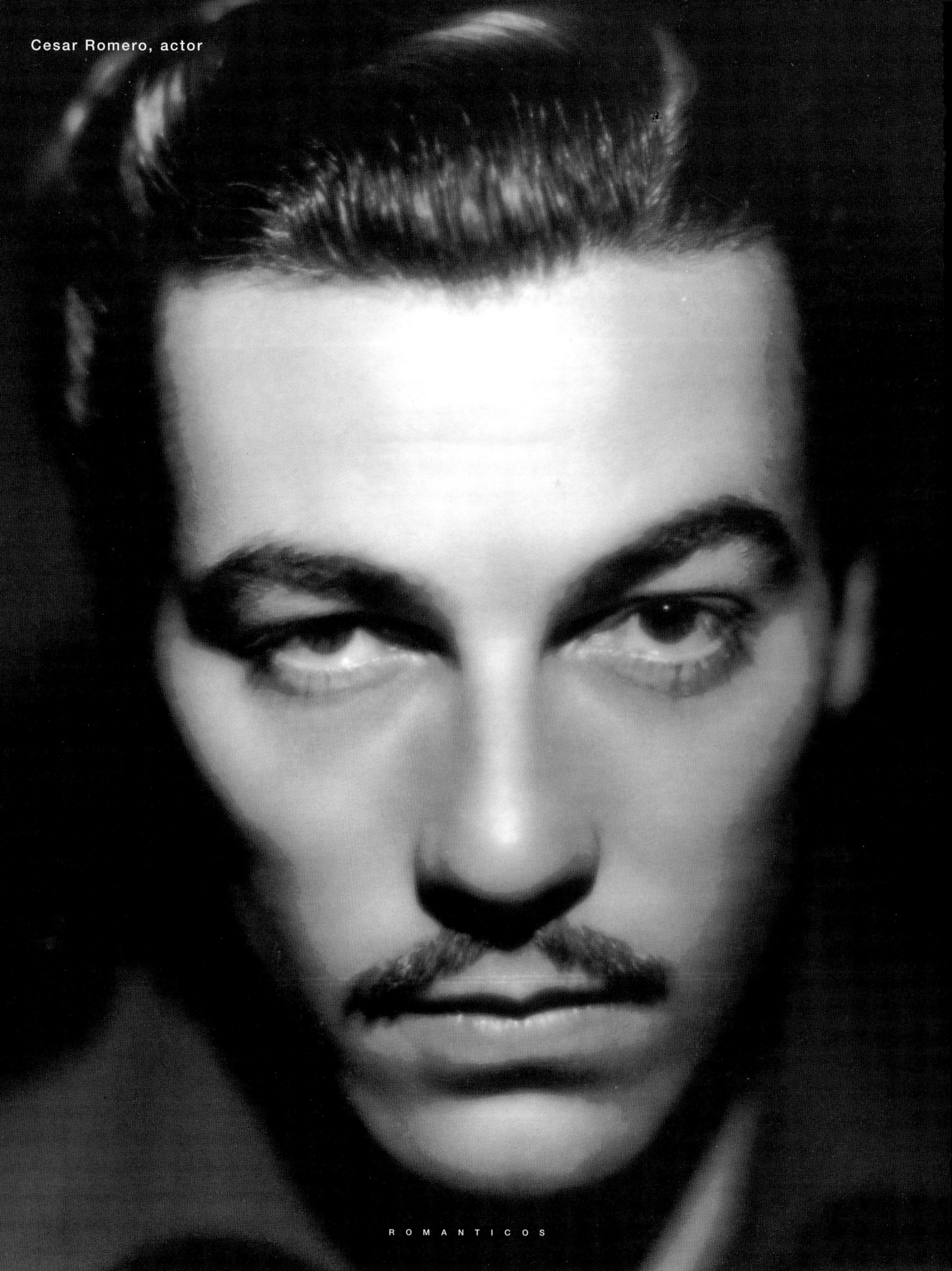
Cesar Romero, actor

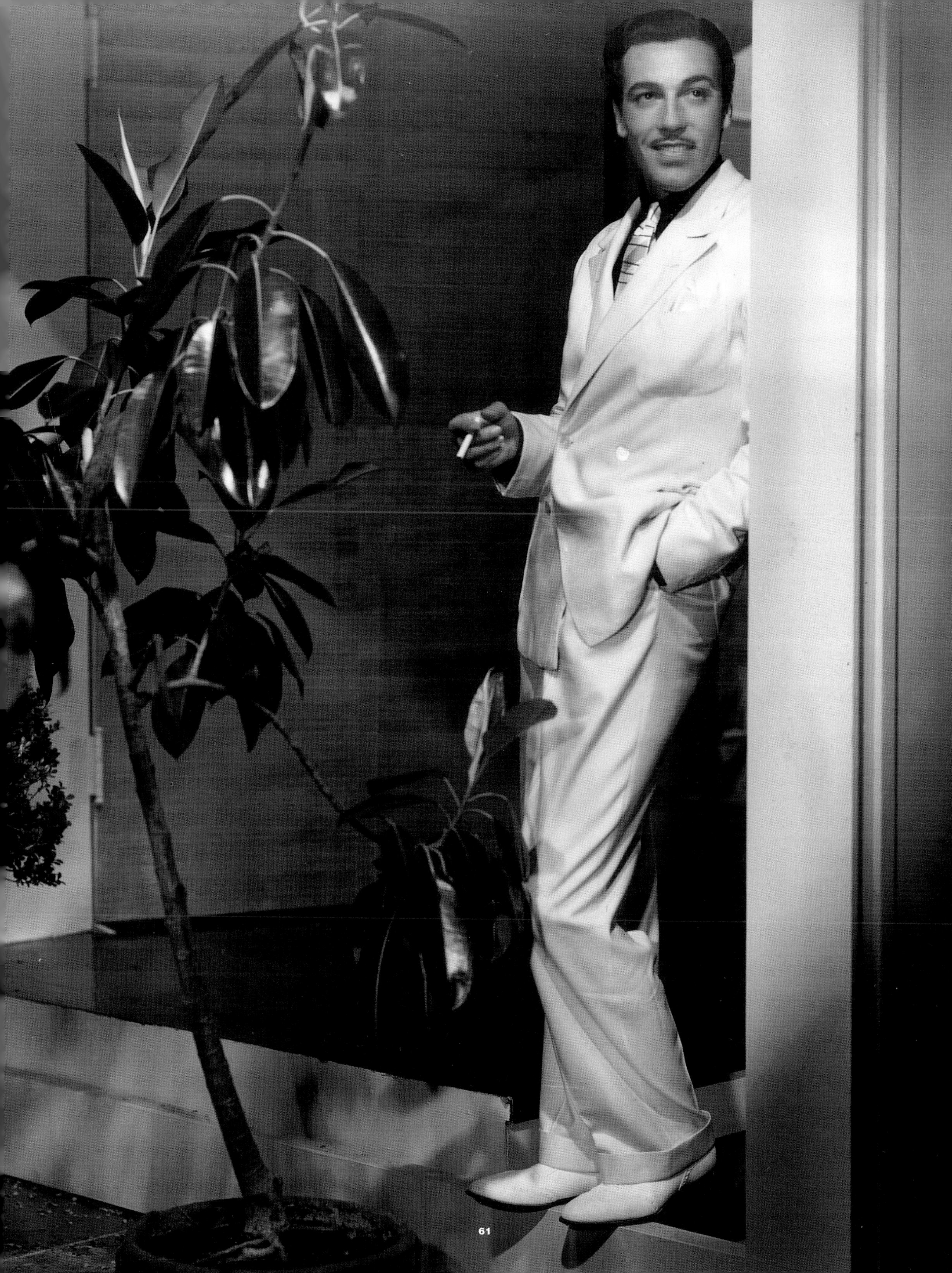

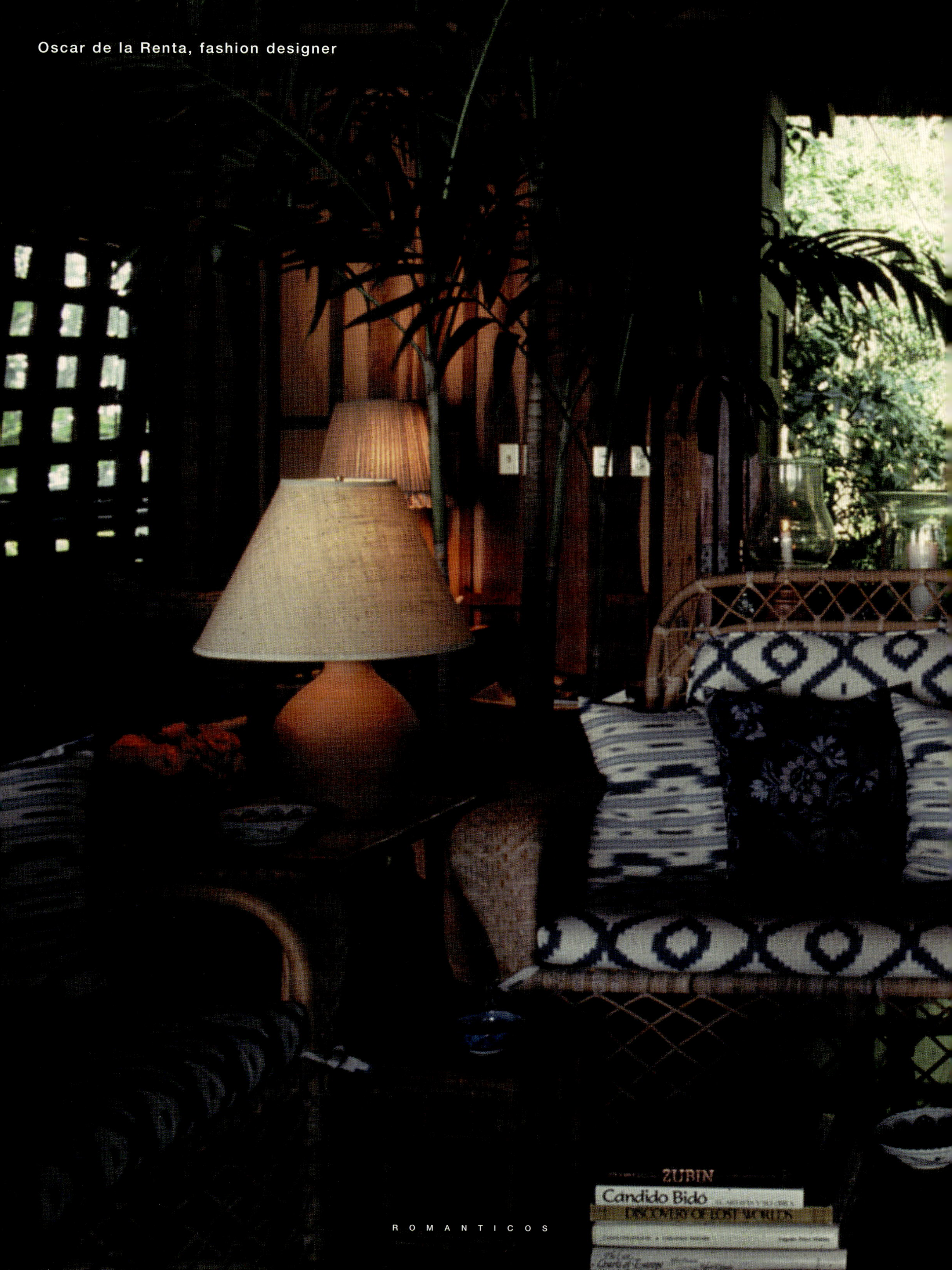

Oscar de la Renta, fashion designer

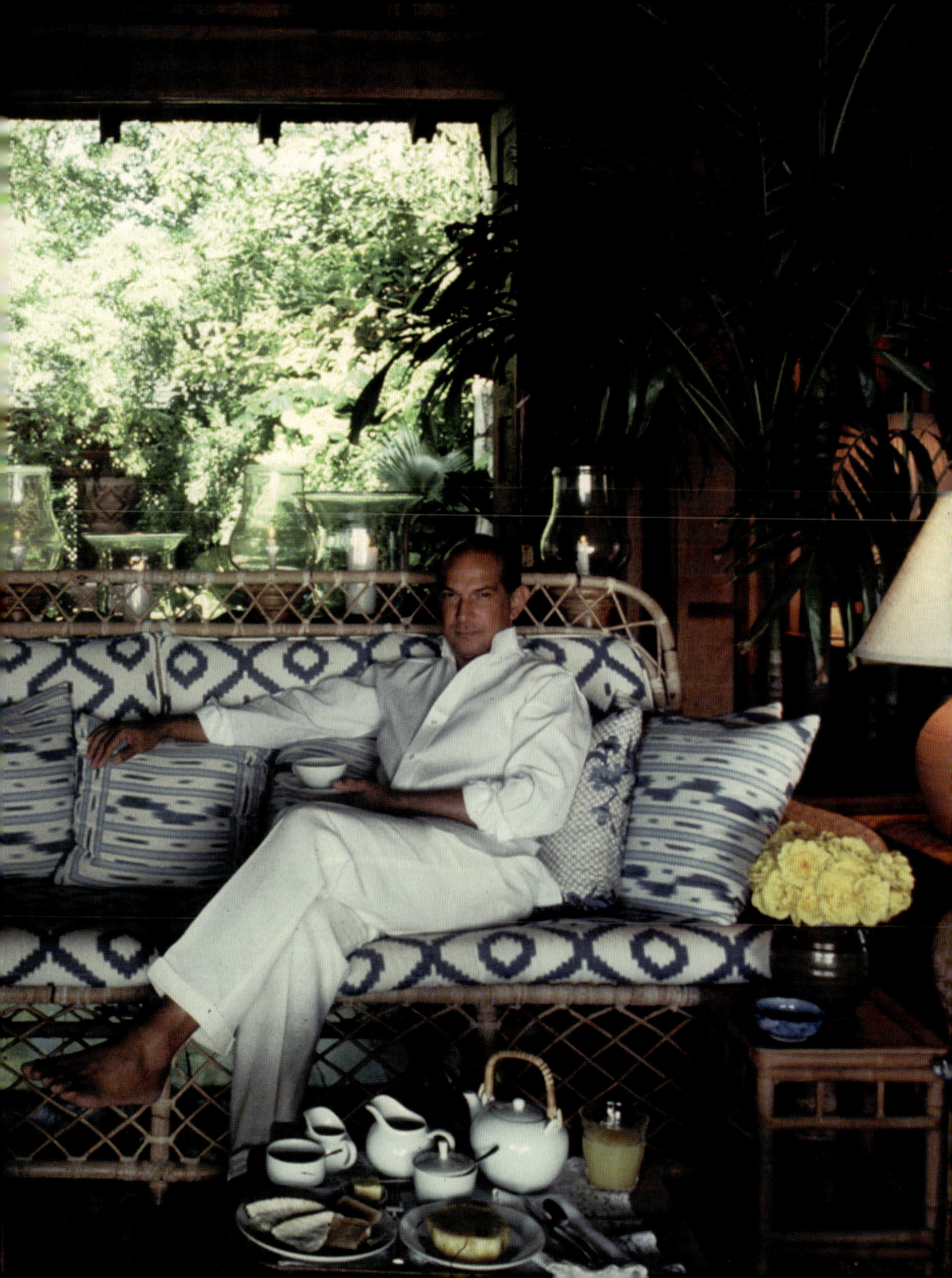

Ruben Toledo, artist

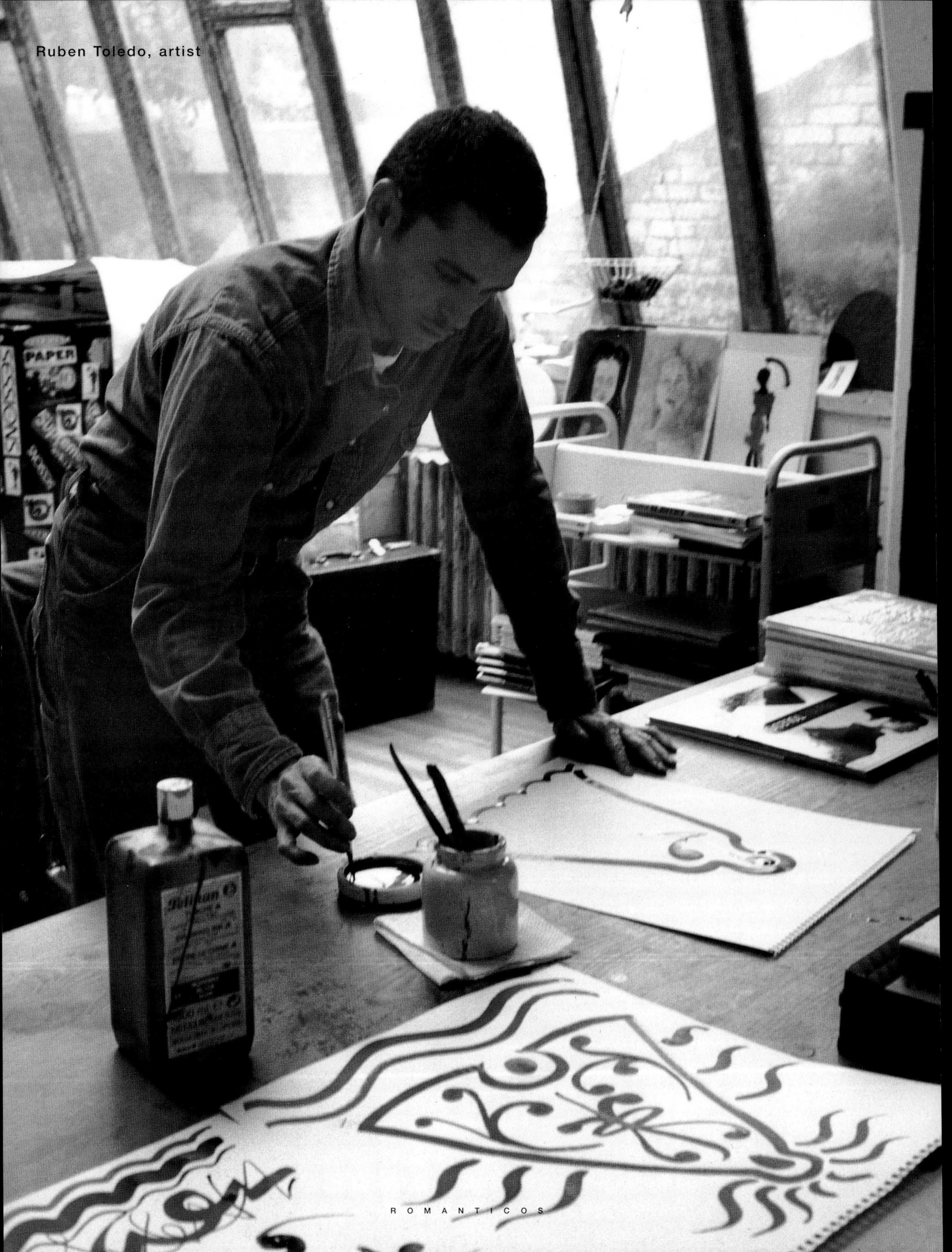

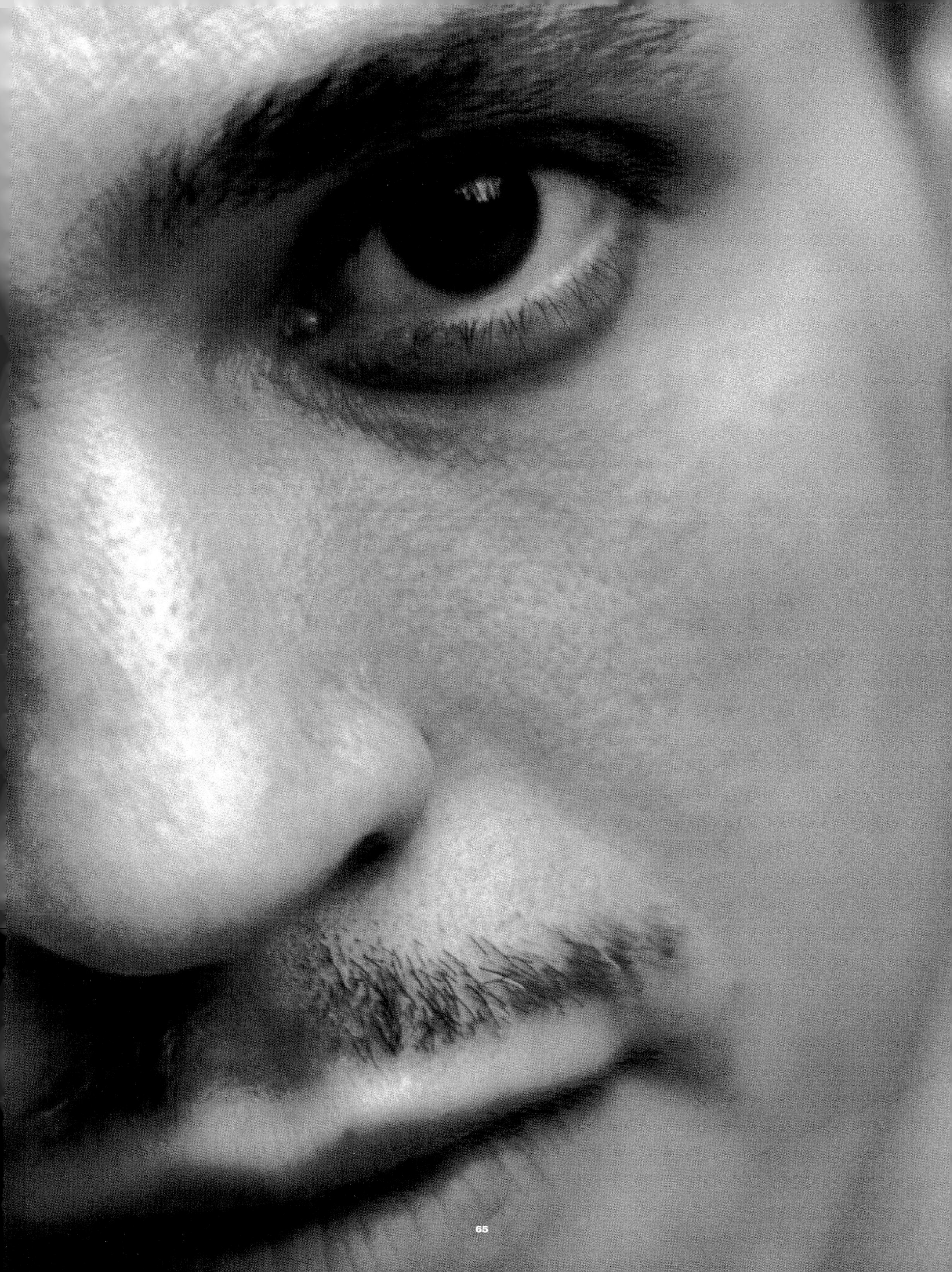

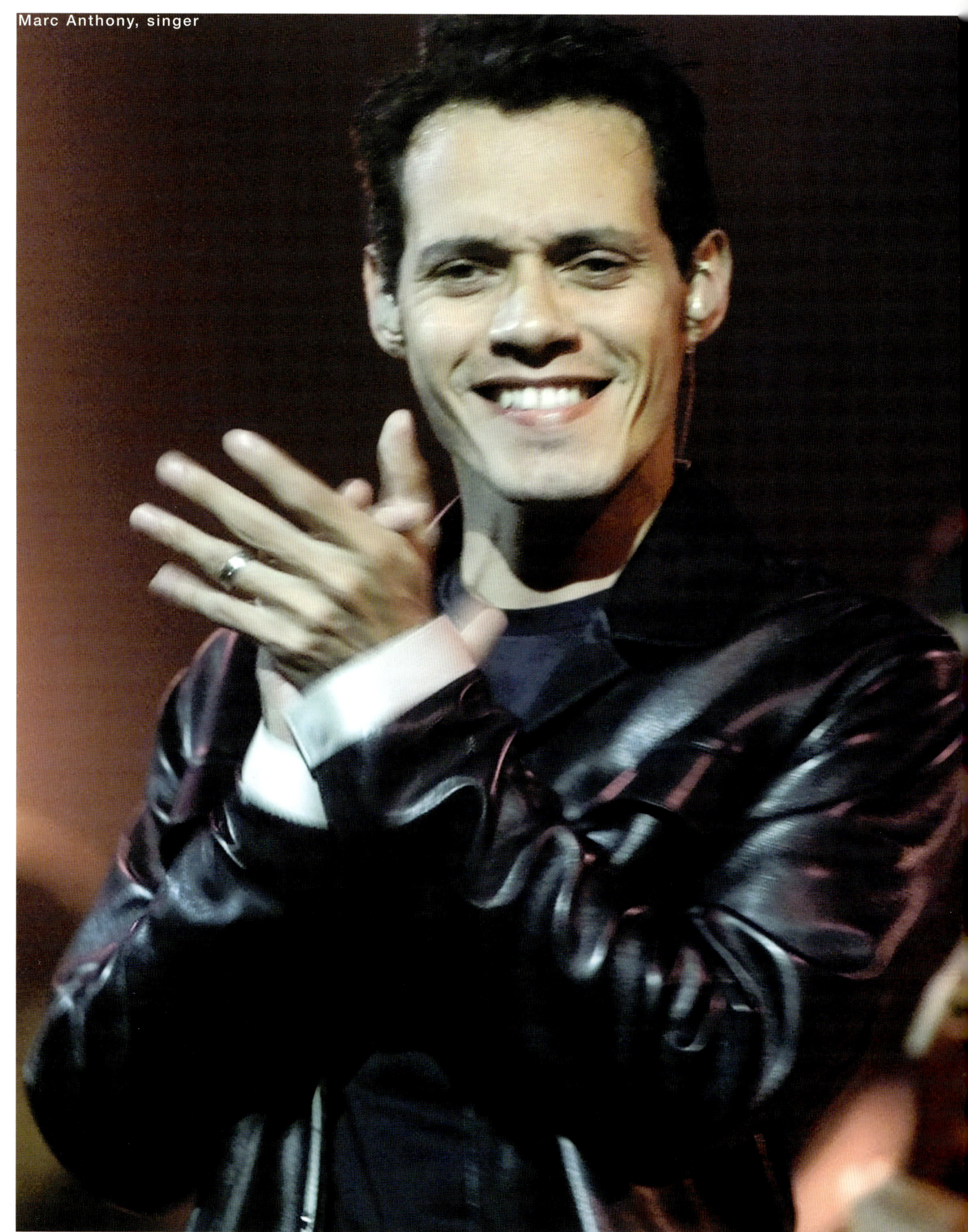

Marc Anthony, singer

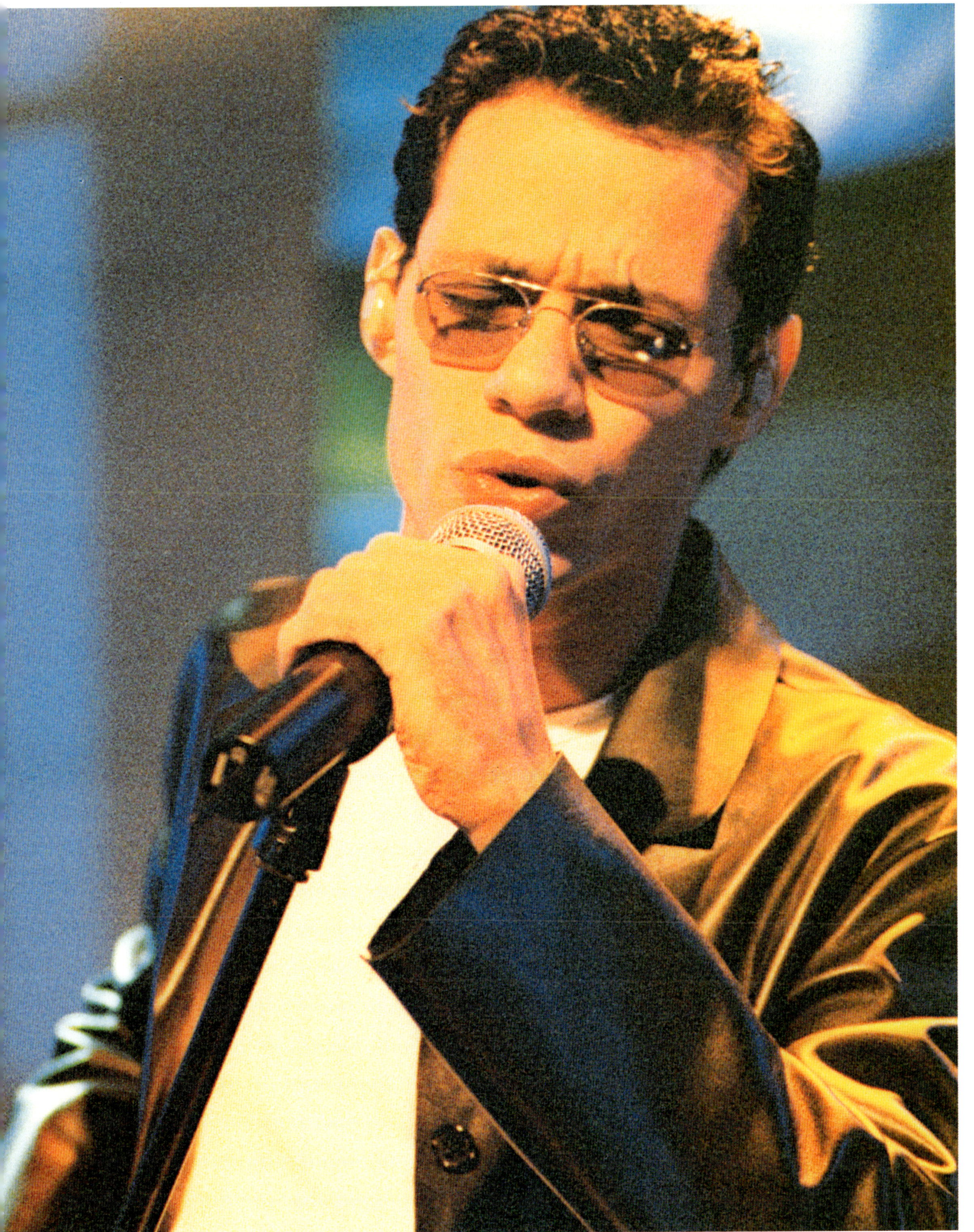

Jon Secada, singer

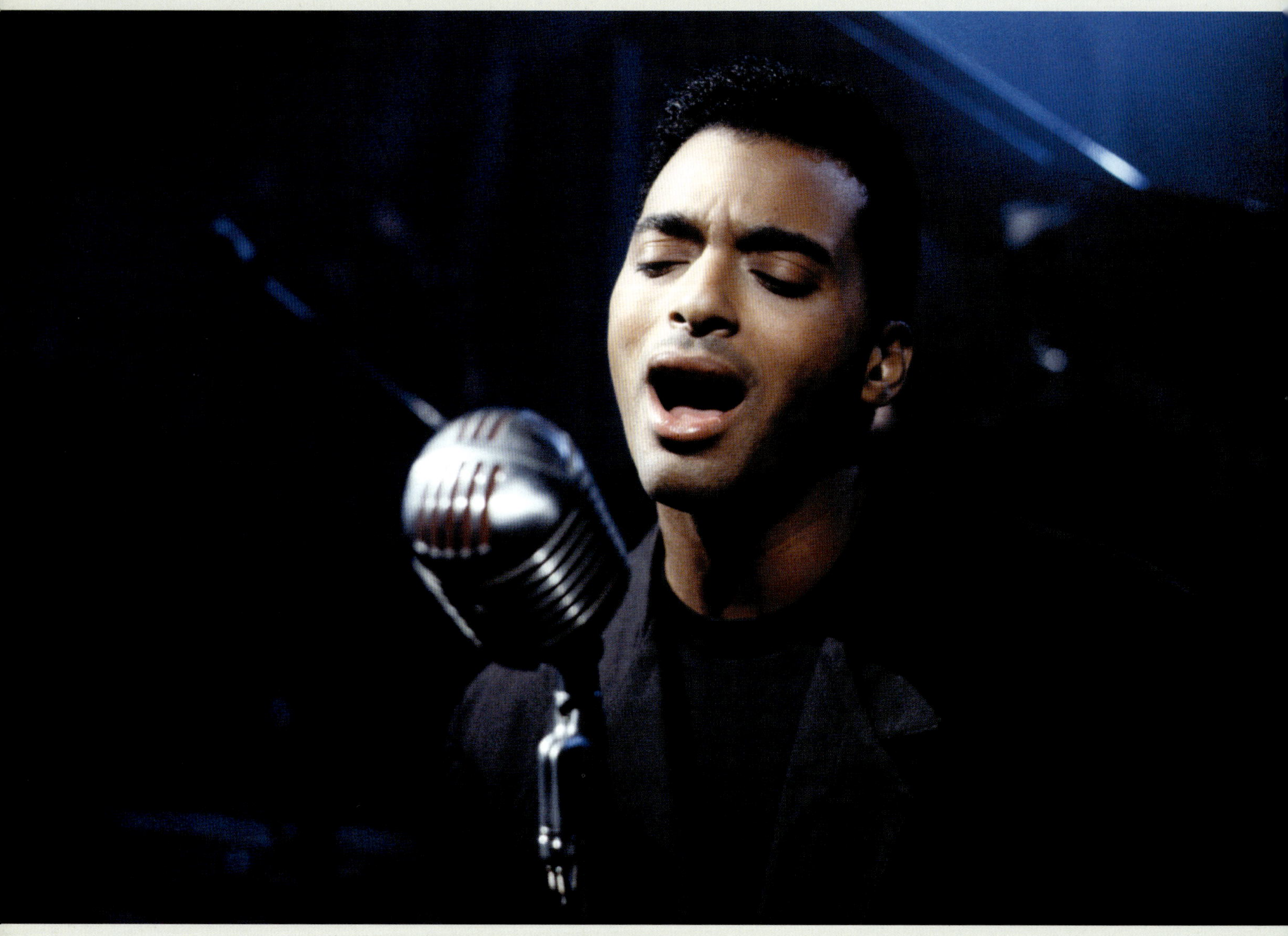

Tito Puente, musician

Rudolph Valentino, actor

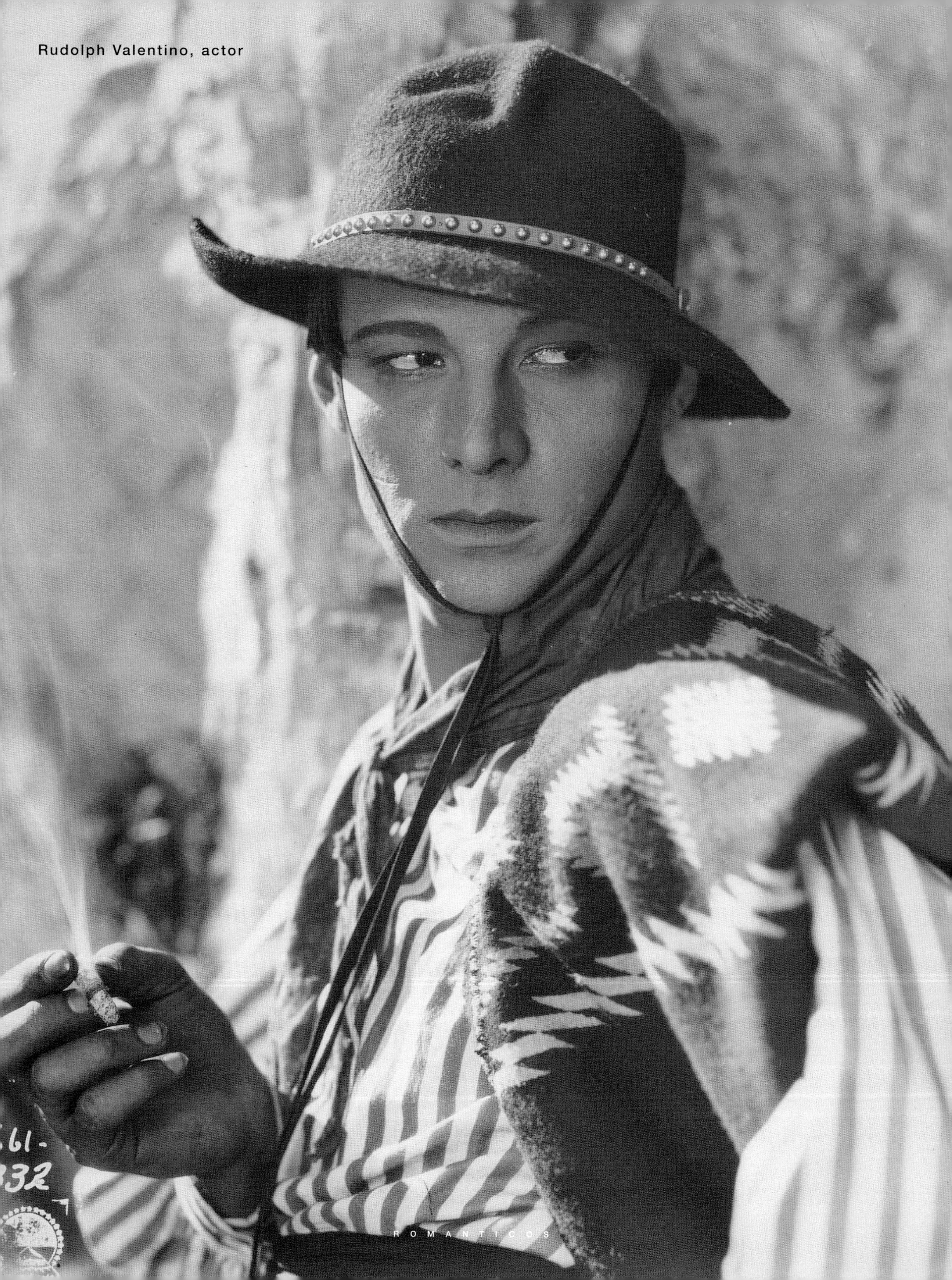

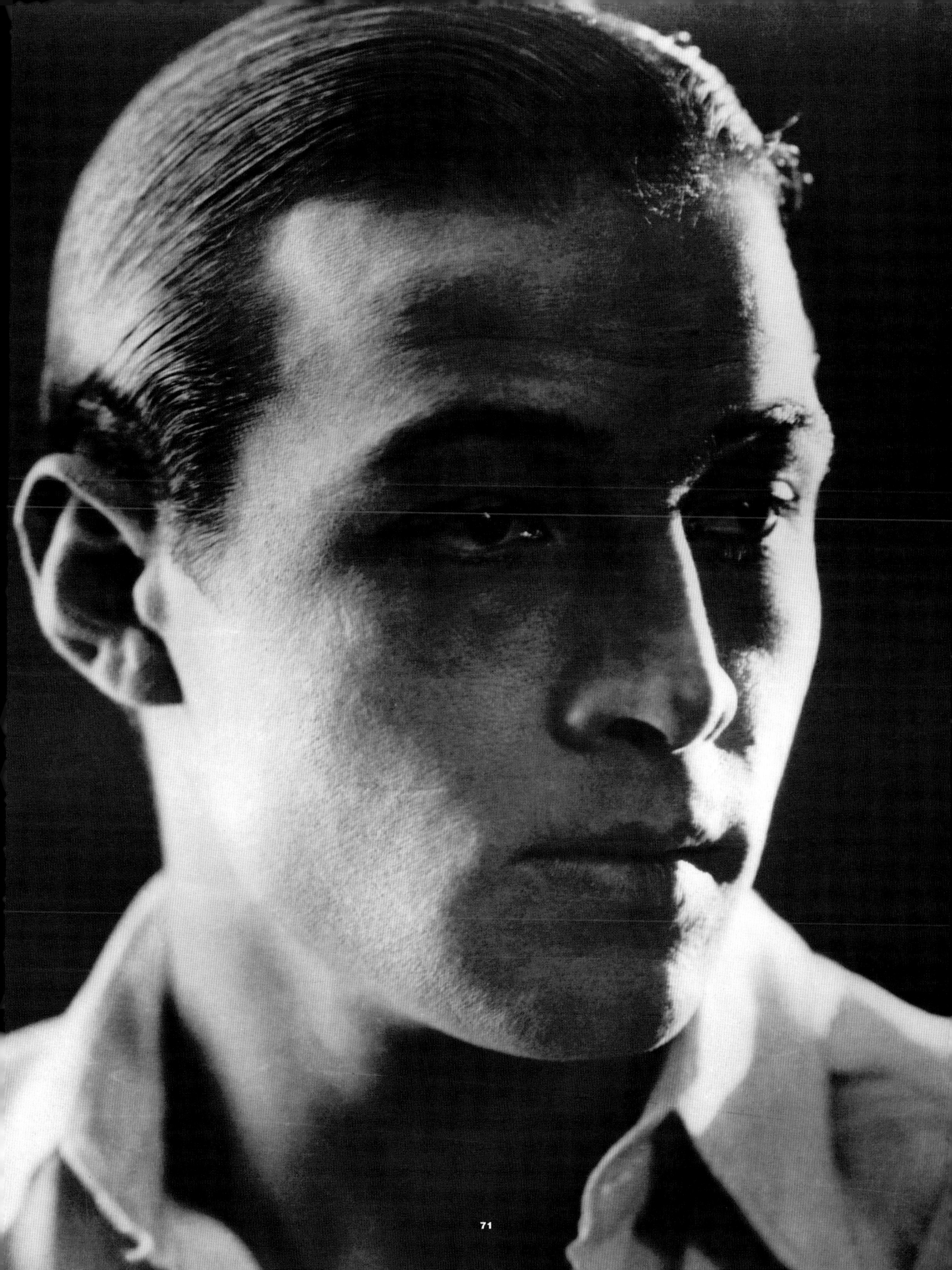

Oscar de la Hoya, boxer

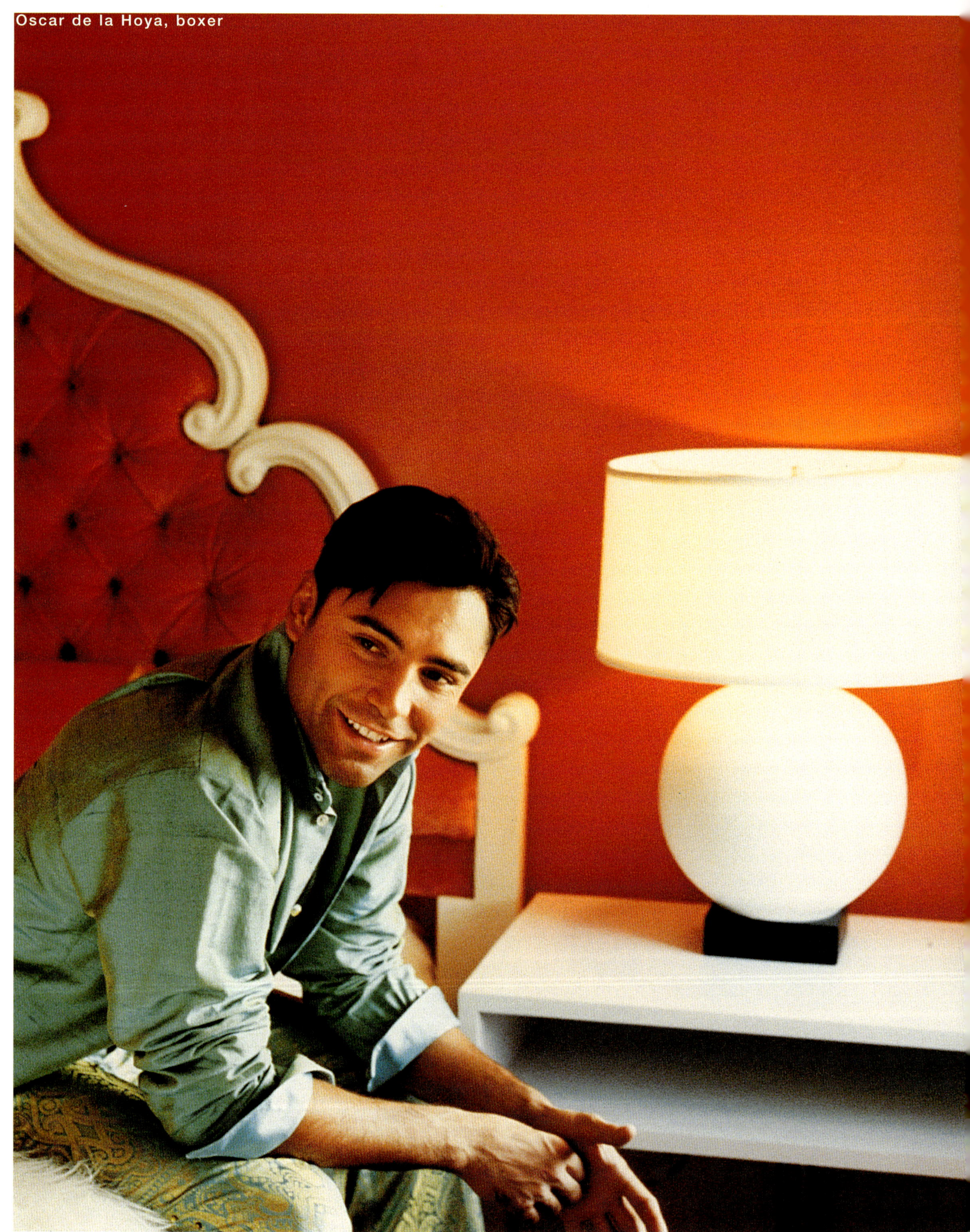

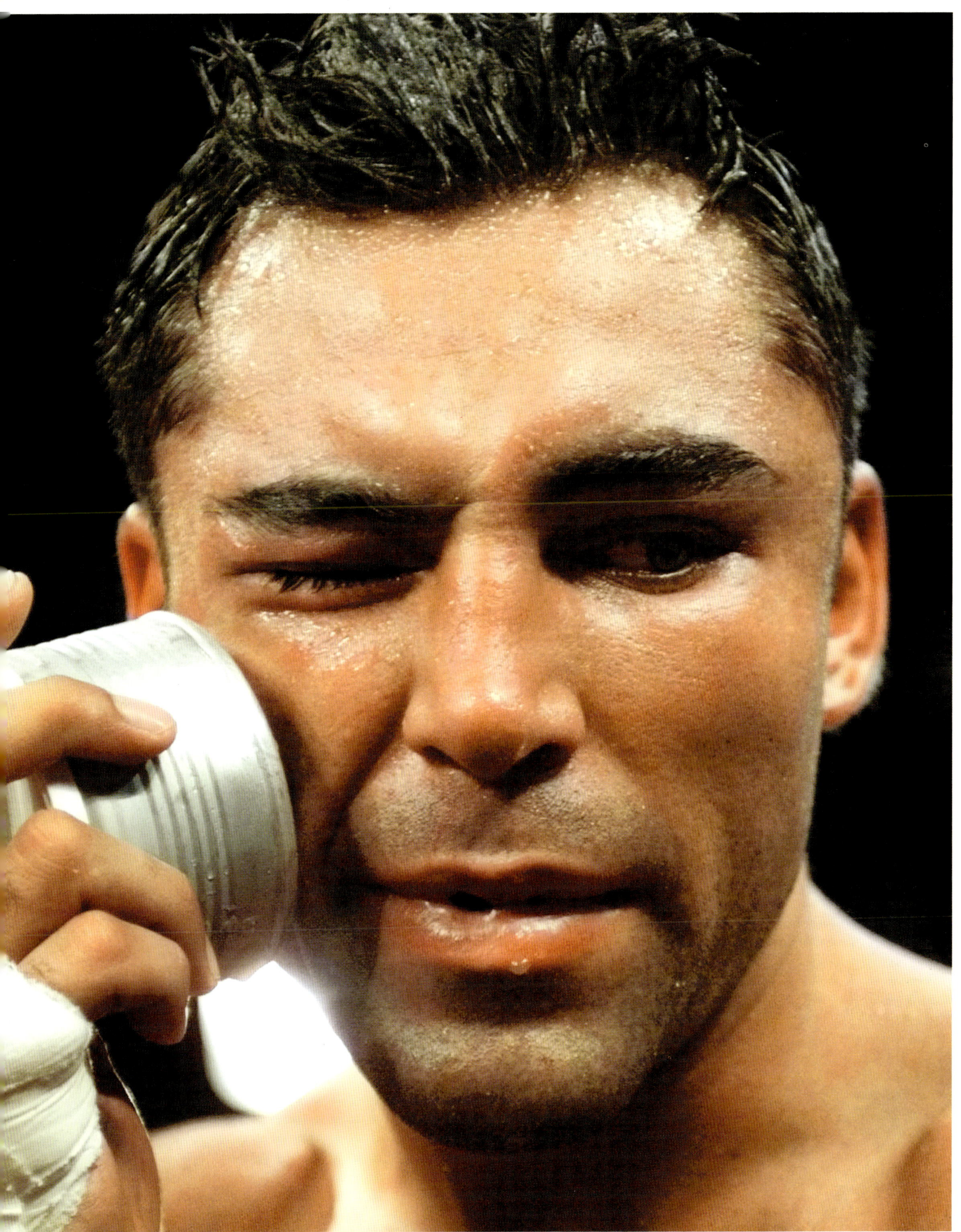

Esai Morales, actor

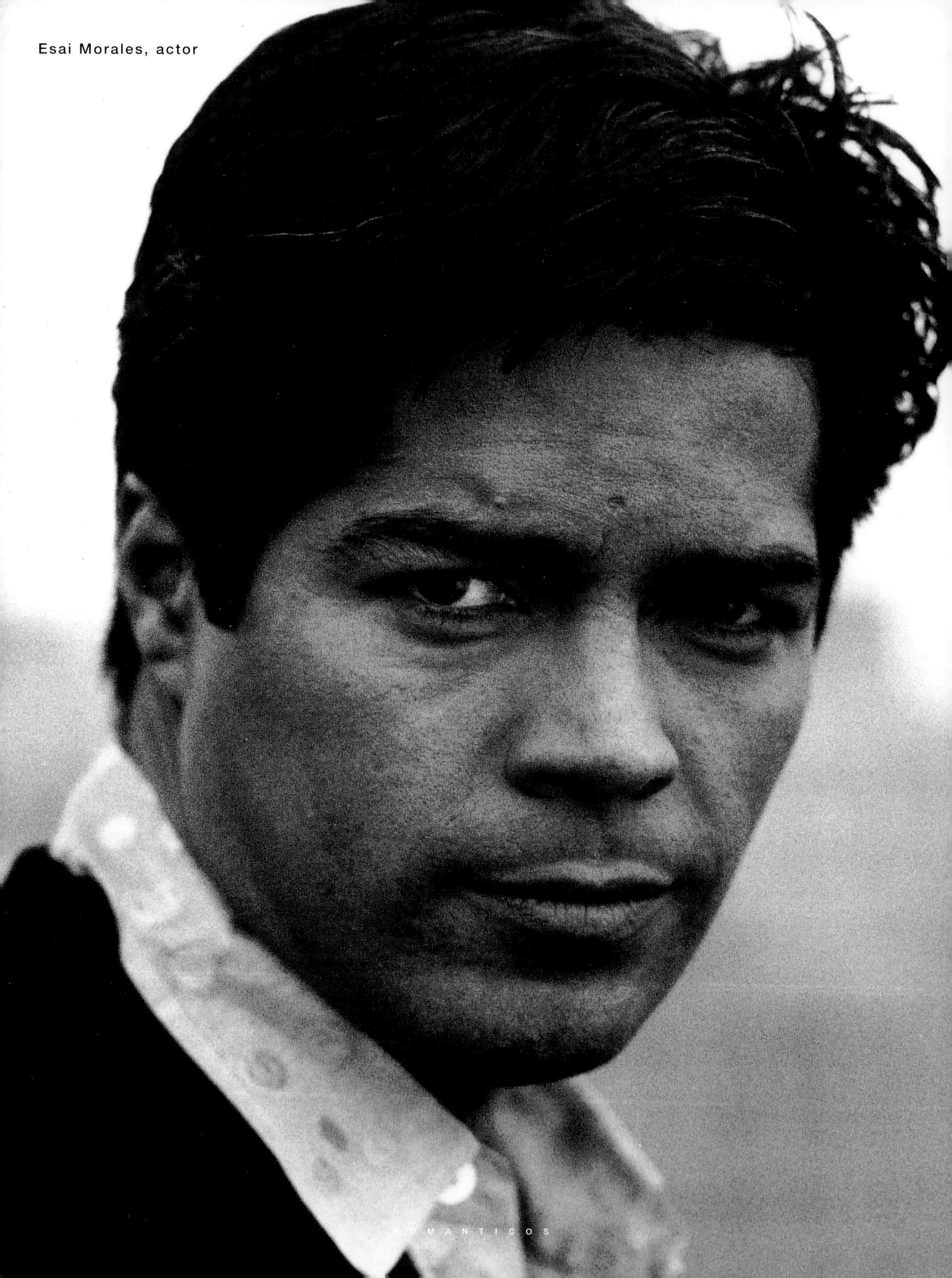

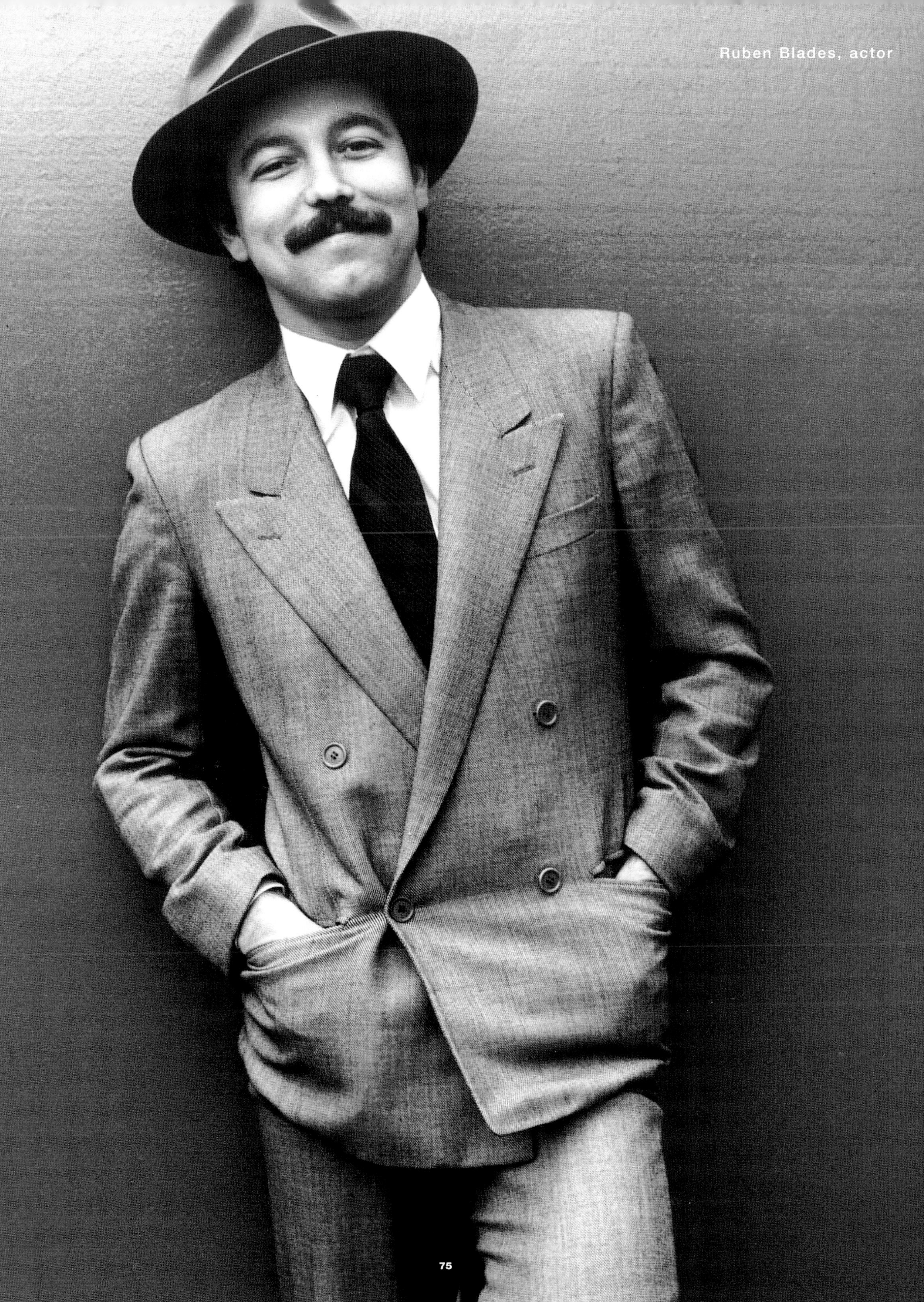

Ruben Blades, actor

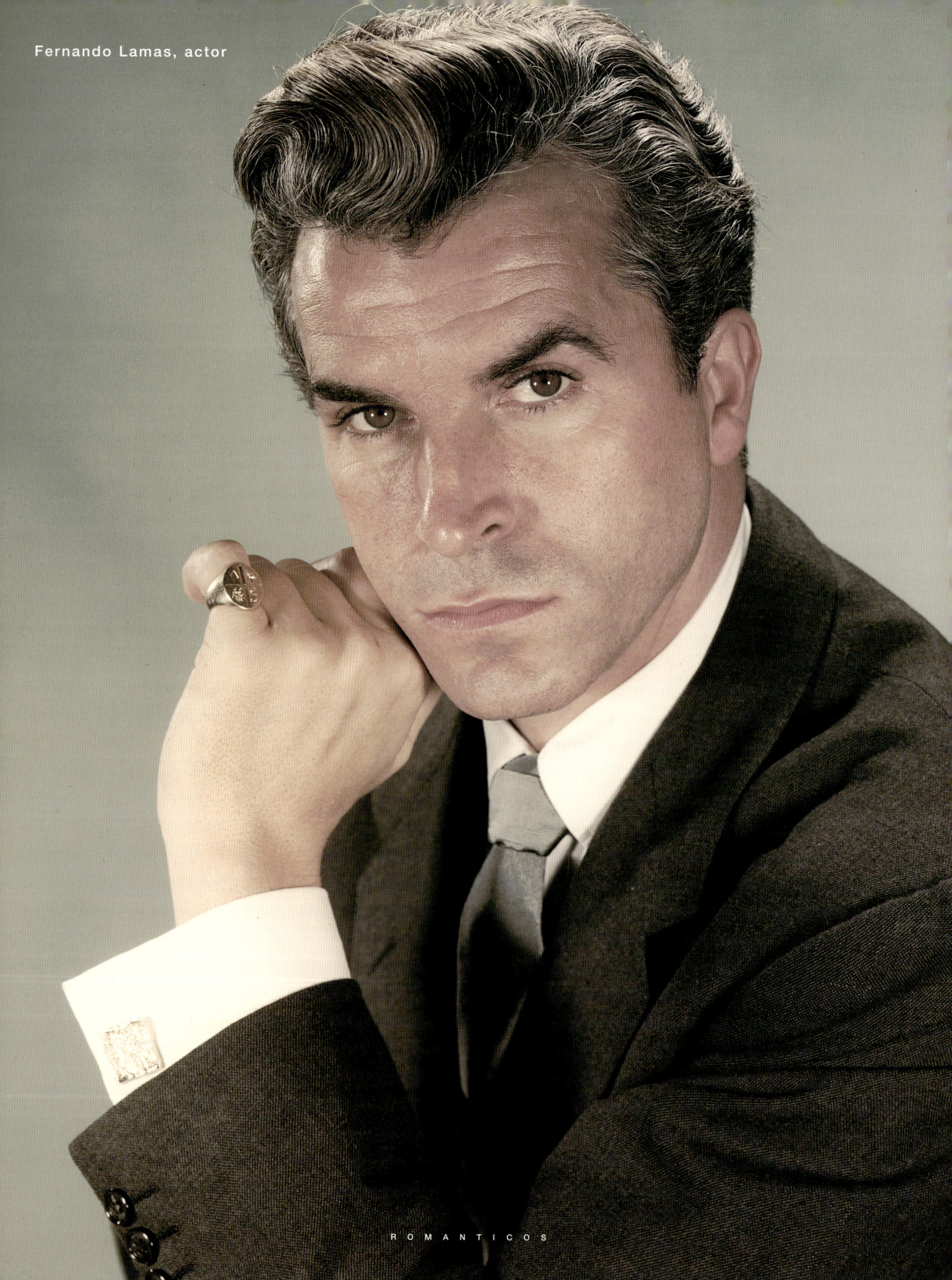
Fernando Lamas, actor

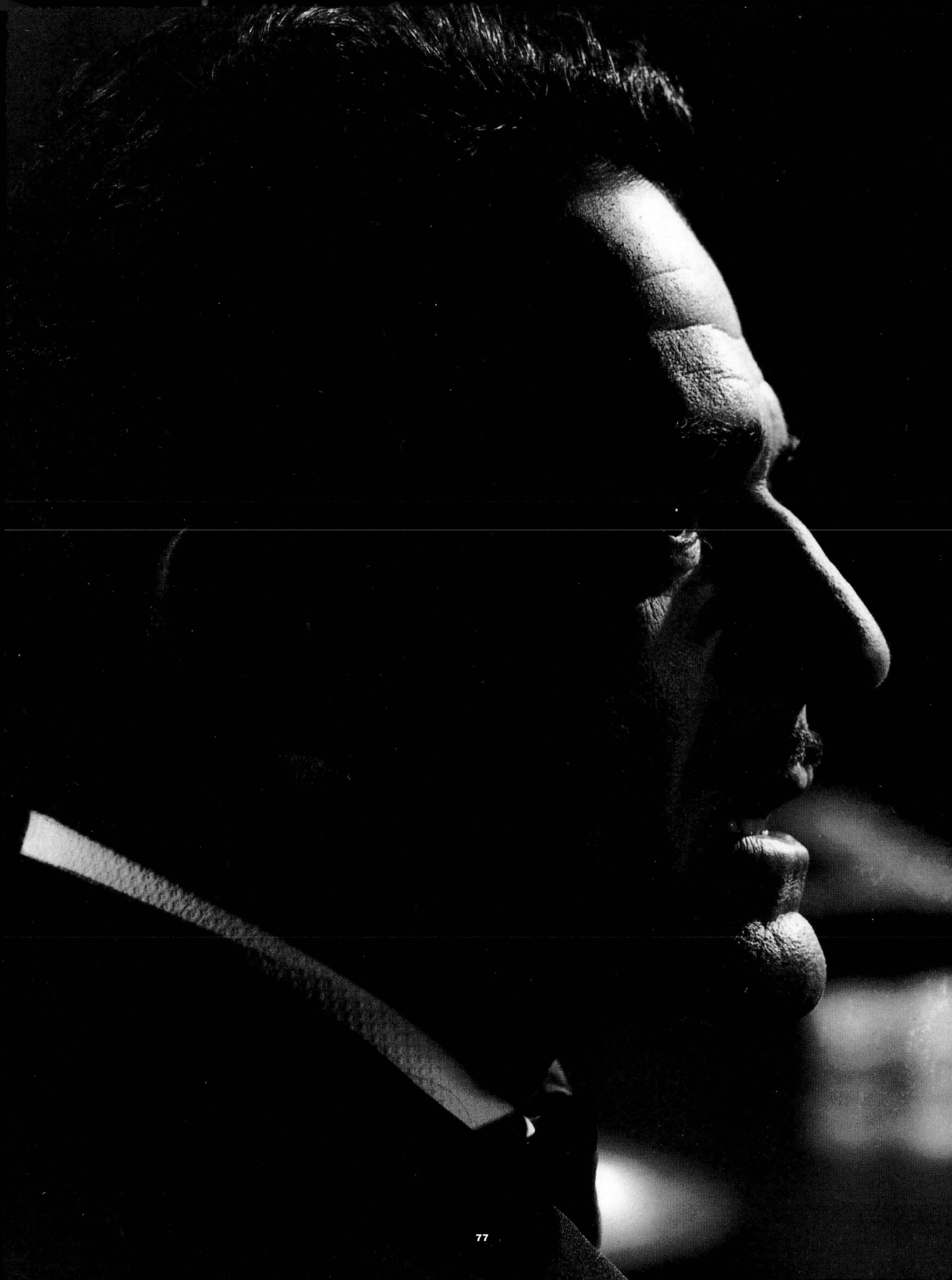

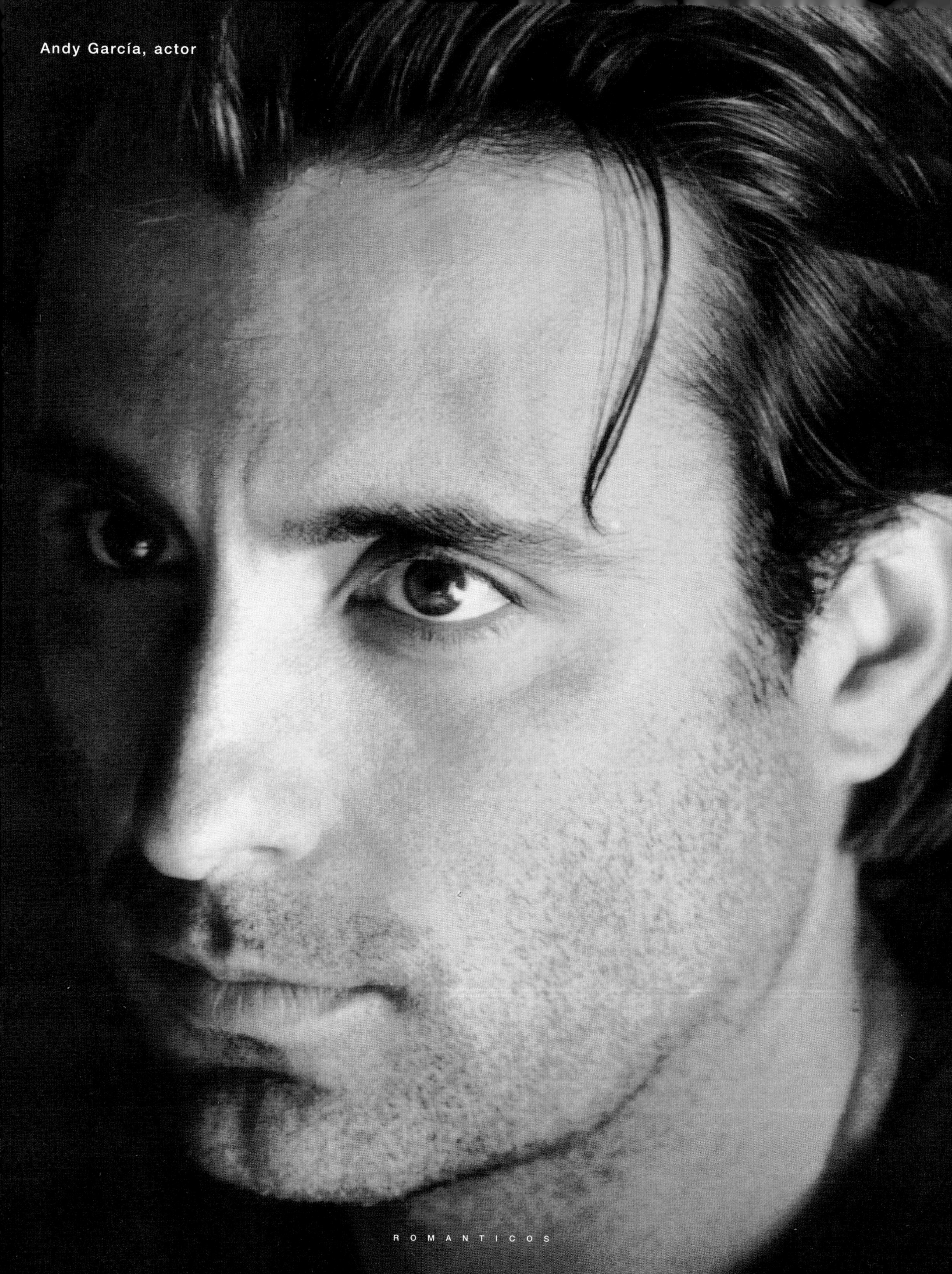
Andy García, actor

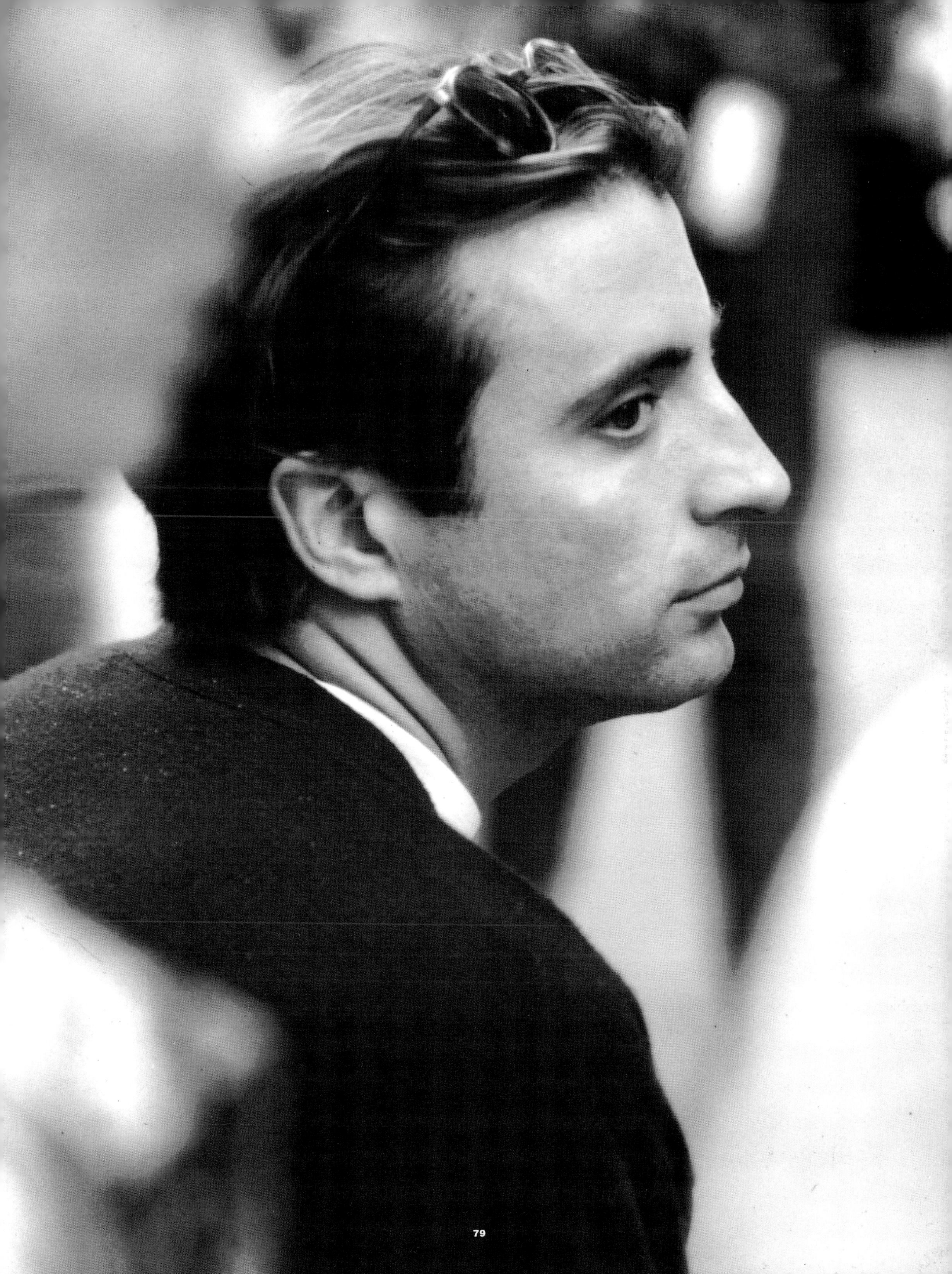

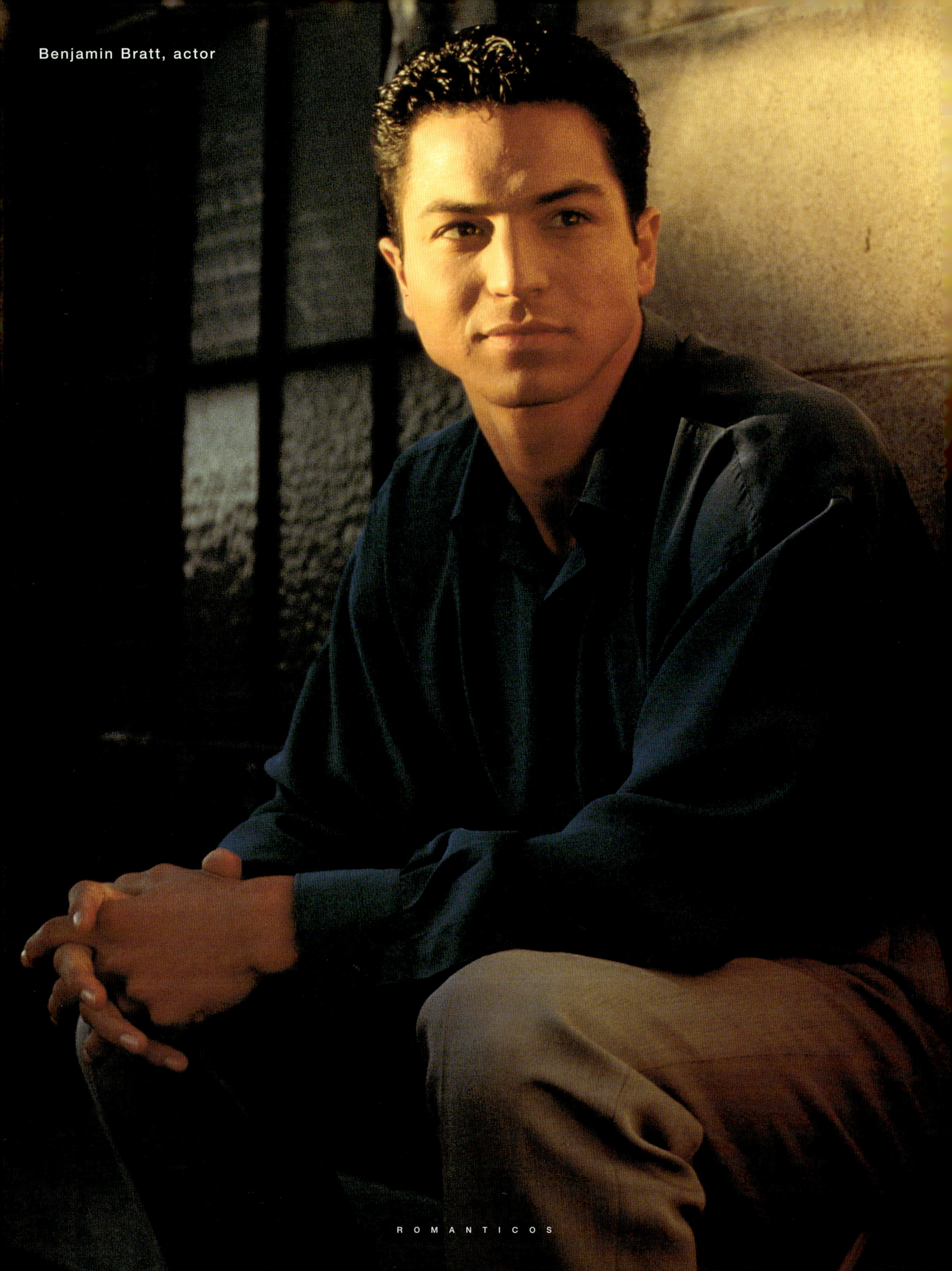
Benjamin Bratt, actor

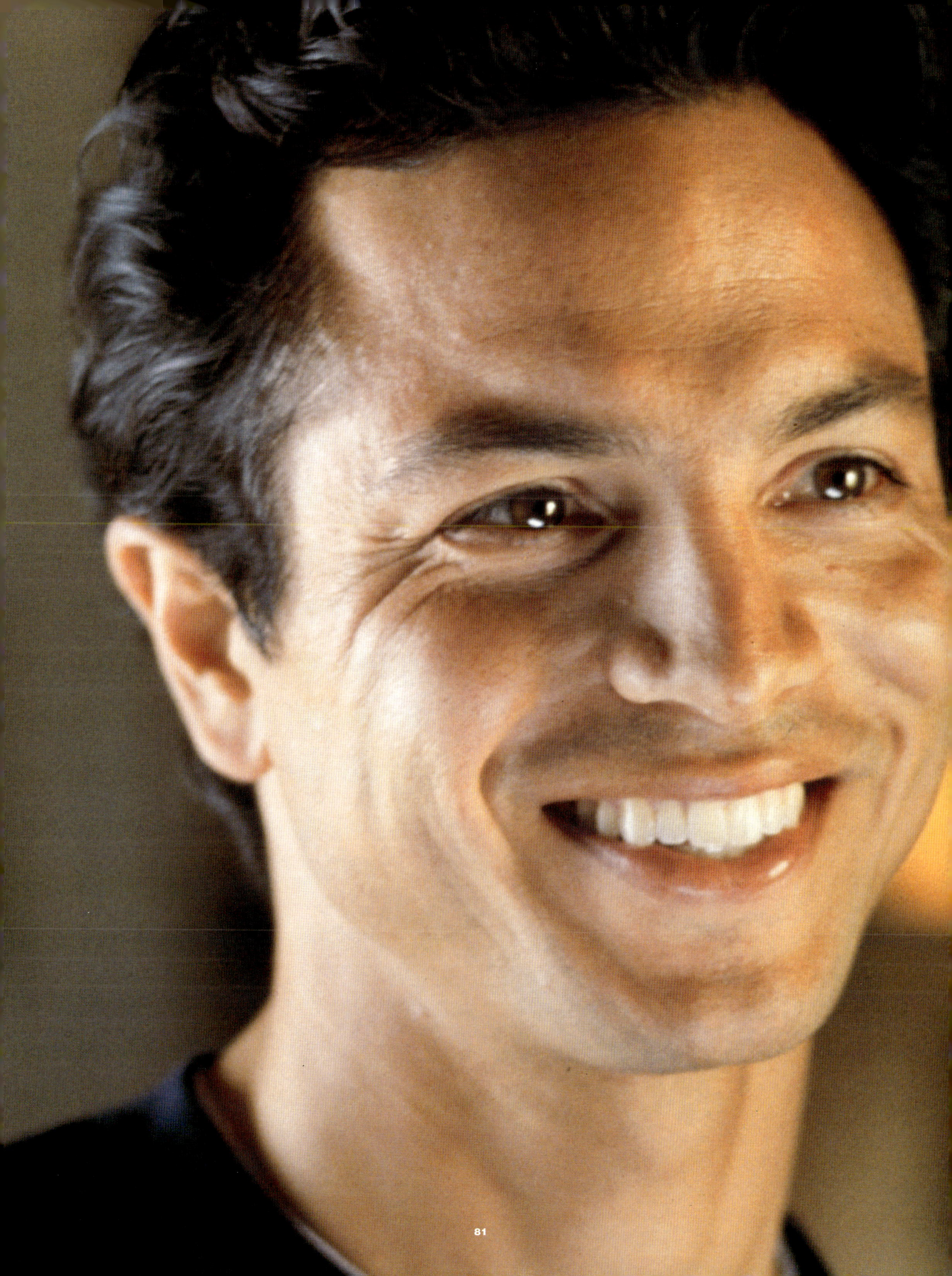

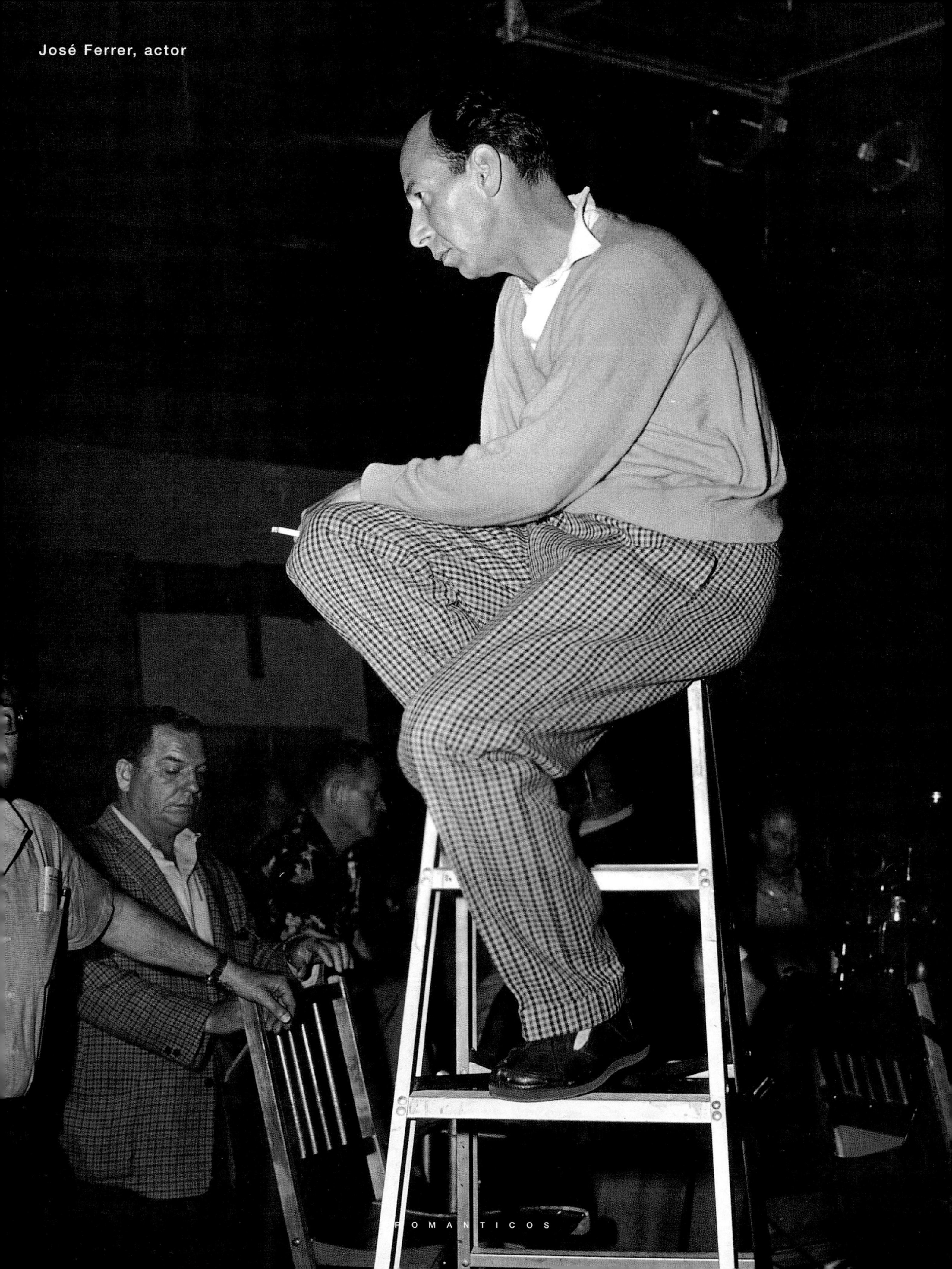
José Ferrer, actor

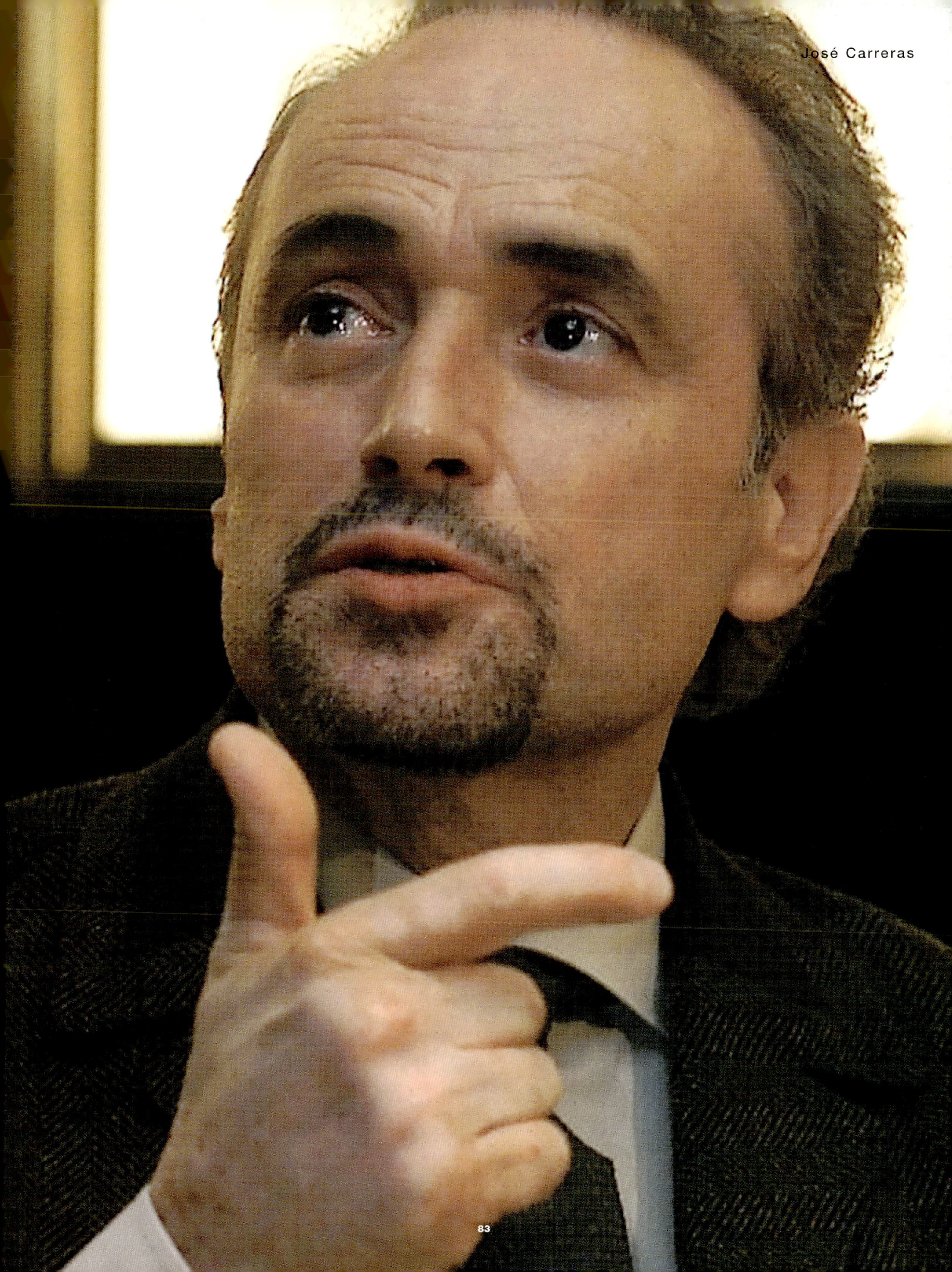

Ricardo Montalban, actor

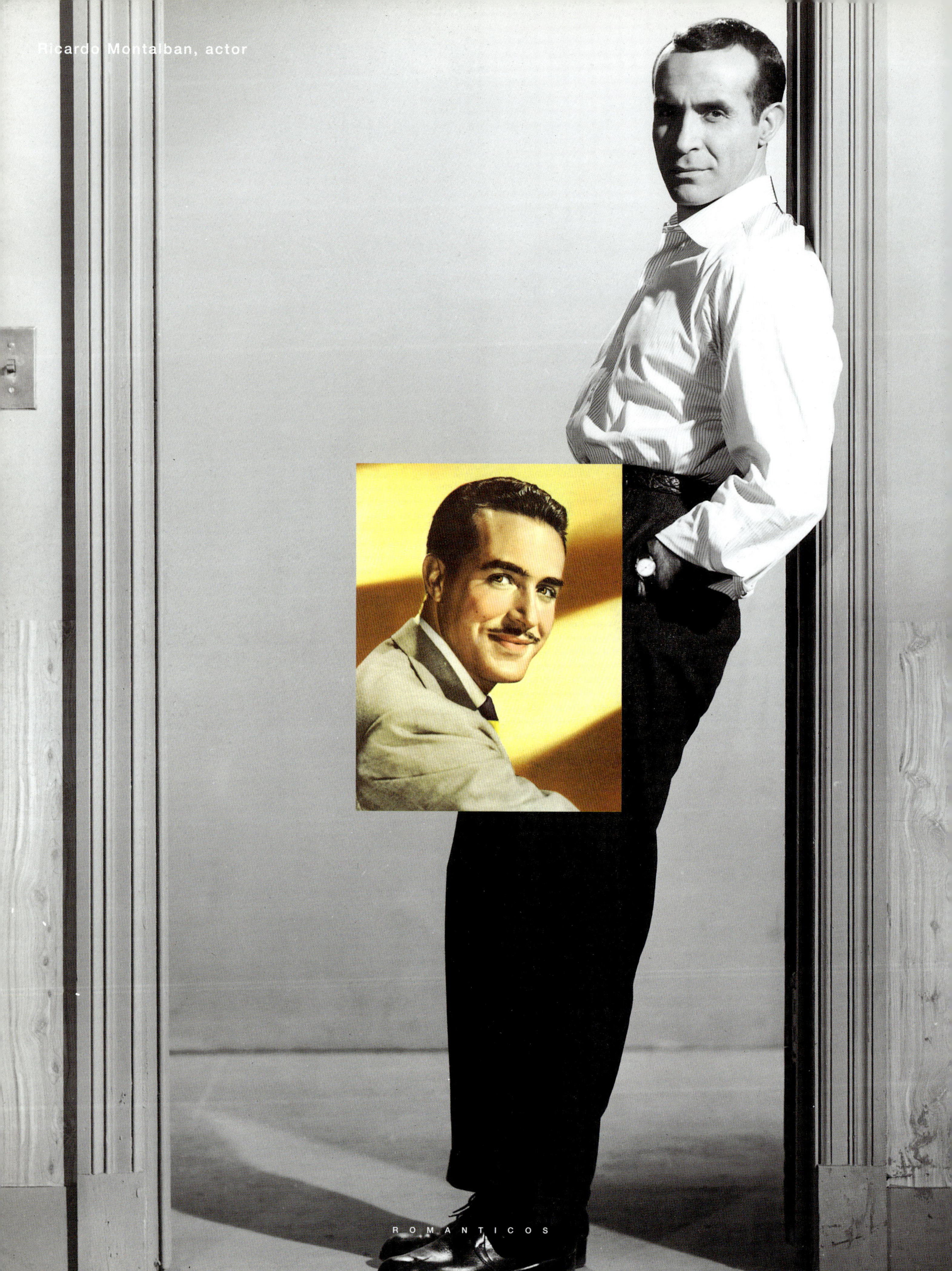

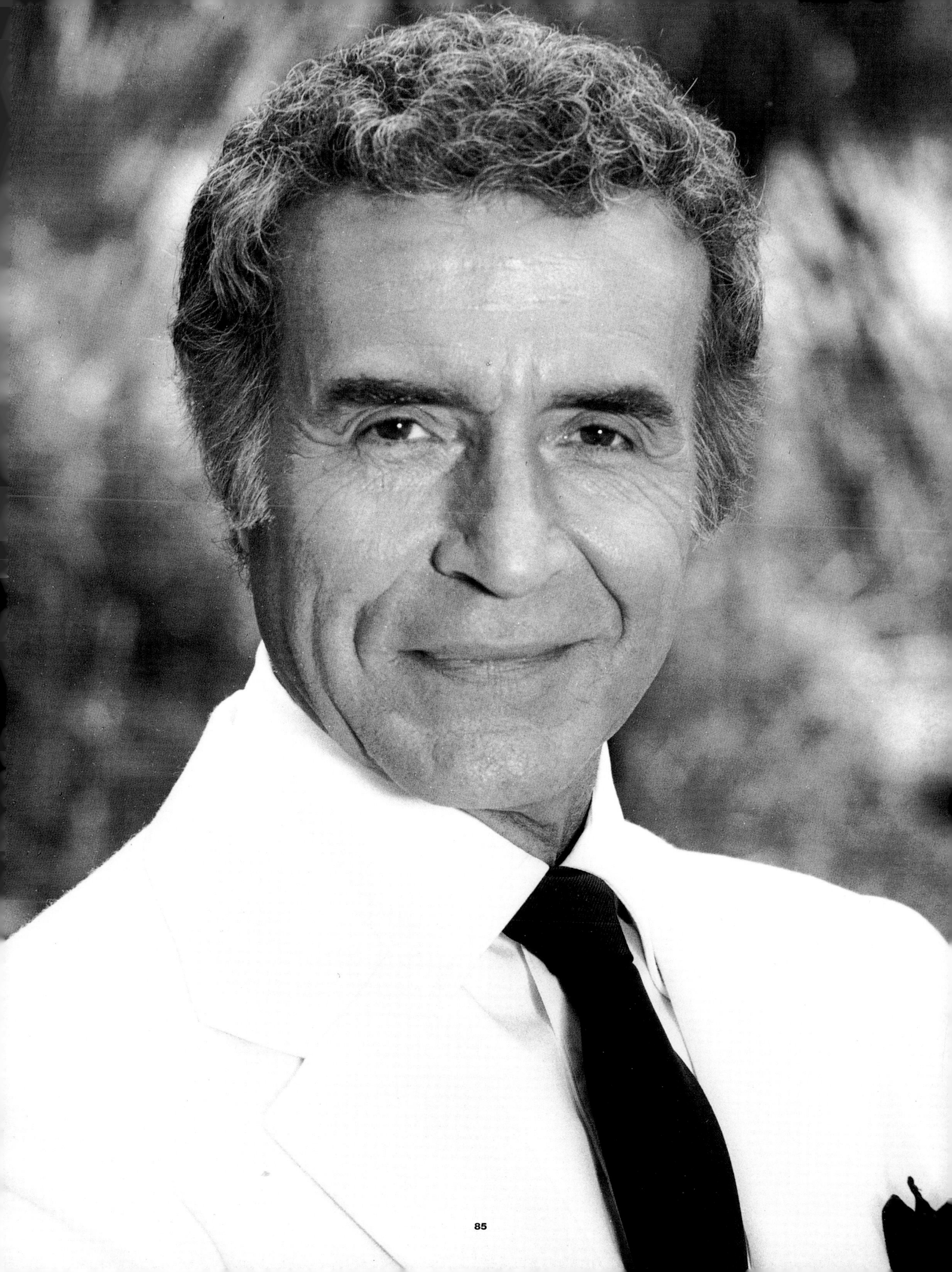

Desí Arnáz, actor

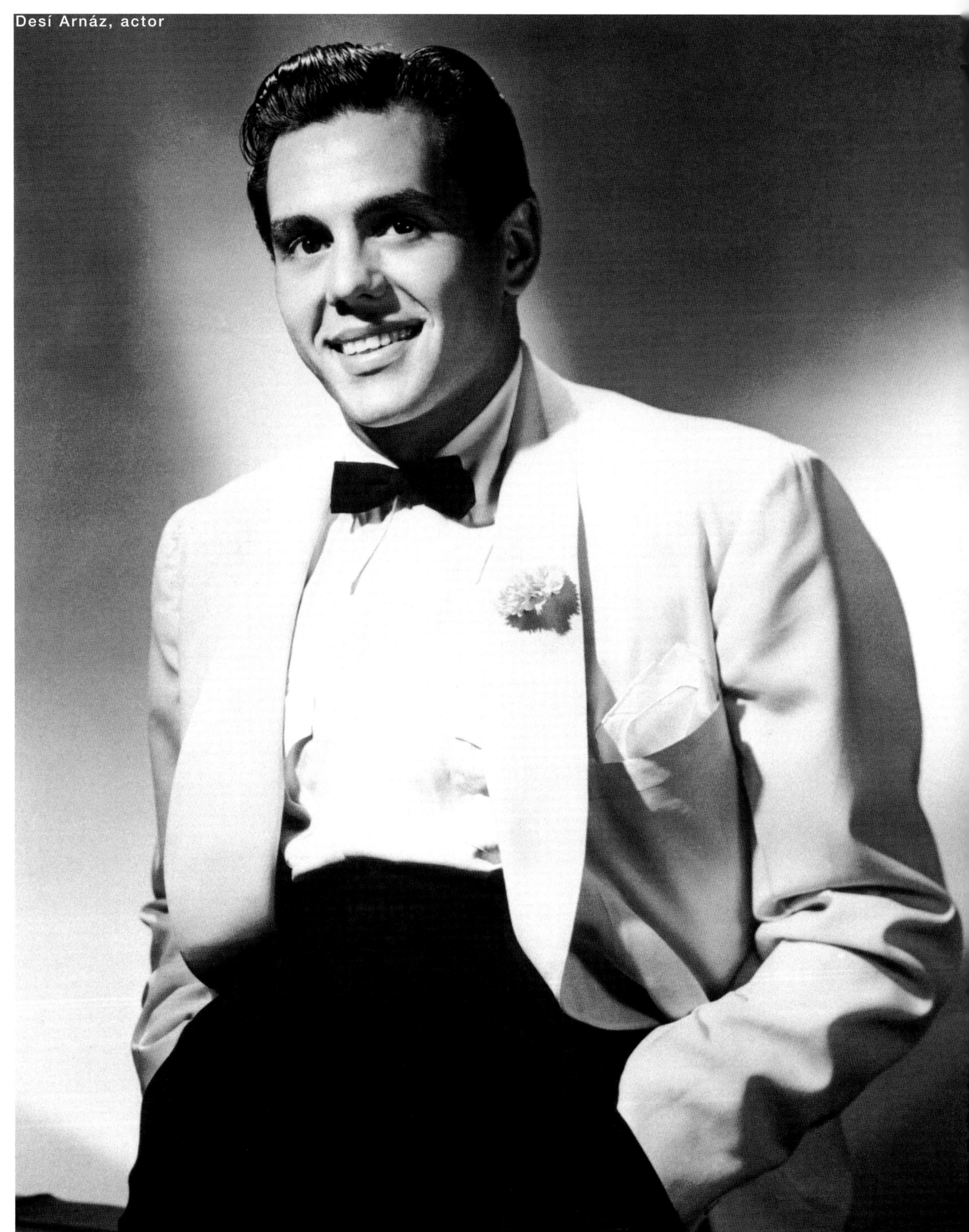

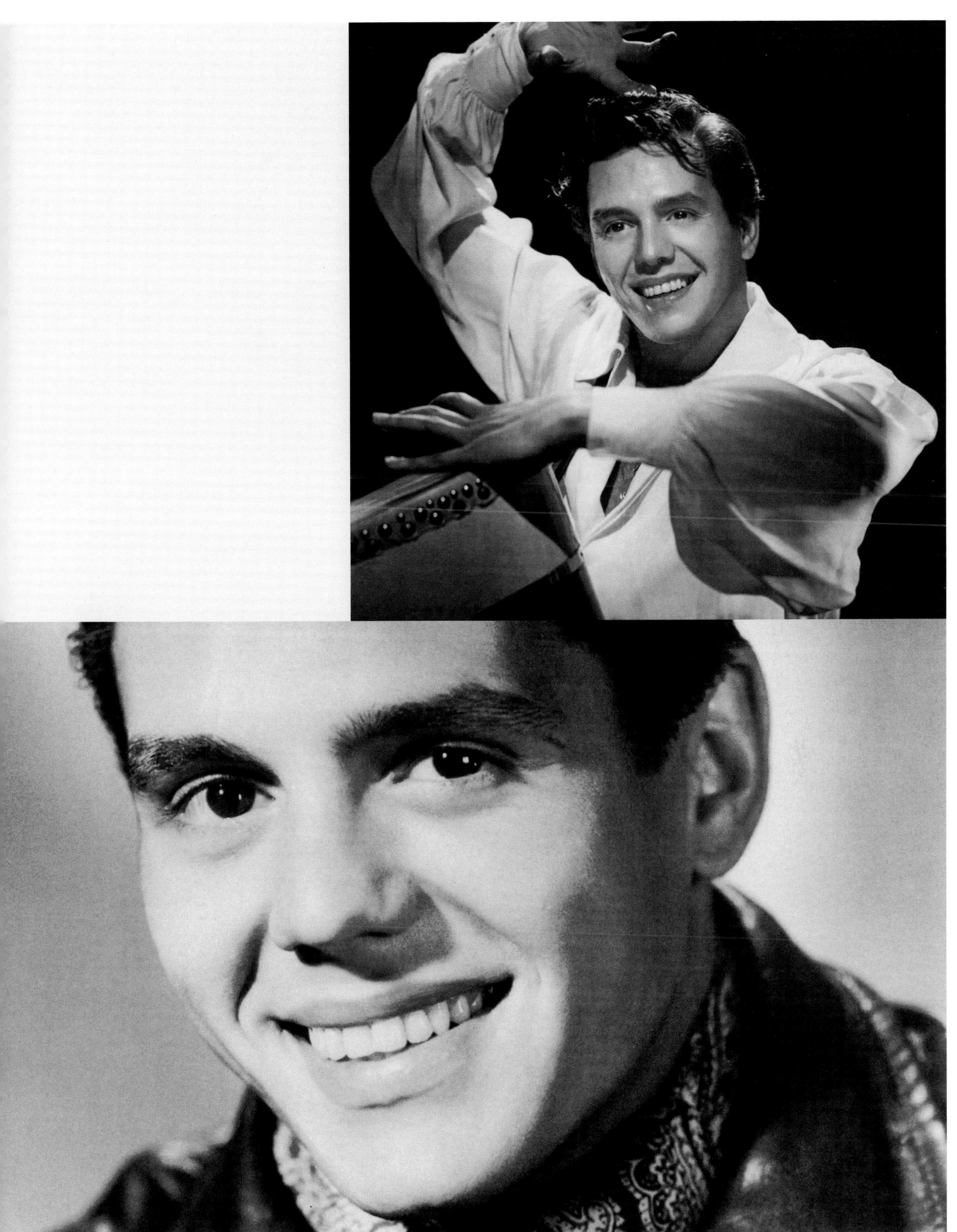

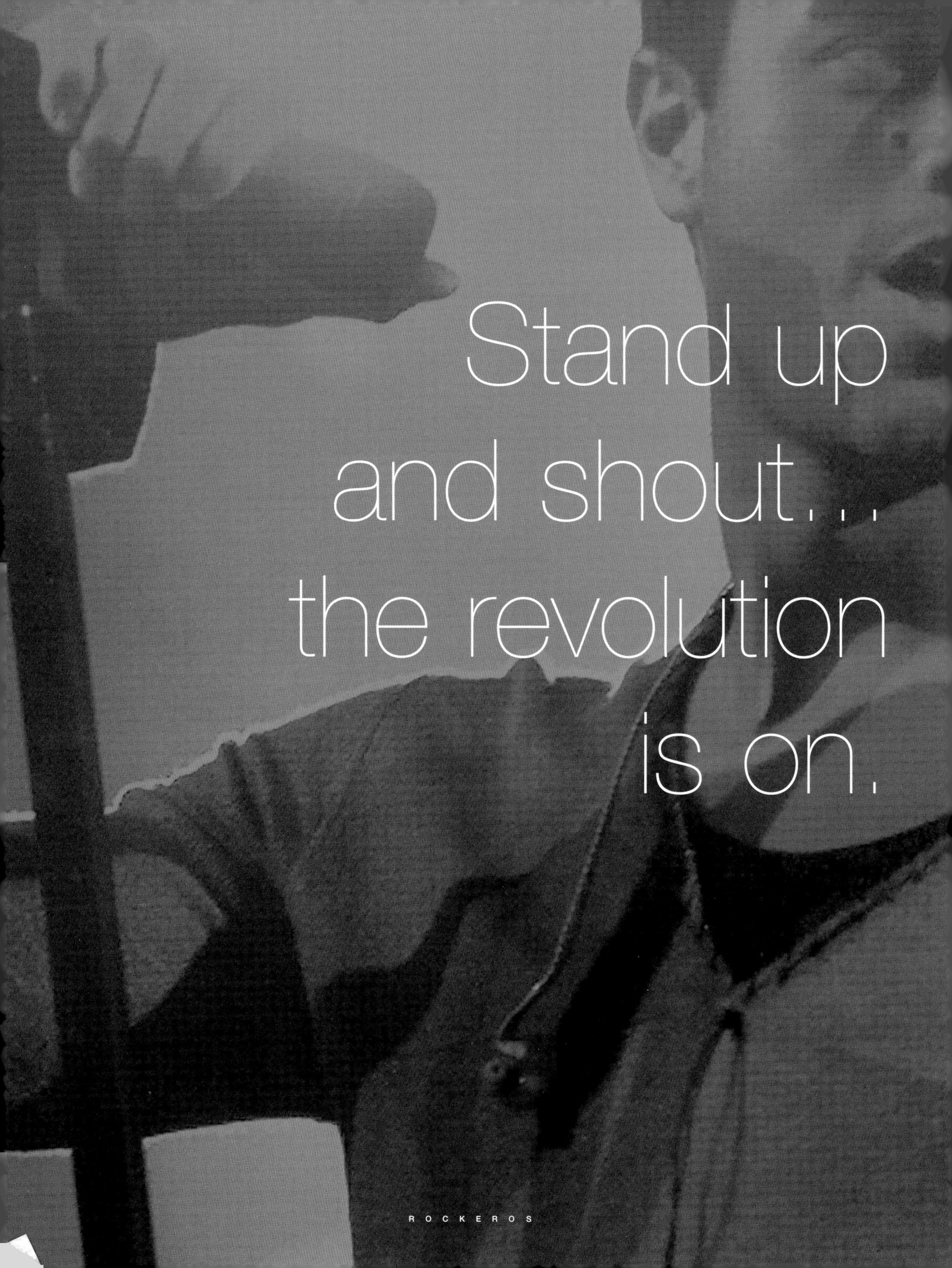

Stand up
and shout...
the revolution
is on.

To say "it's only rock-and-roll" is to rashly misrepresent an idea that has come to stand for so much more than just music. Named after a slang expression for sex, this raw, energetic music has always represented danger, revolution—a way of undermining the status quo, the death rattle of established ways and ideas. But whether the threat comes from unadulterated animal magnetism, the free spirit of youthful rebellion, or social conscience and upheaval, it always takes that special spark to blaze a trail, a sharper edge to leave your mark. Musically inclined or not, the individual who isn't afraid to stand up and shout, "Here's who I am, take it or leave it," is a real rocker.

Take Cuban poet Reinaldo Arenas: The embodiment of freedom under any system, rather than give up his gift, he chose to accept the consequences that came with it. At odds with Castro's revolution because he was gay, when he smuggled his second book out of the country, he was rewarded with both the 1969 National Book Award in Paris for best novel and imprisonment in Cuba. The only people allowed to read his works were, ironically, his oppressors: government agents. But neither harassment, poverty, or obscurity could keep him from his vision, from expressing his true voice.

Of course, one doesn't have to live under a totalitarian regime to experience or understand. Zack de la Rocha was well schooled in this matter by both his radical Chicano artist father and the taunts of "wetback" from his not-so-enlightened playground instructors in the school of life. As front man for his former rap-rock band, Rage Against the Machine, de la Rocha had a platform to do just that, railing against institutionalized racism and corporate and governmental corruption, among other social ills—a post-modern folkie with dreadlocks, a Ché Guevara t-shirt, and a conspiratorial cynicism cranked all the way up to "Eleven"—shouting out for those with a voice too repressed, too disenfranchised to be heard: "We've all been put to sleep . . .[by] a system that would rather see all of you at that bar . . .being put to sleep with beer or drugs, rather than acting against it."

While there are those fiery spirits like de la Rocha and the iconoclastic Argentine revolutionary, who set out to stir up the social order, there are those who do so simply by virtue of being themselves, by refusing to see any limitations. The Puerto-Rican born, New York raised José Feliciano, probably best known for his ubiquitous Spanish-language Christmas song "Felíz Navidad," had already helped to fling open one previously closed door when he crossed over from bolero music, (one of the first Latin stars to do so), in 1968 with his soulful remake of The Doors' "Light My Fire." But when he gave the same treatment to "The Star-Spangled Banner" during Game 5 of the World Series that year, he rocked the mainstream. The revolution was on, and it was being televised. After the controversy died down, however, it became apparent most people were ready for the change, and the voices of dissent were in the minority: Recorded live, his rendition would go on to become the first time the national anthem was a Top 40 hit.

It's this melding of influences that makes rock-'n'roll so disarmingly powerful. "I look at the Rolling Stones," says Benicio del Toro, "who took this fusion of country blues, added some reggae, and turned it into the best rock'n'roll. They fused everything. And I fuse things." This uncompromising method actor draws from his Italian and Spanish heritage and his experiences growing up in Puerto Rico and Pennsylvania, where it wasn't always easy being different and music often served as his only cultural bridge and ally, to create uniquely appealing characters. The personification of rock 'n' roll, del Toro is the amalgamation of disparate influences, the mysterious stranger and the everyman, the rebel shaking up the social order, the outsider looking in, making us look at ourselves.

Dave Navarro, musician

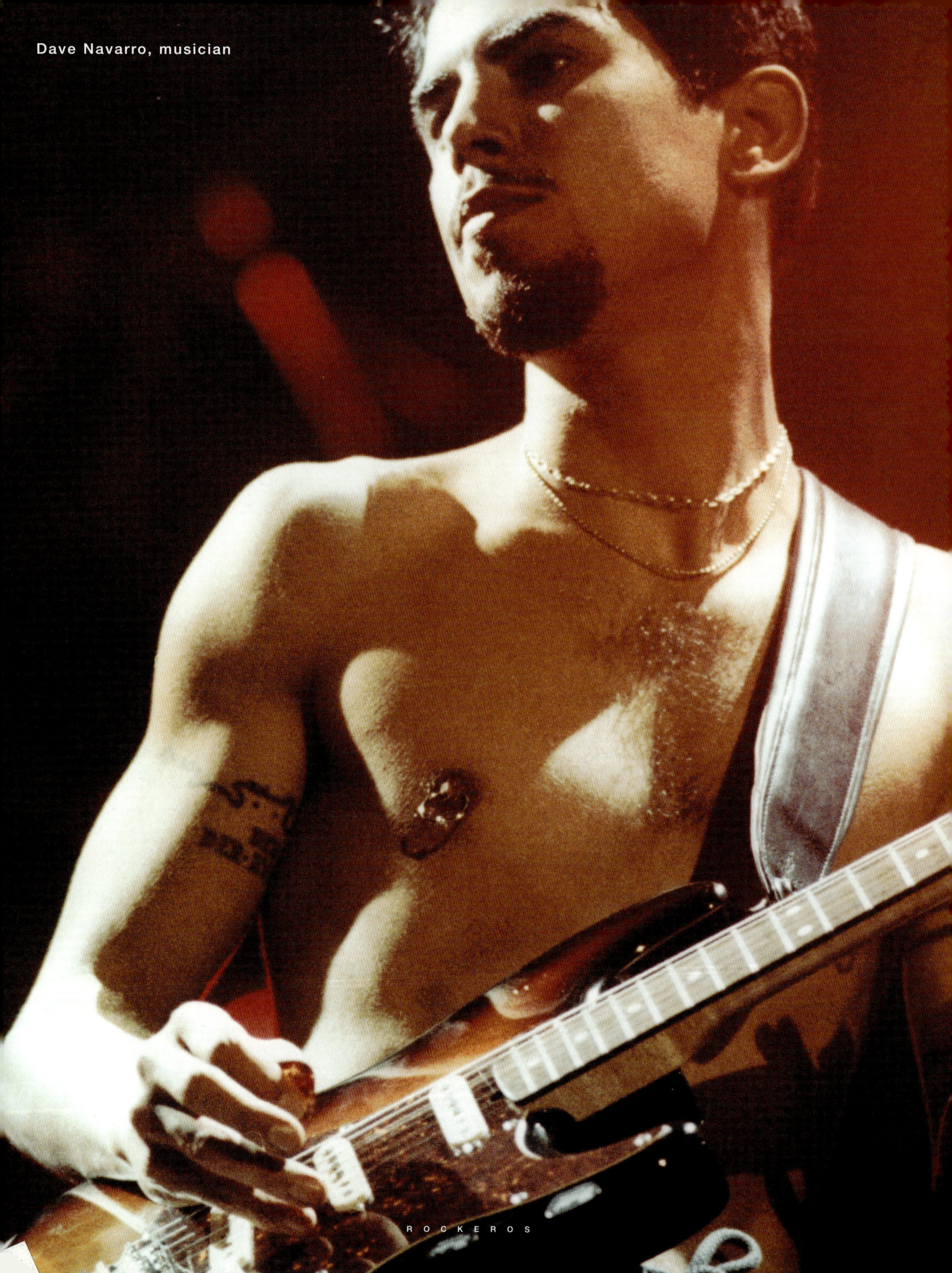

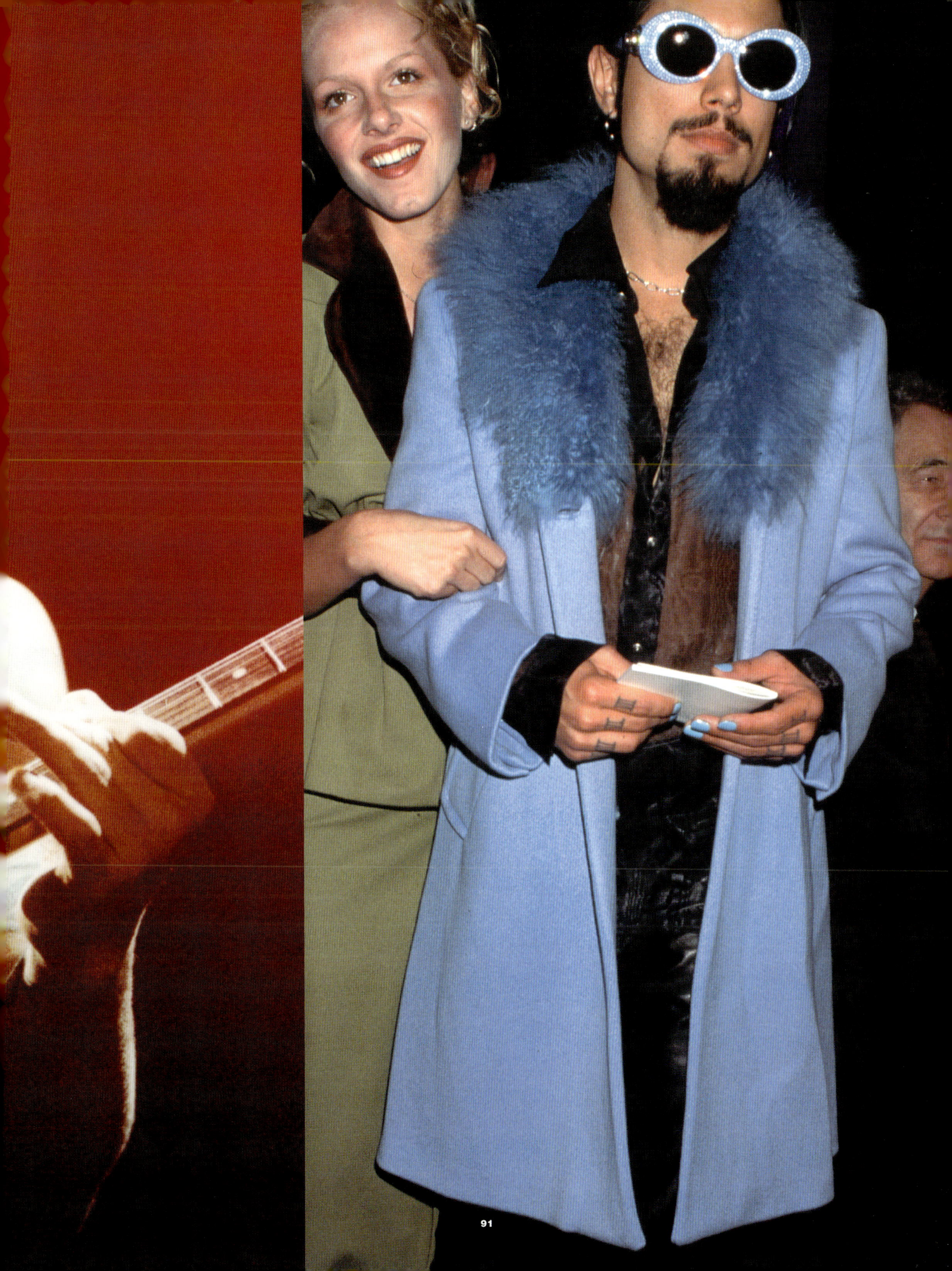

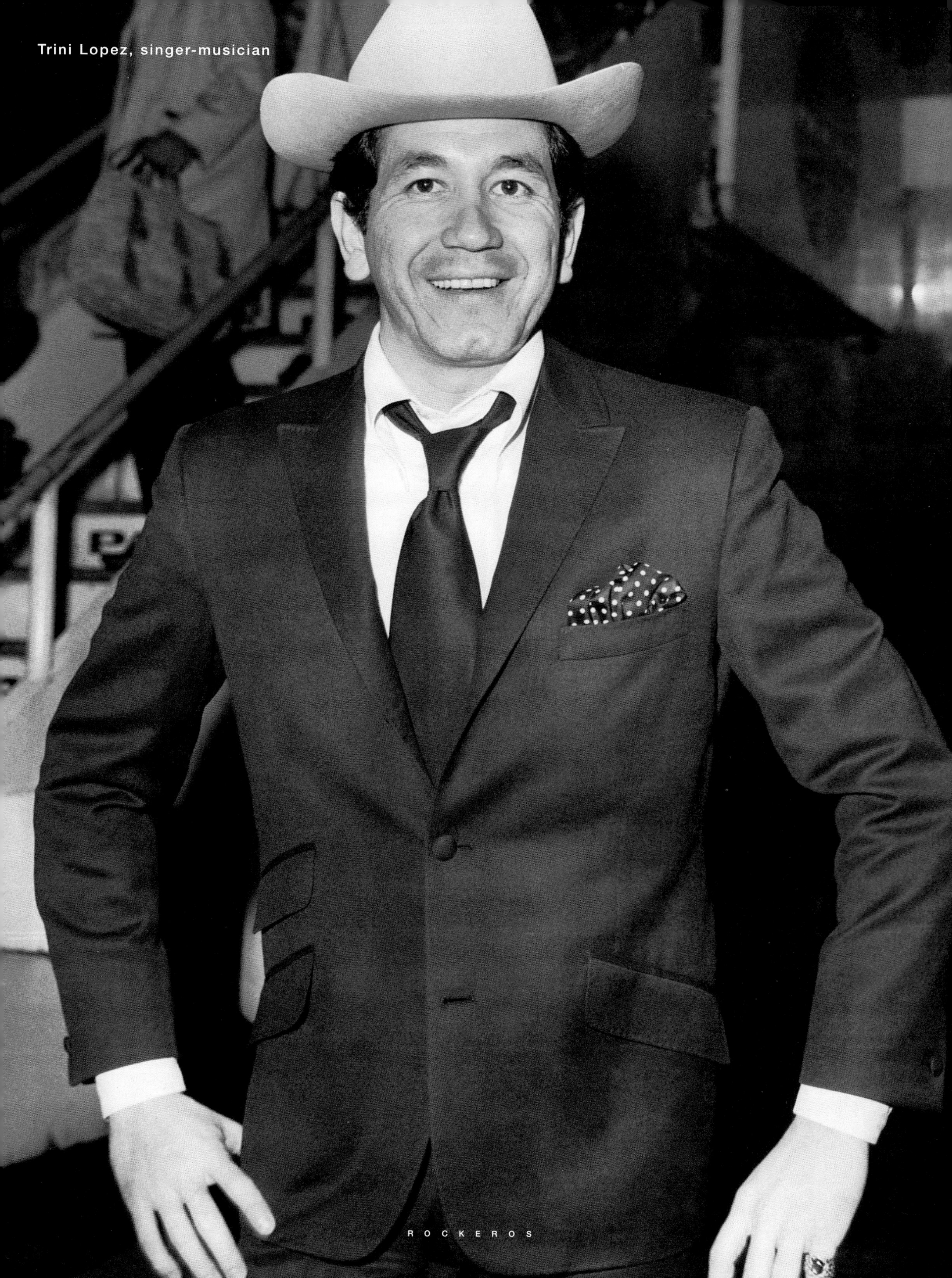

Trini Lopez, singer-musician

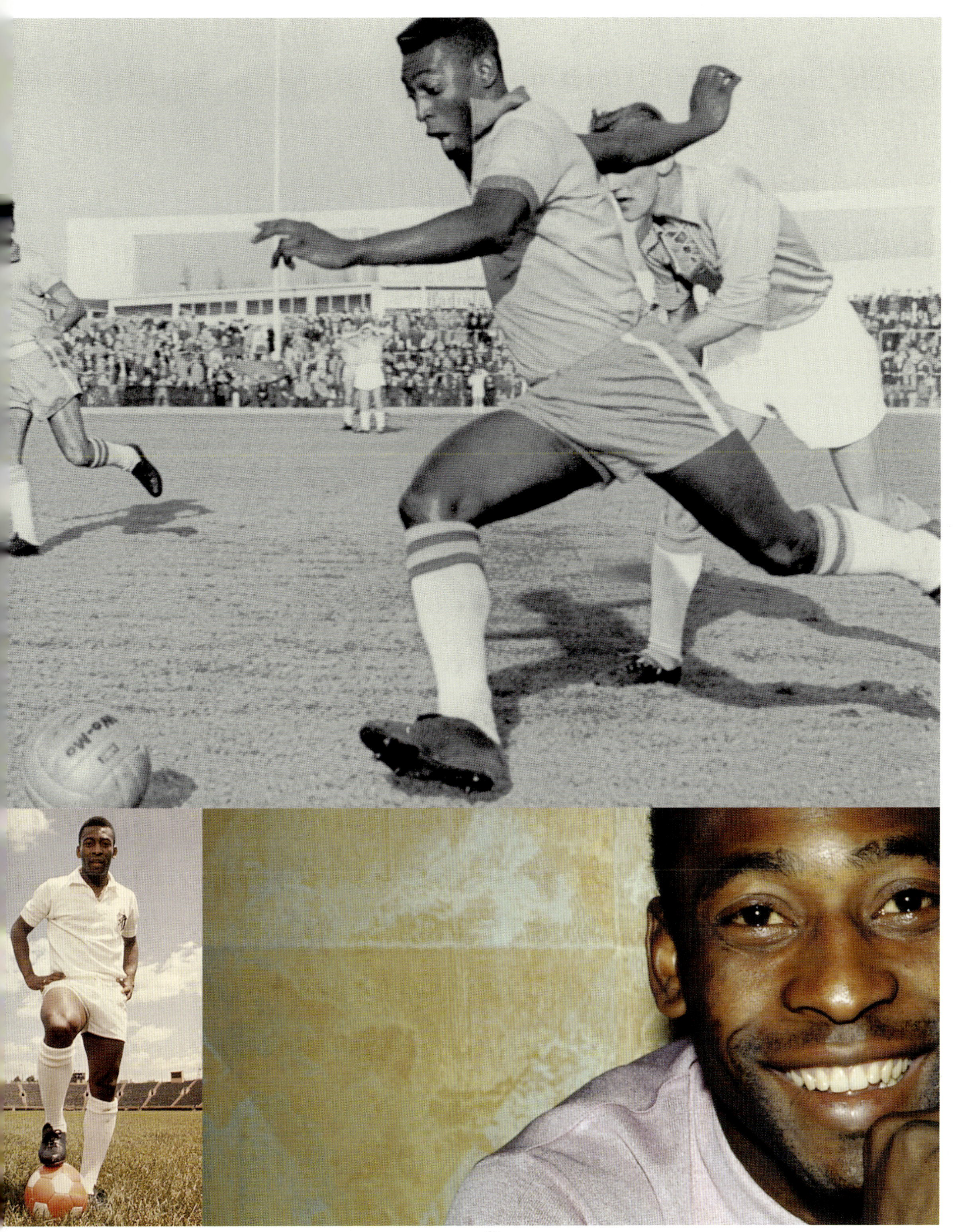
Wo-Mo

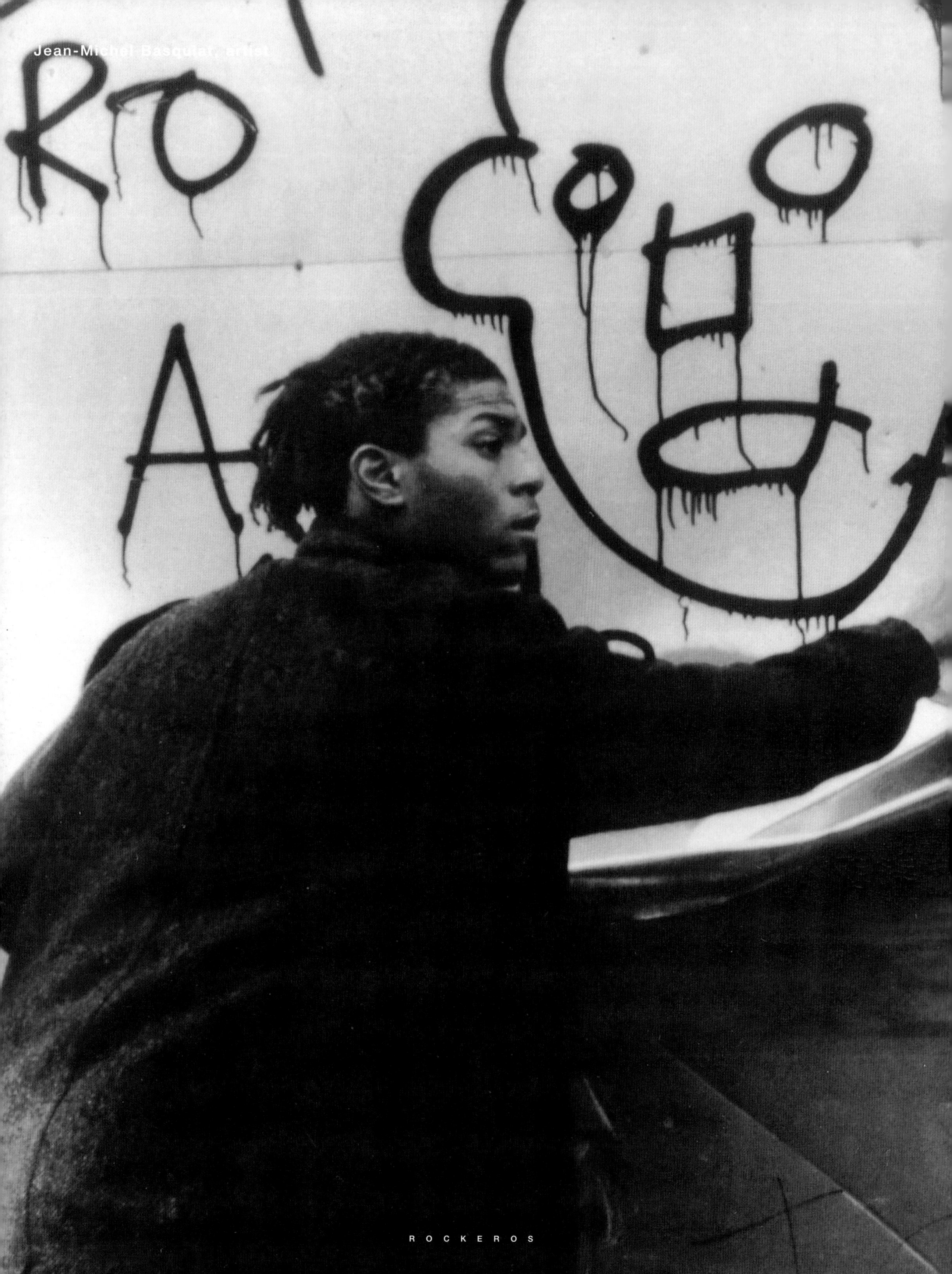

Jean-Michel Basquiat, artist

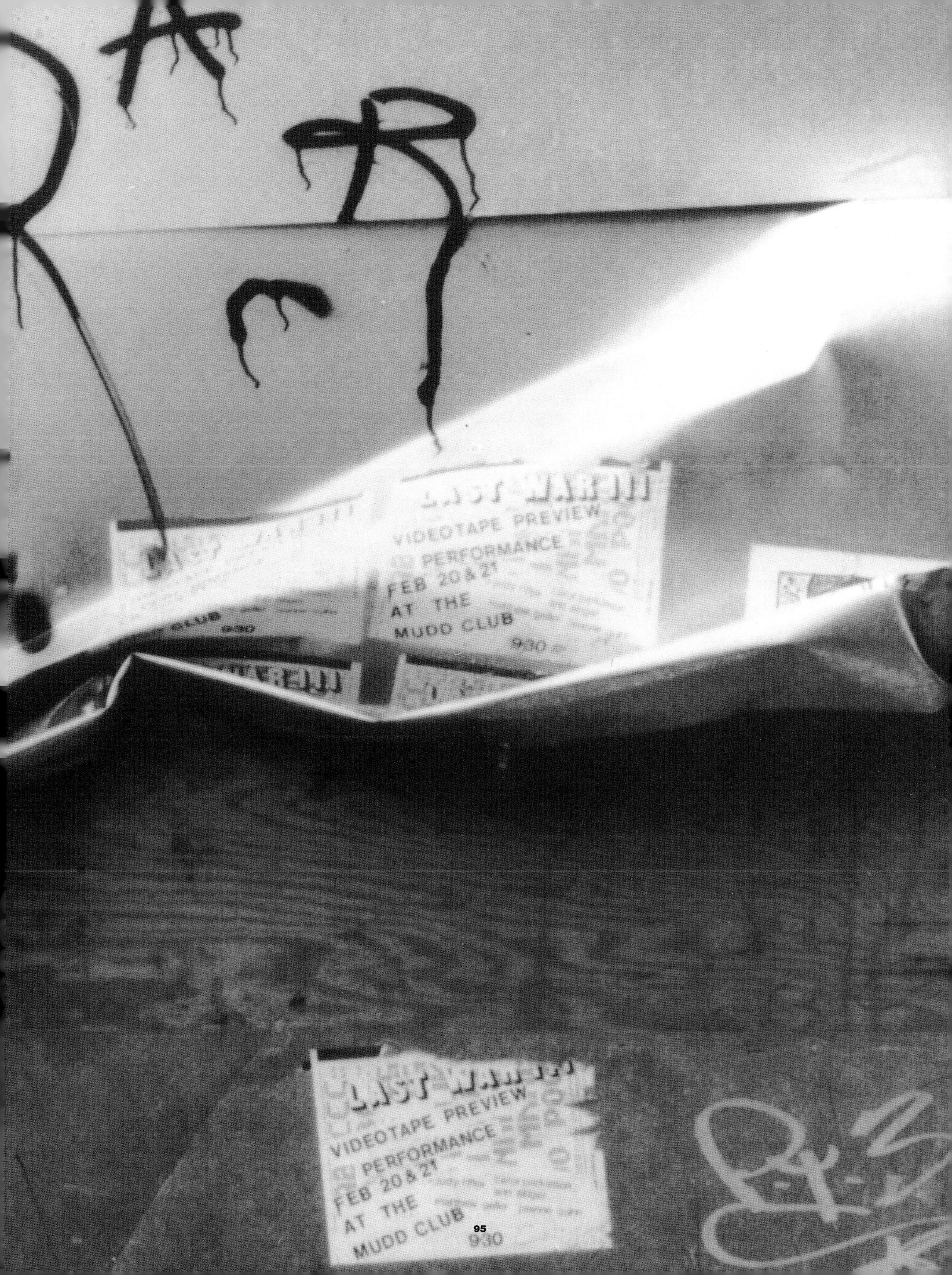

LAST WAR III
VIDEOTAPE PREVIEW
PERFORMANCE
FEB 20 & 21
AT THE
MUDD CLUB
930

LAST WAR III
VIDEOTAPE PREVIEW
PERFORMANCE
FEB 20 & 21
AT THE
MUDD CLUB
930

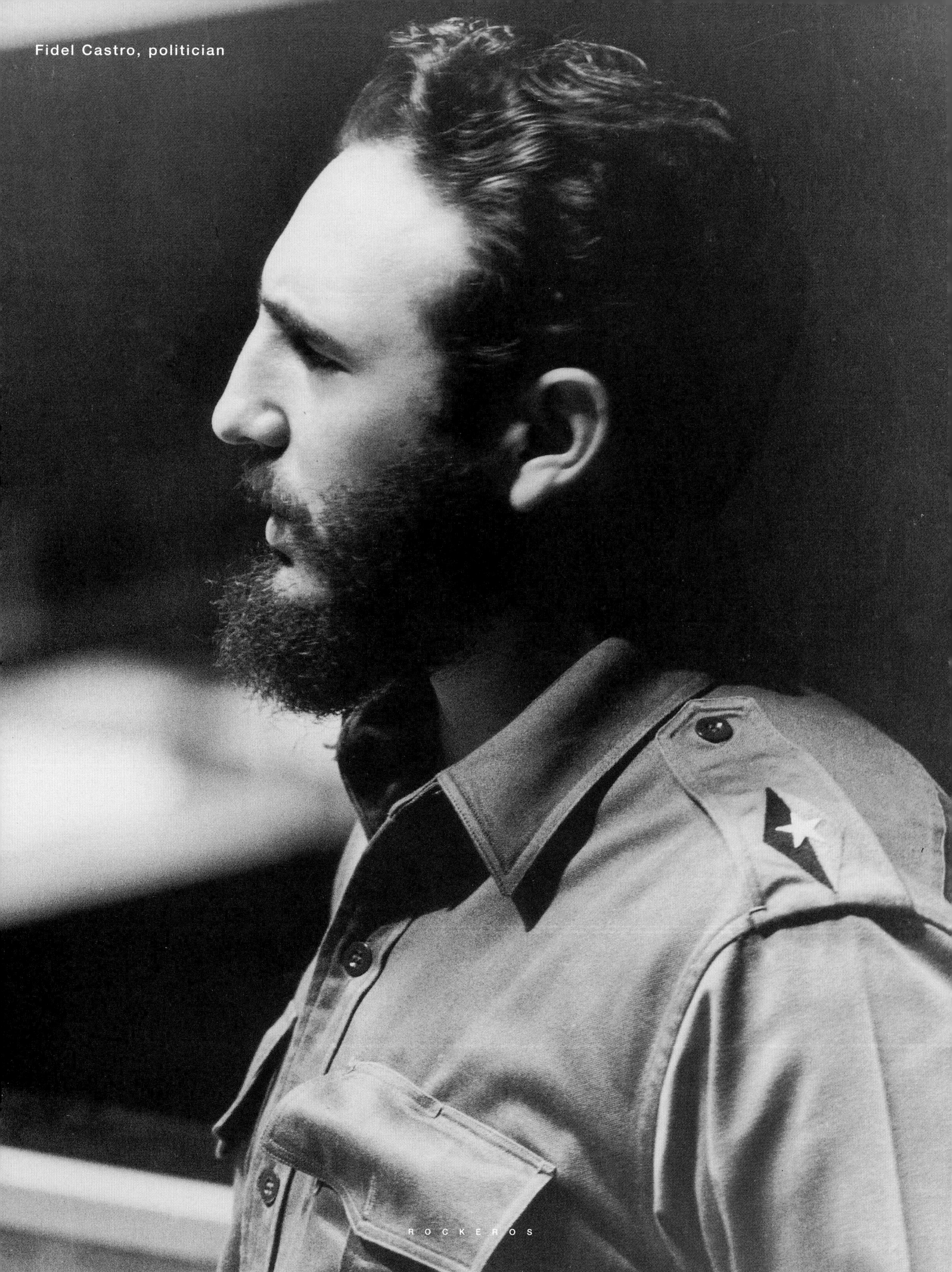

Fidel Castro, politician

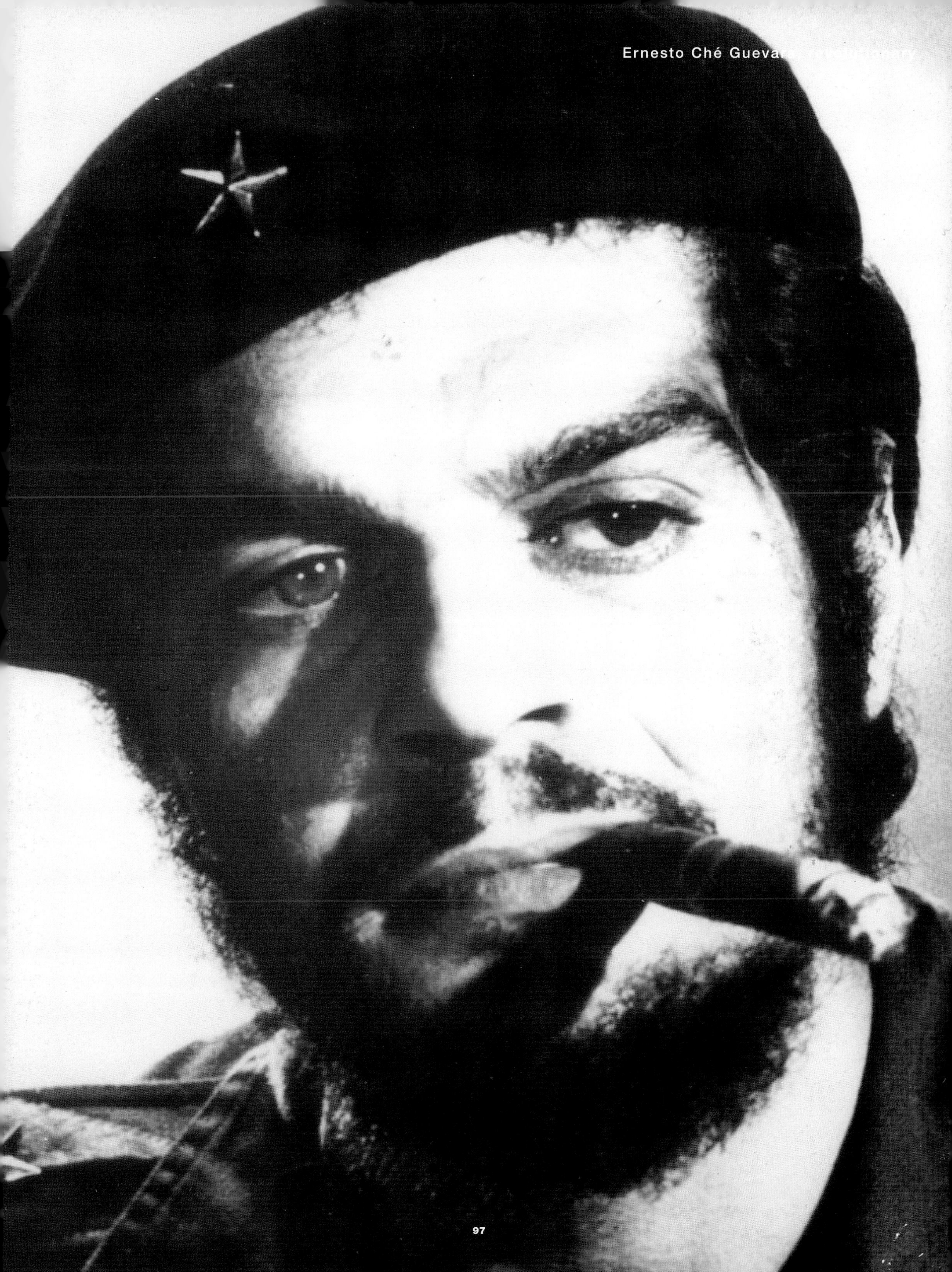

Ernesto Ché Guevara: revolutionary

Cypress Hill, hip-hop artists

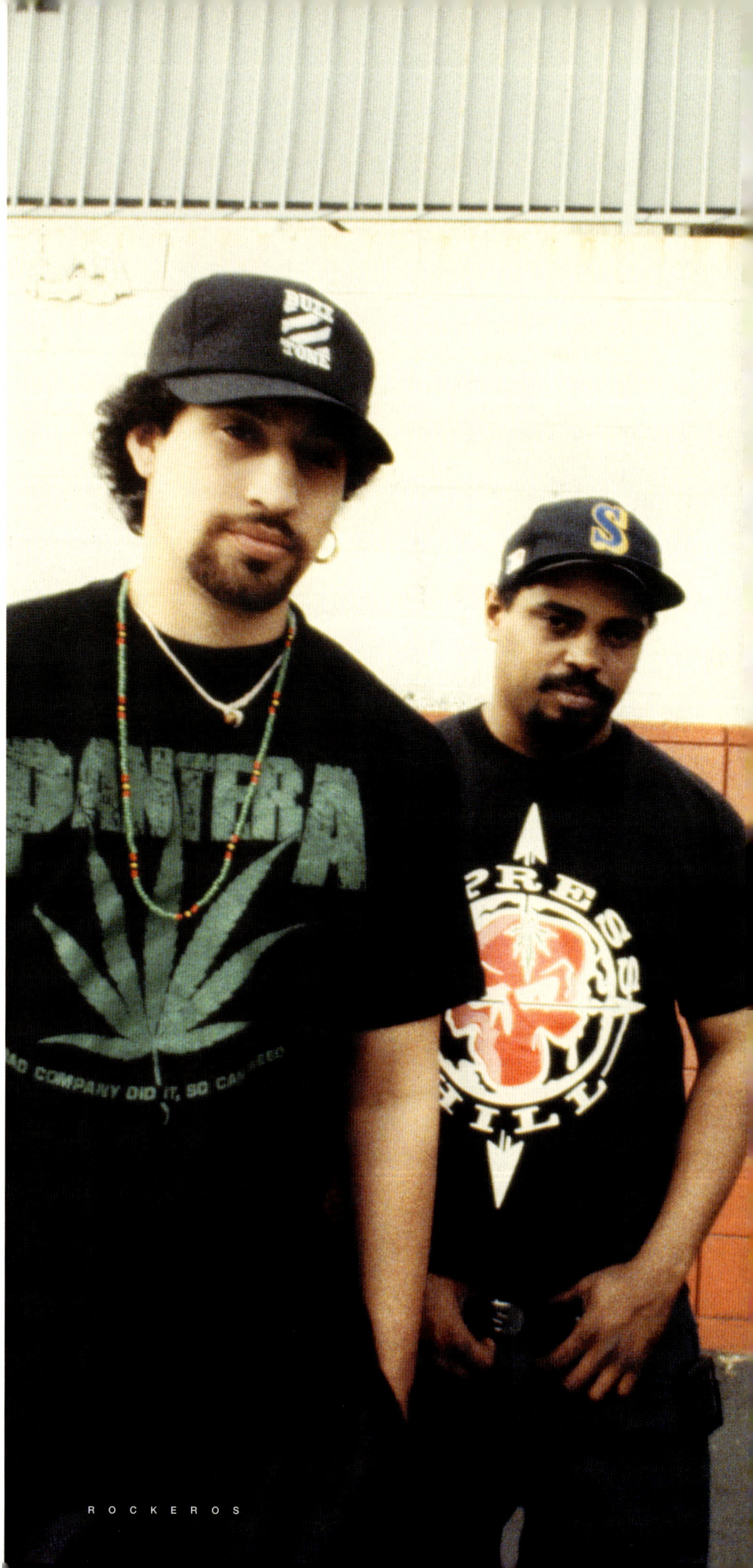

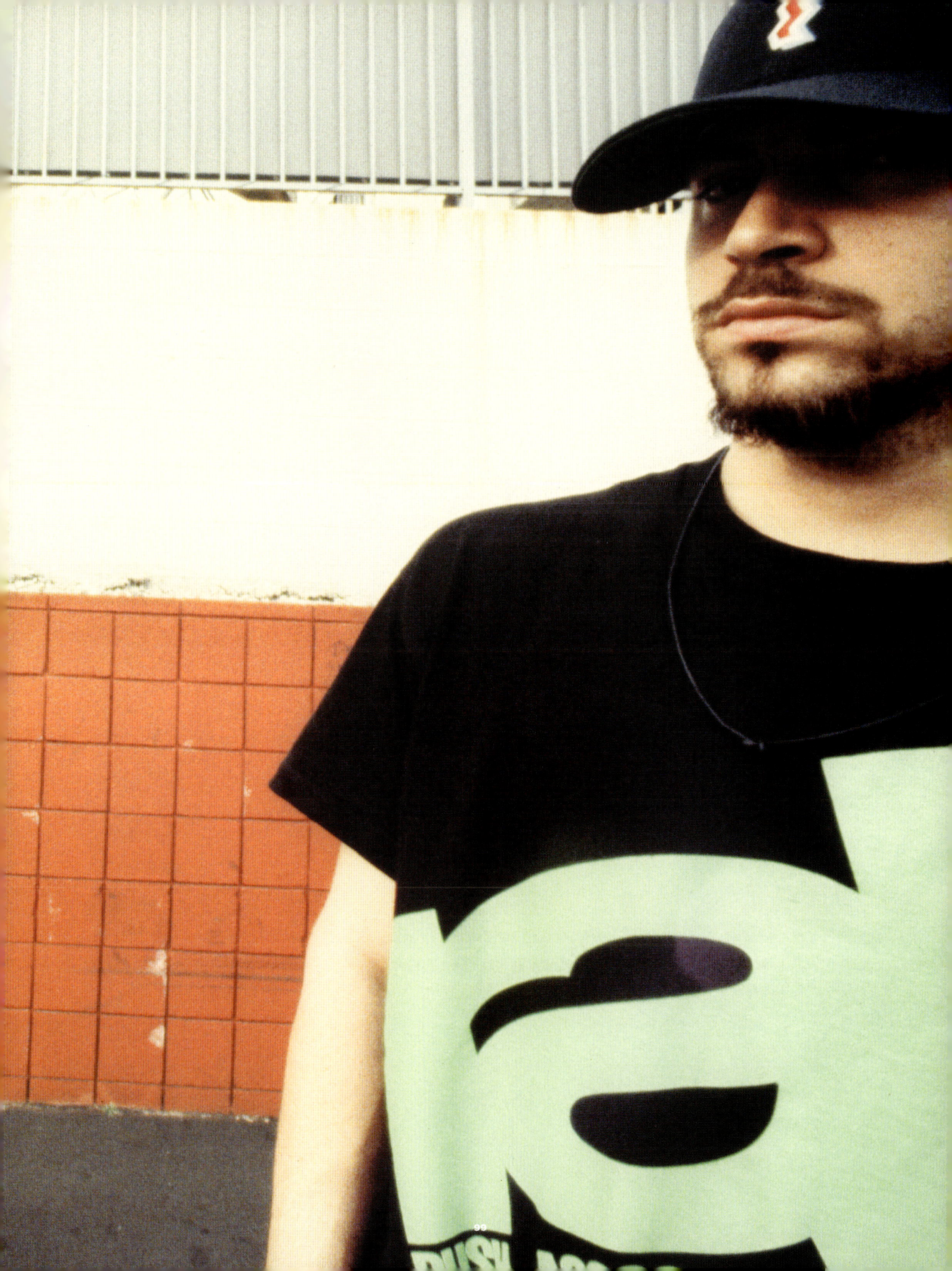

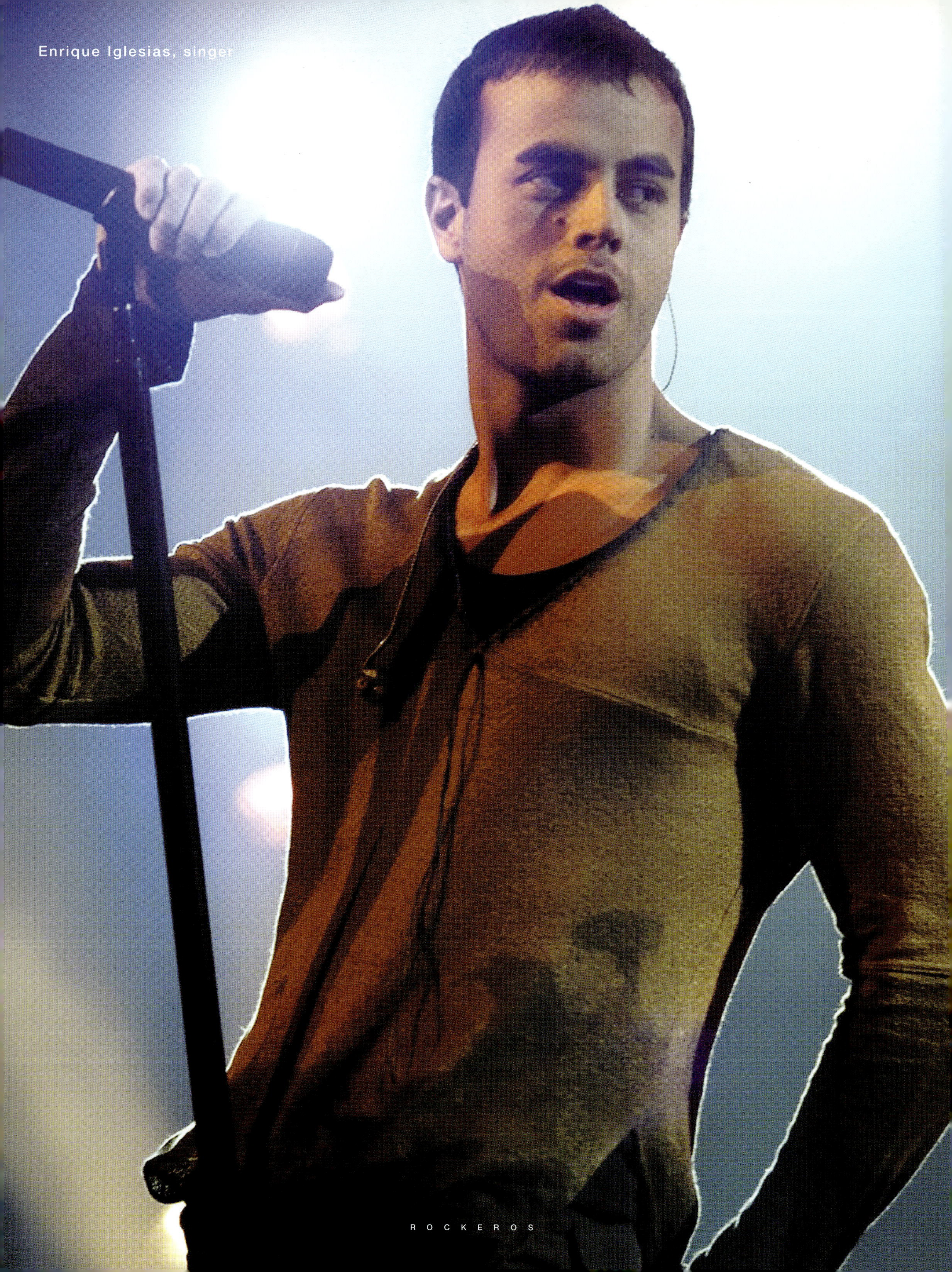

Enrique Iglesias, singer

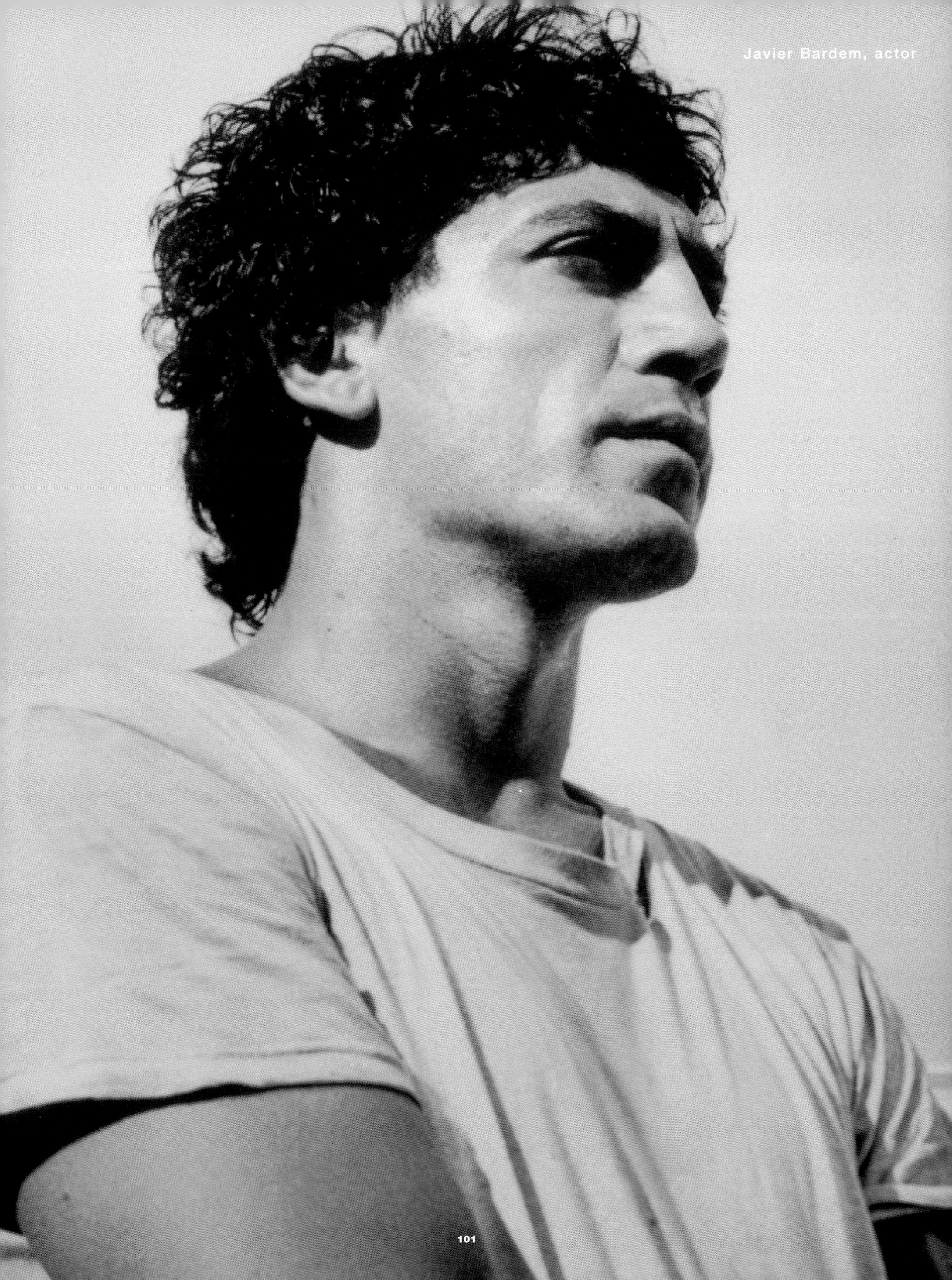
Javier Bardem, actor

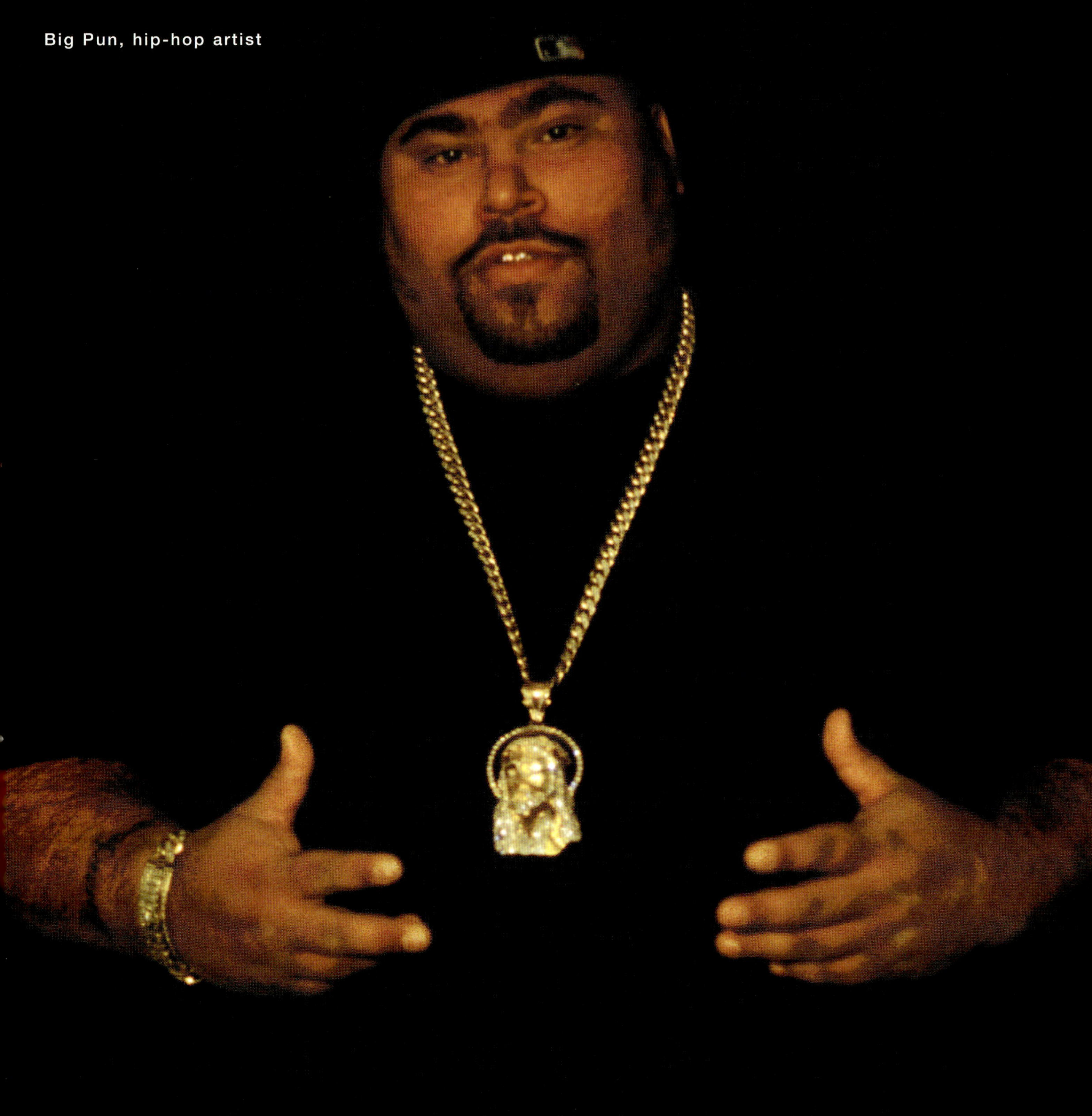

Big Pun, hip-hop artist

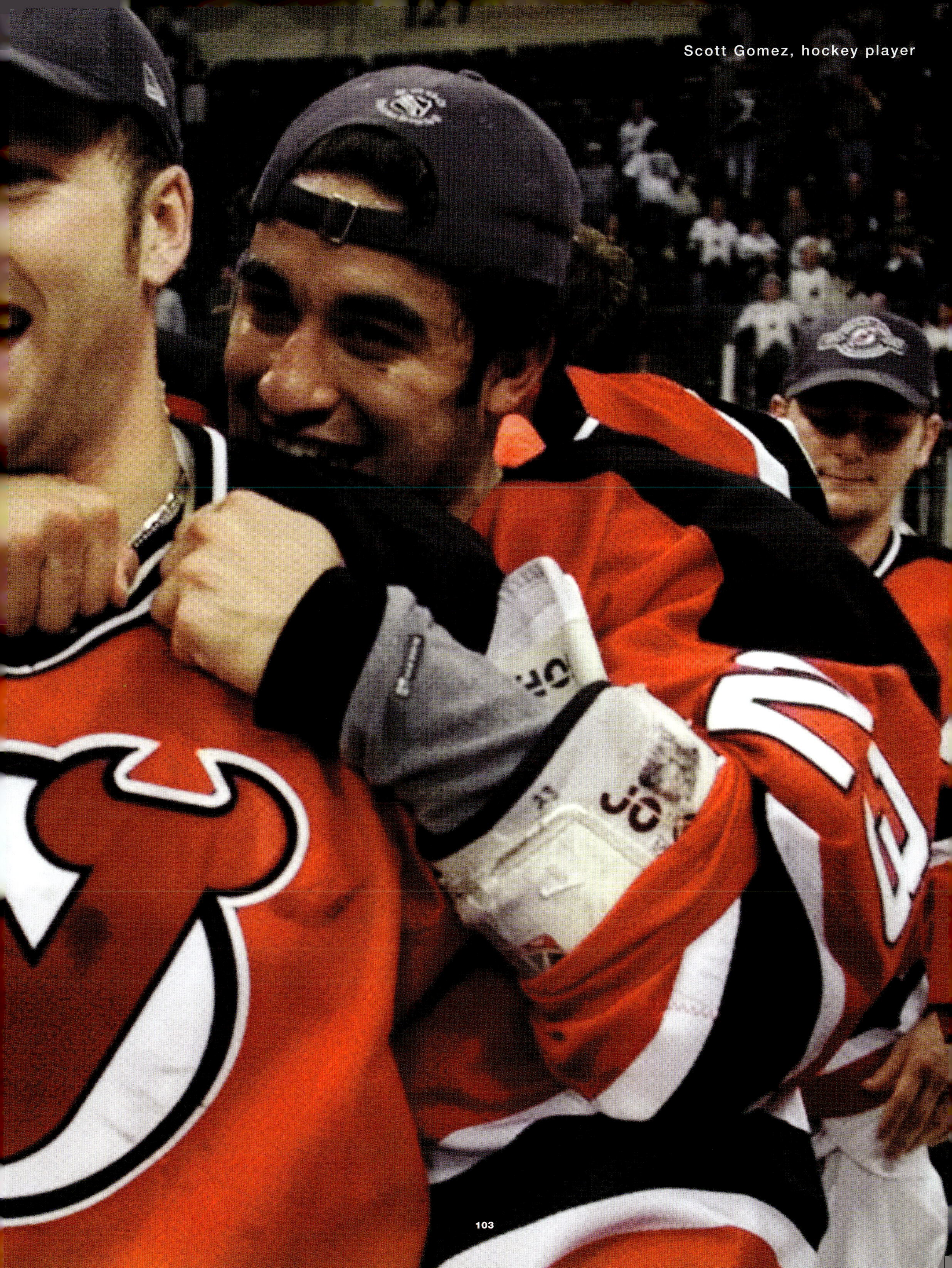

Scott Gomez, hockey player

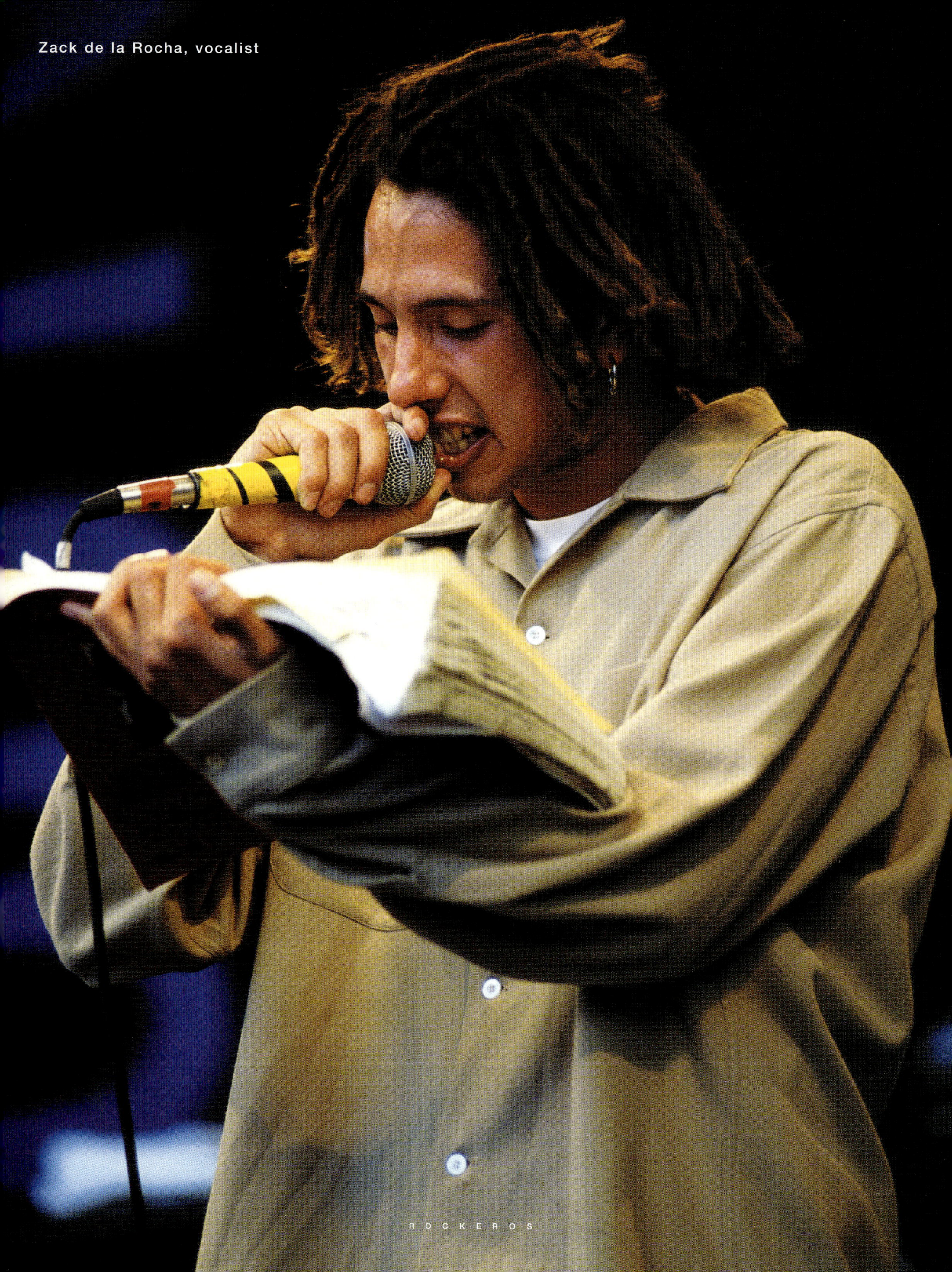

Zack de la Rocha, vocalist

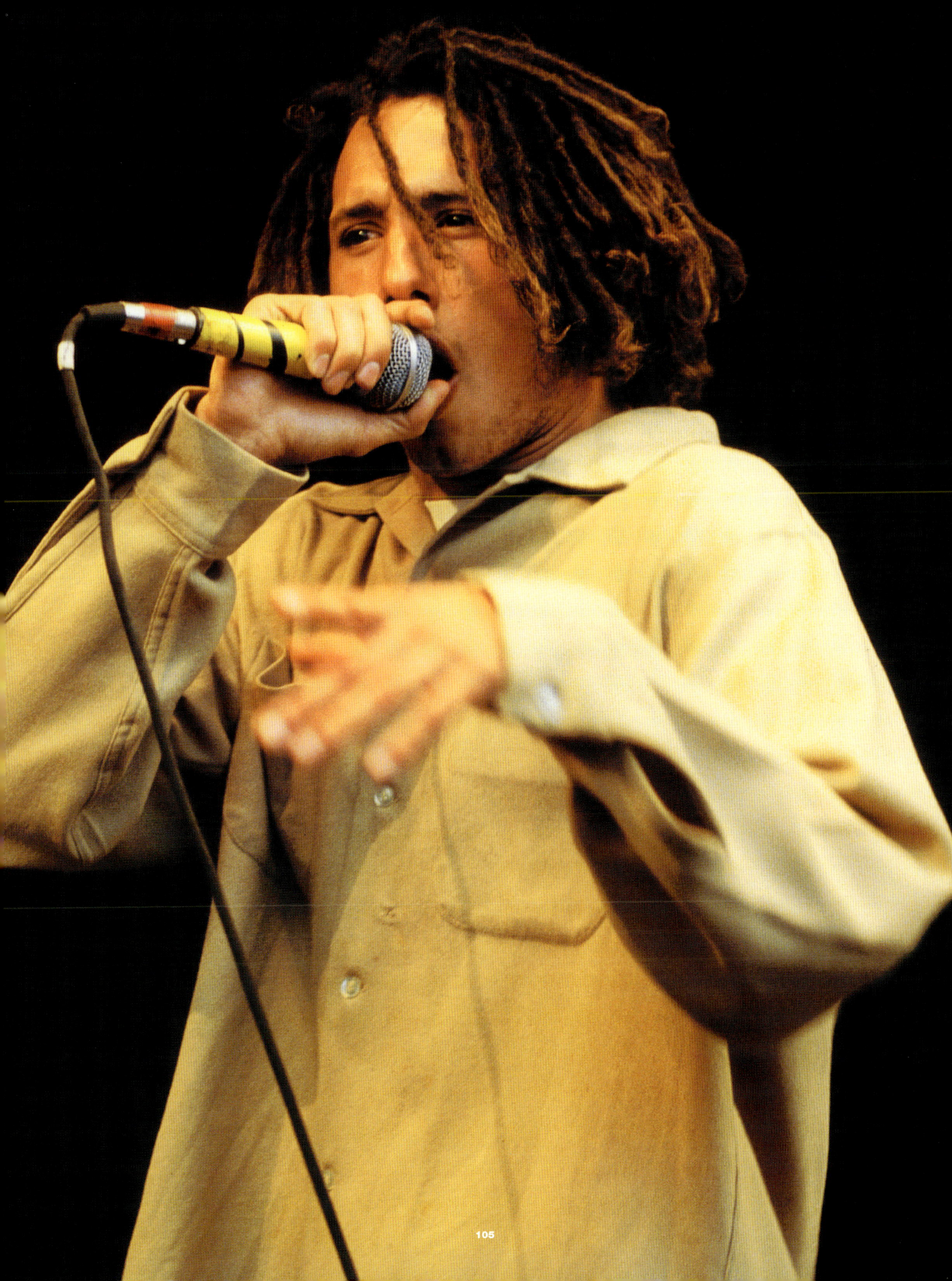

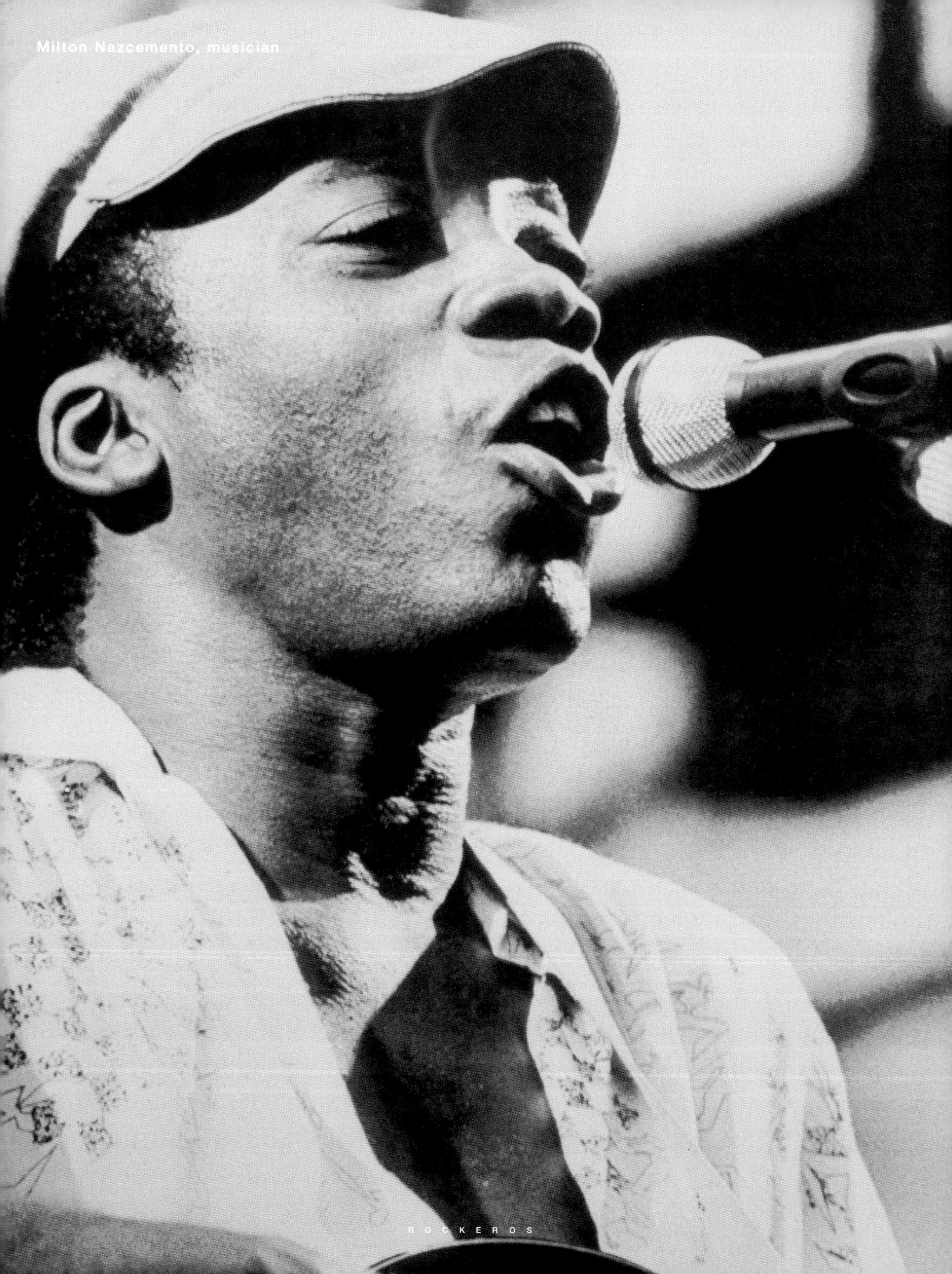
Milton Nazcemento, musician

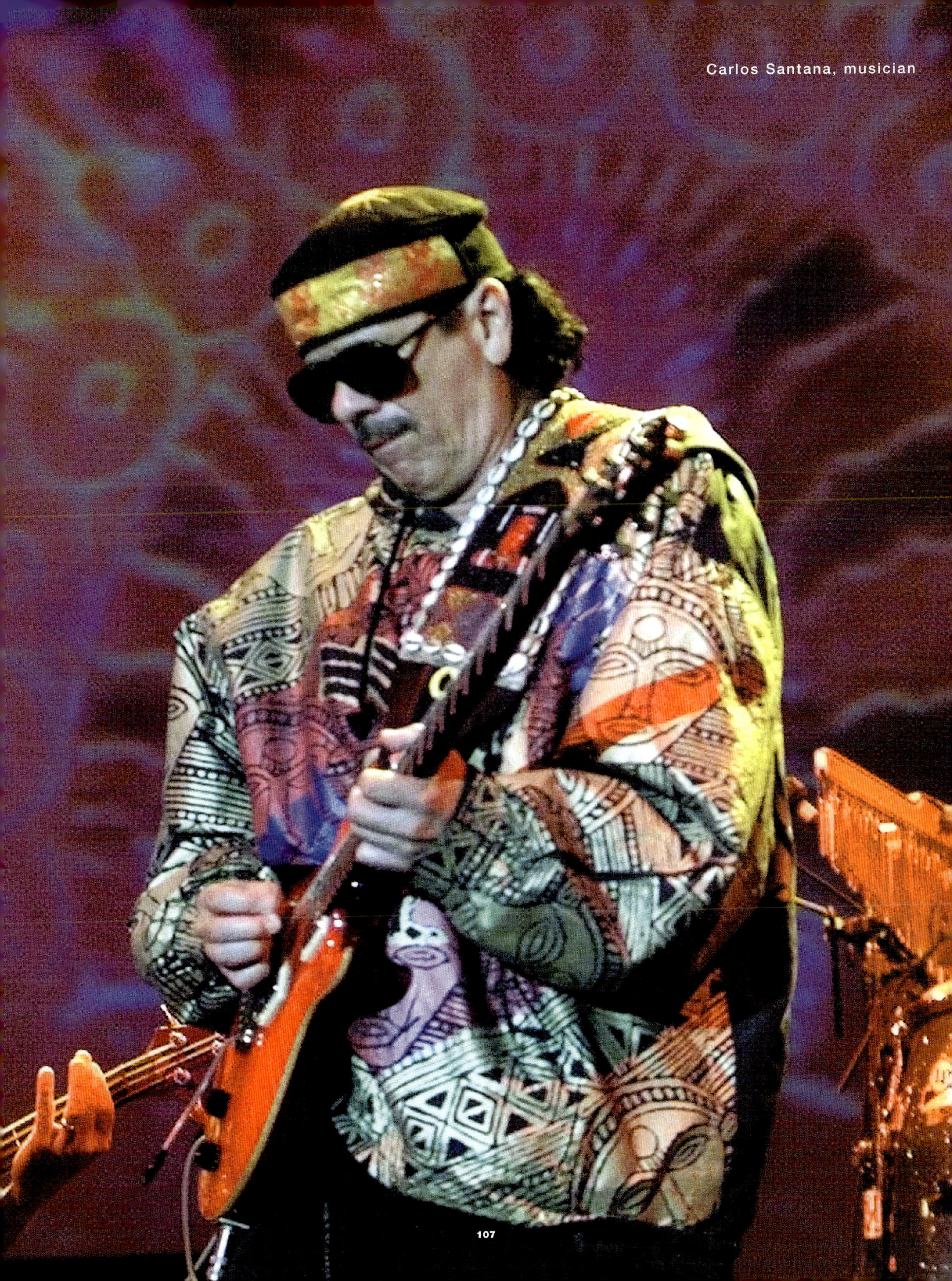

Carlos Santana, musician

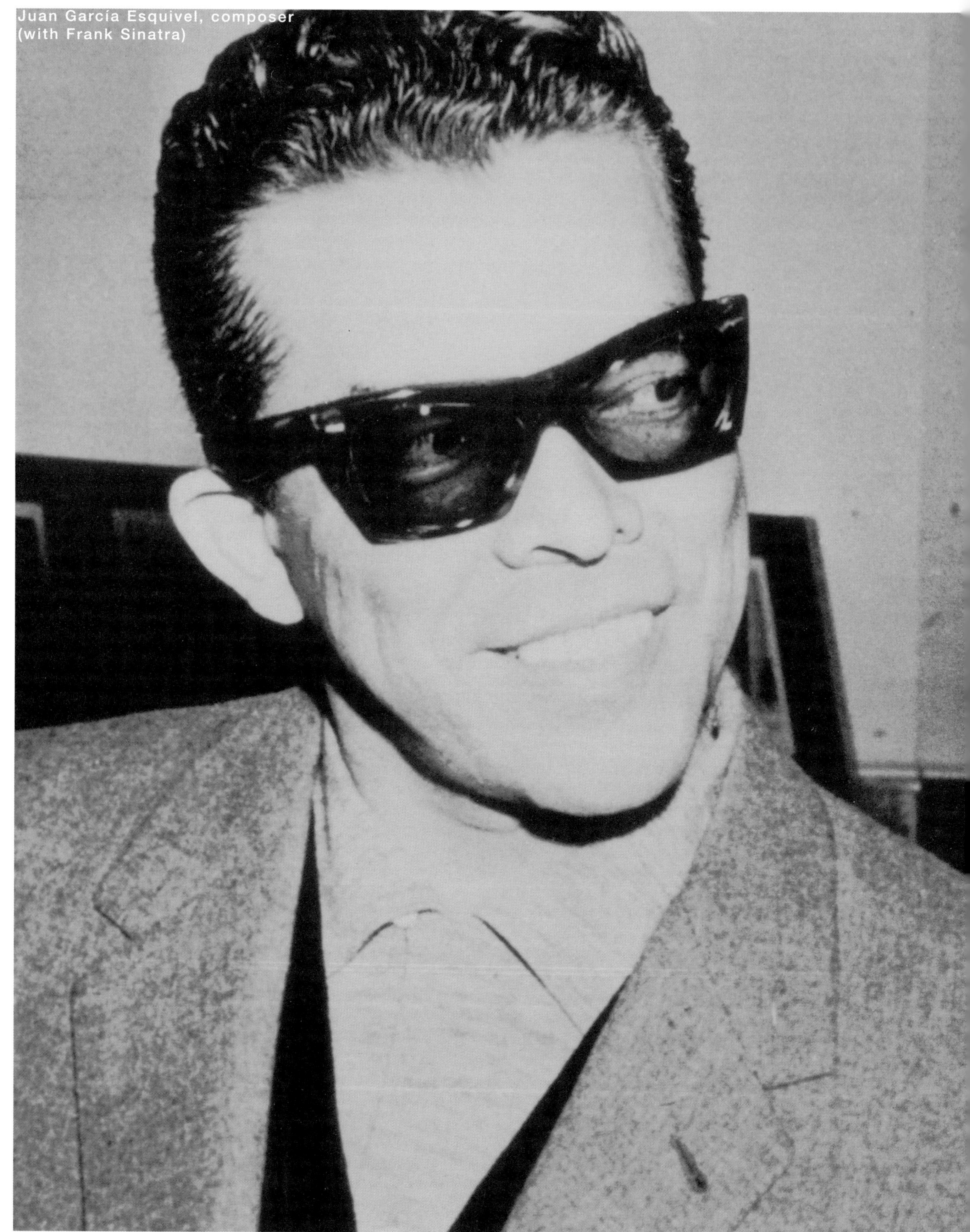

Juan García Esquivel, composer
(with Frank Sinatra)

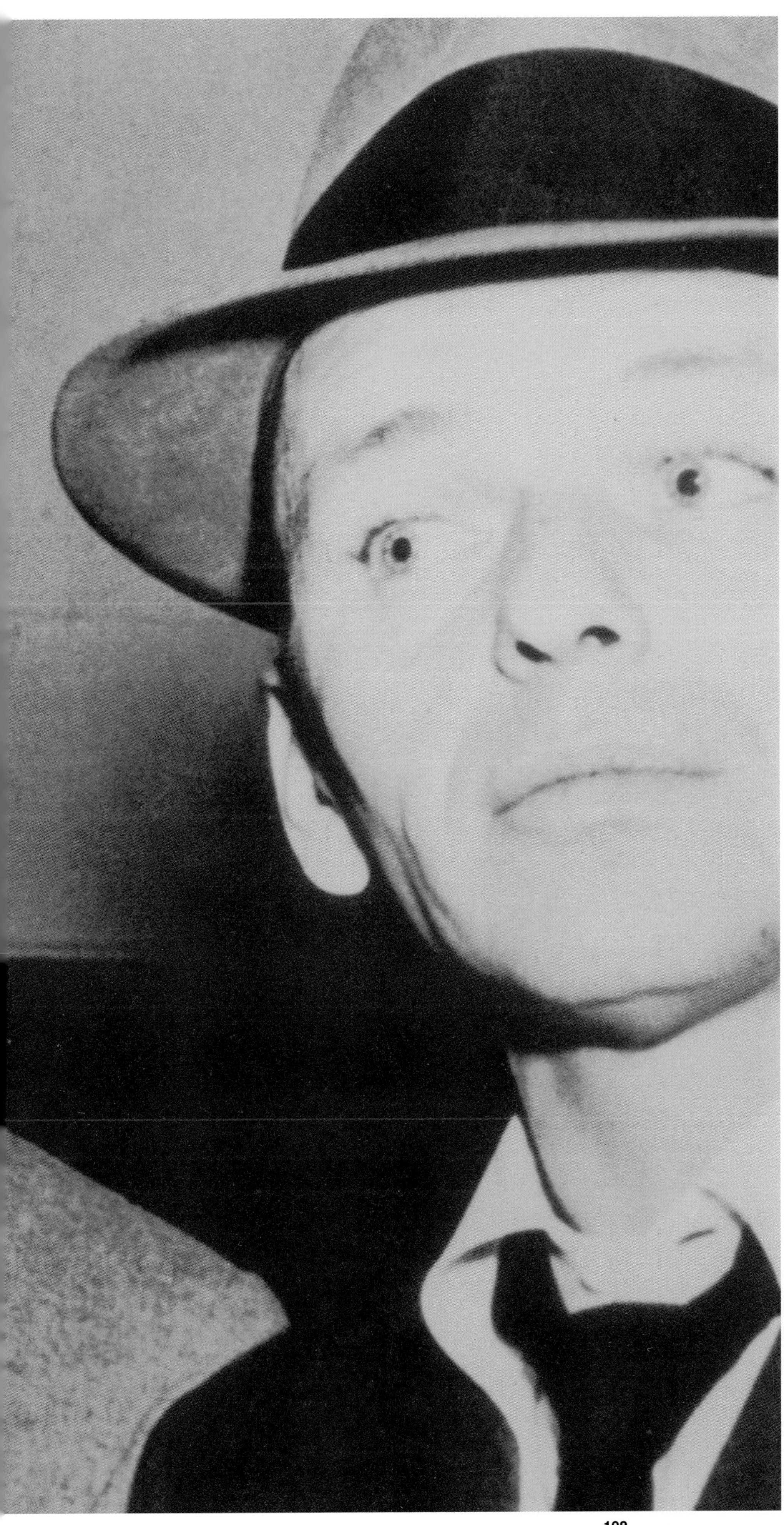

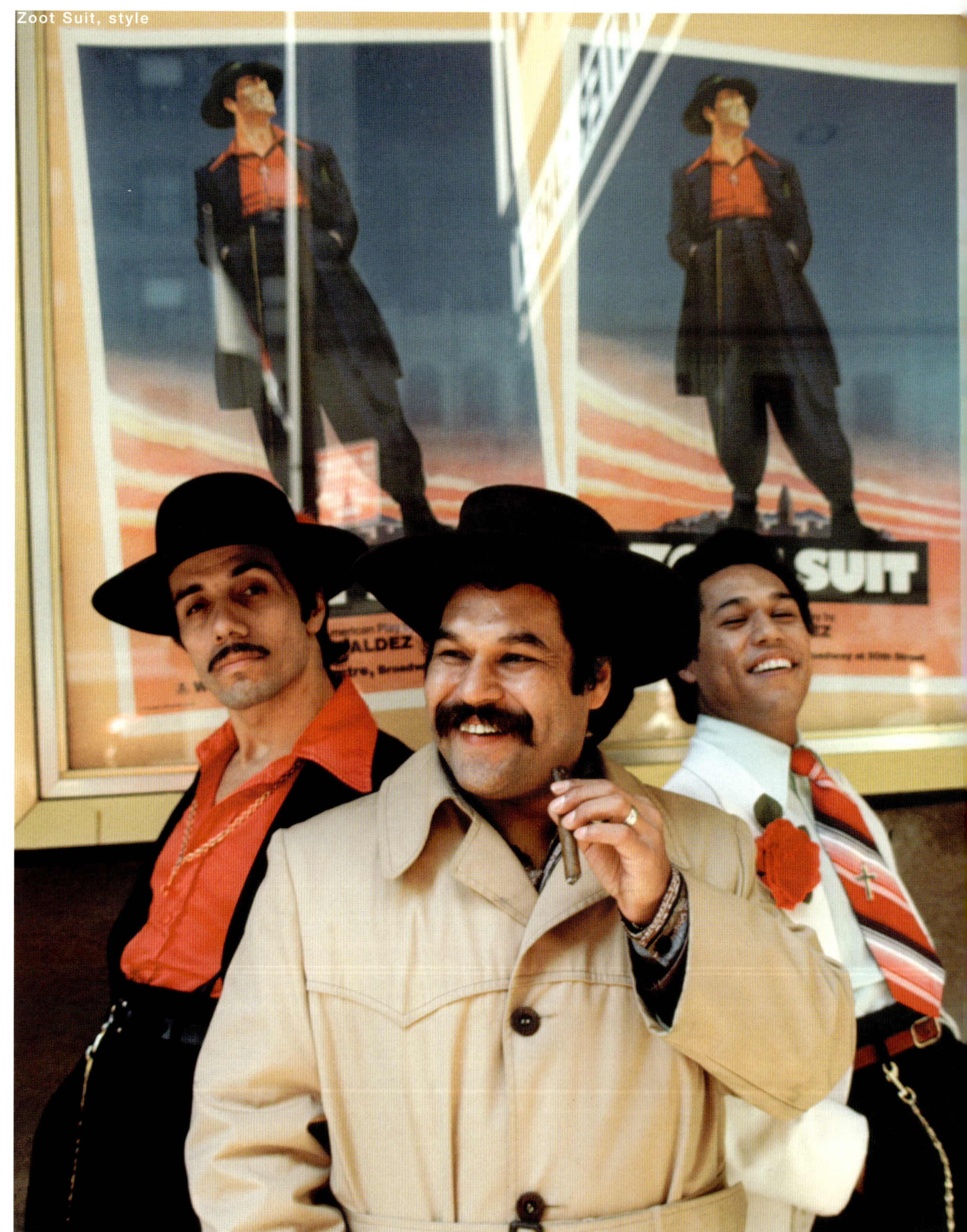

Zoot Suit, style

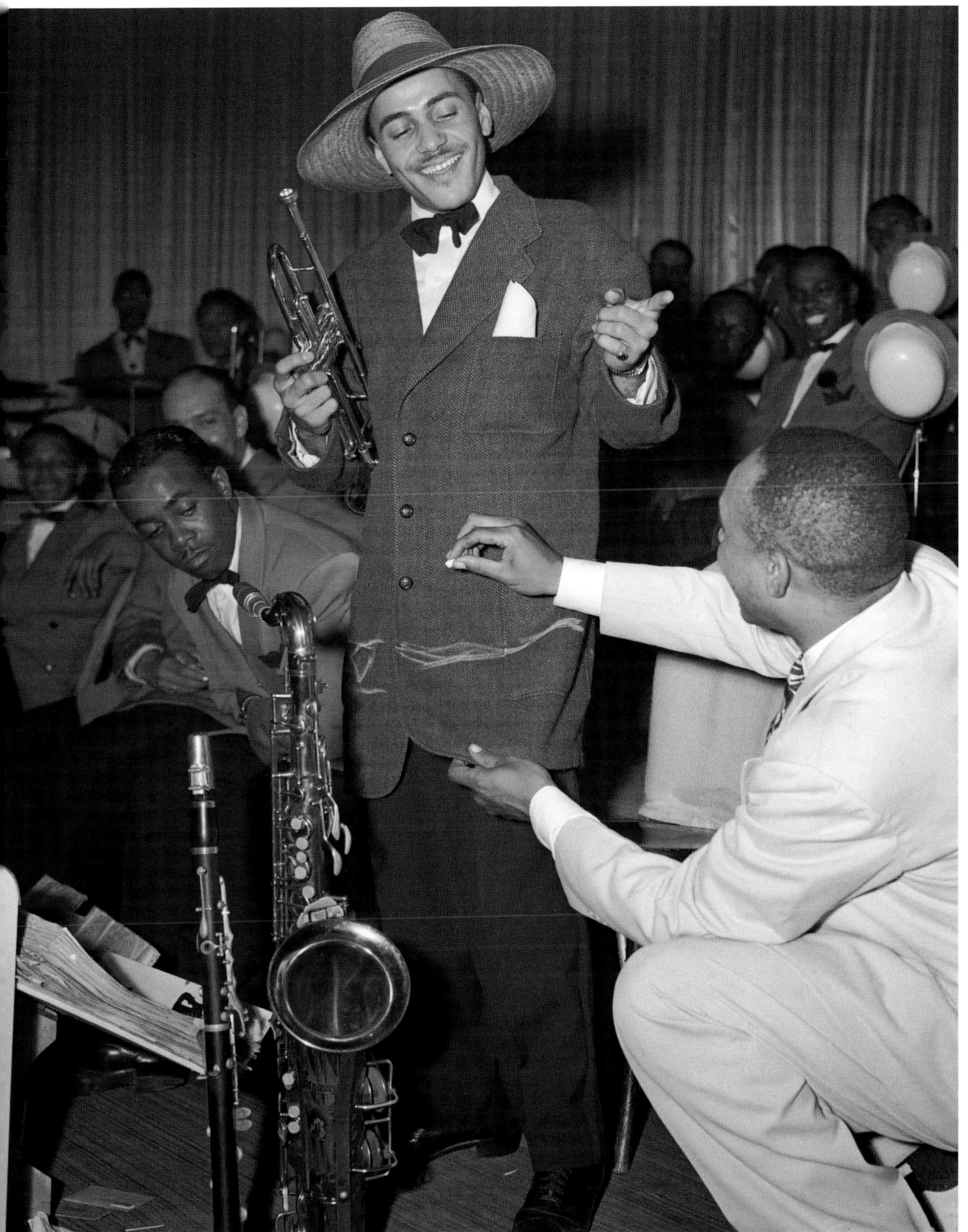

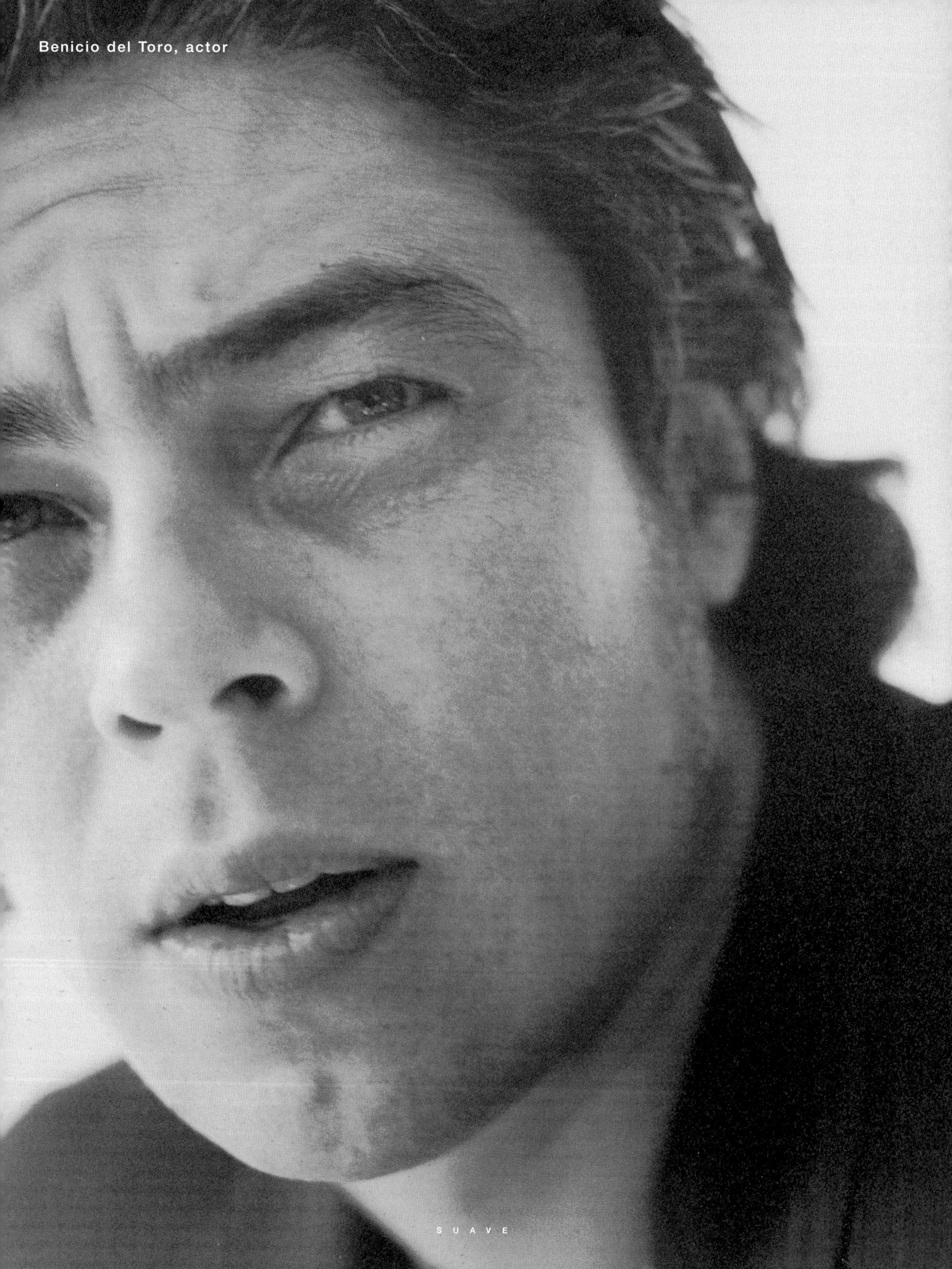

Benicio del Toro, actor

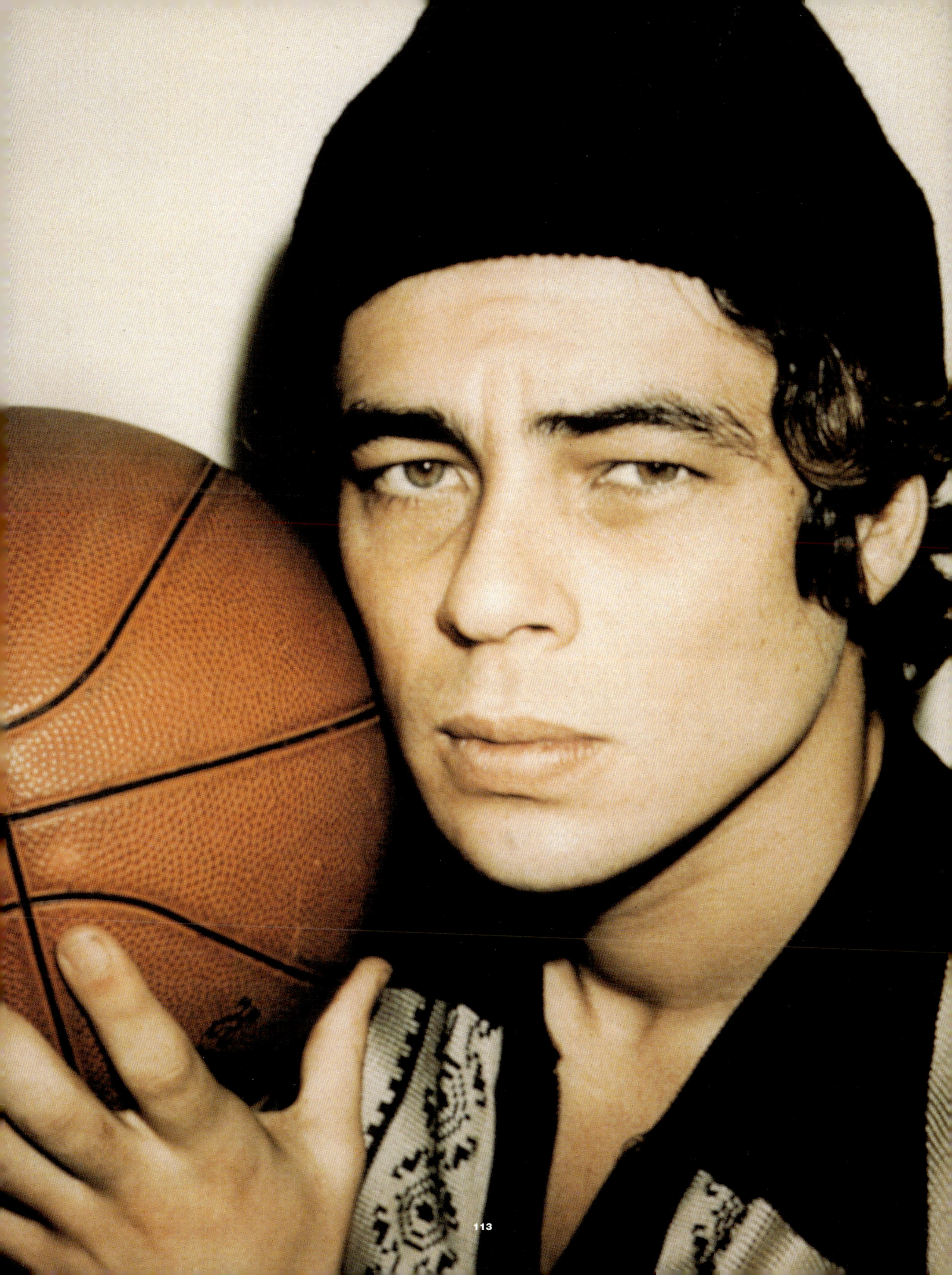

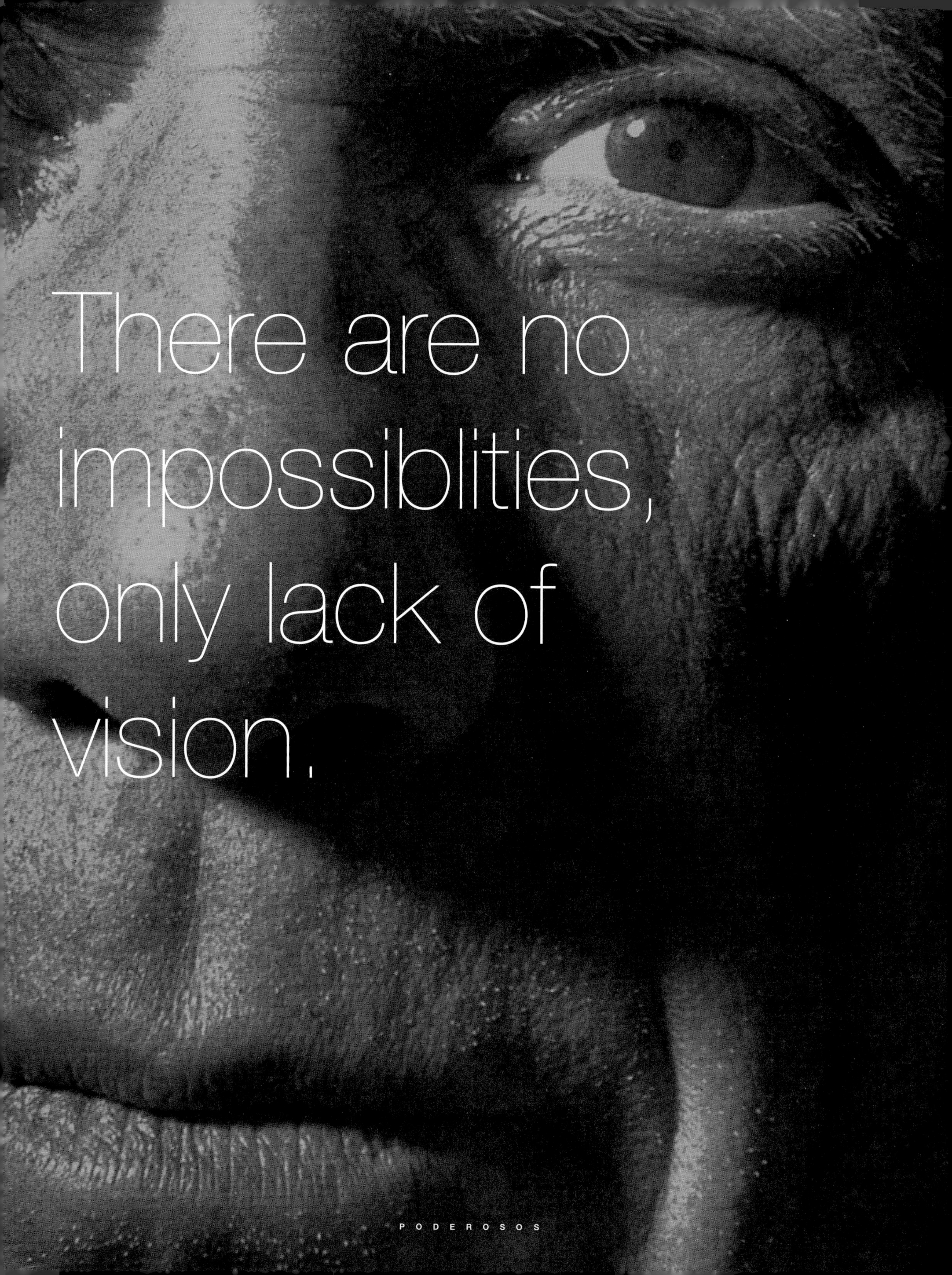

There are no impossiblities, only lack of vision.

Whether strutting like a peacock in an electric Zoot suit or lounging languidly in white linen, Latin men have always possessed a singular sense of style.

Poderosos transcend stereotypes. The powerful Latin man's strength is expressed with his overwhelming style. Regardless of the medium the *poderoso* employs to channel his power it's the stroke of a pen or the turn of a phrase that conveys the *poderoso's* signature style and individuality.

The outlaw image of Emiliano Zapata, a true *poderoso*, is forever embedded in popular culture. He glamorized a peasant chic at a time when aspiring Mexican cosmopolites were coveting the French ideal of sophistication. Zapata's ranchero clothing represented his agrarian politics, but he quickly shattered the image of a passive farmer by donning weapons and using them. In the midst of a war, when Mexico was grappling with it's identity, Zapata became the face of the indigenous masses, and raised the *mestizo* consciousness

Whether eliciting outrage or inspiration, the *poderoso* never evokes indifference.

Adored or hated, Fidel Castro is one of the most stylish leaders of our era. With his trademark beard, fatigues, and cigar, Castro exemplifies power. Absolute power. The dictator has adroitly used his military garb as a means of intimidation. Recognizing the profound effect of fashion on the classes, Castro minimized the importance of clothes, a sign of class distinctions. He encouraged Cuban men to wear the subtle, cotton *guayabera*, symbolizing membership in the proletariat, instead of a dress shirt and tie, hallmarks of the middle and ruling classes. In this respect, Castro may even parallel fashion designer Cristobal Balenciaga, in the Latin influence on fashion.

Poderosos exude the extraordinary, and their stature implies that there are no impossibilities, only lack of vision. While some men execute their vision by force, others express their passions with poignancy.

Federico García Lorca was a Spanish poet who was killed because General Francisco Franco's hard-line regime failed to see the vision in his works. Lorca was murdered in his beloved Grenada because the Fascists contended he did more damage with his pen than others do with pistols. Genteel in appearance, he looked the part of the Spanish bourgeoise dressed in a white suit and bow tie. But the poet's writings were darker and more controversial than he allowed his public persona to appear. While Lorca may not have represented the virile image of a Spaniard, the Chilean poet Pablo Neruda lauded Lorca as the perfect representative of Spain's vitality and profundity.

A truly wise man, César Chávez shrouded himself in a cloak of dignity. Dressed modestly in button-down shirts and tennis shoes, Chávez believed his appearance should accurately symbolize the people he represented, impoverished laborers. But his humble presence did not detract from his honest character; it only lent sincerity to his cause. When questioned about the respect farm workers had for him, Chávez simply replied, "Because the feeling is mutual."

Poderosos are powerful personalities whose imprint on the world is, "I was here." They are irrepressible spirits who, through an independence movement, epic mural, or magic realism revolutionize with a style all their own.

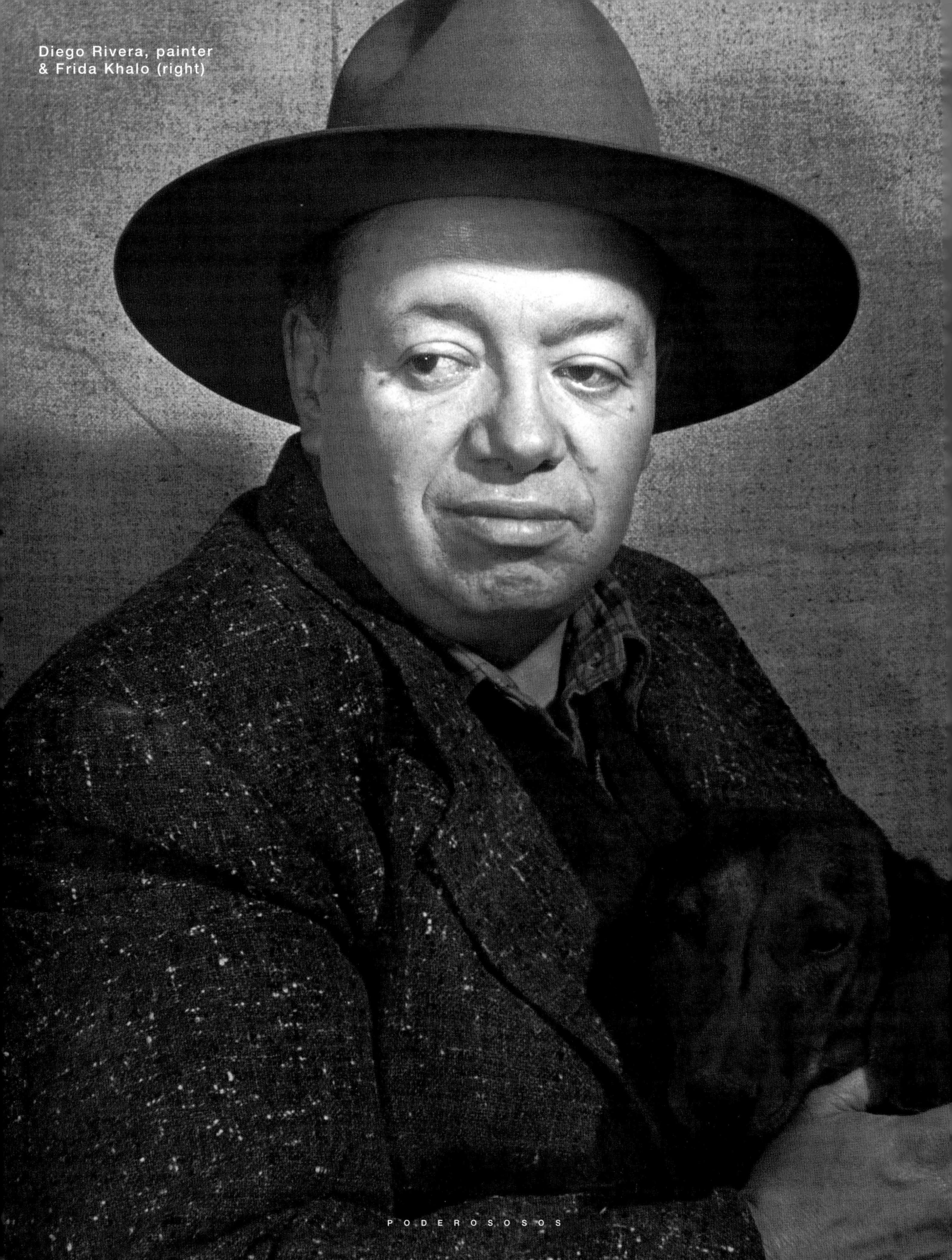

Diego Rivera, painter
& Frida Khalo (right)

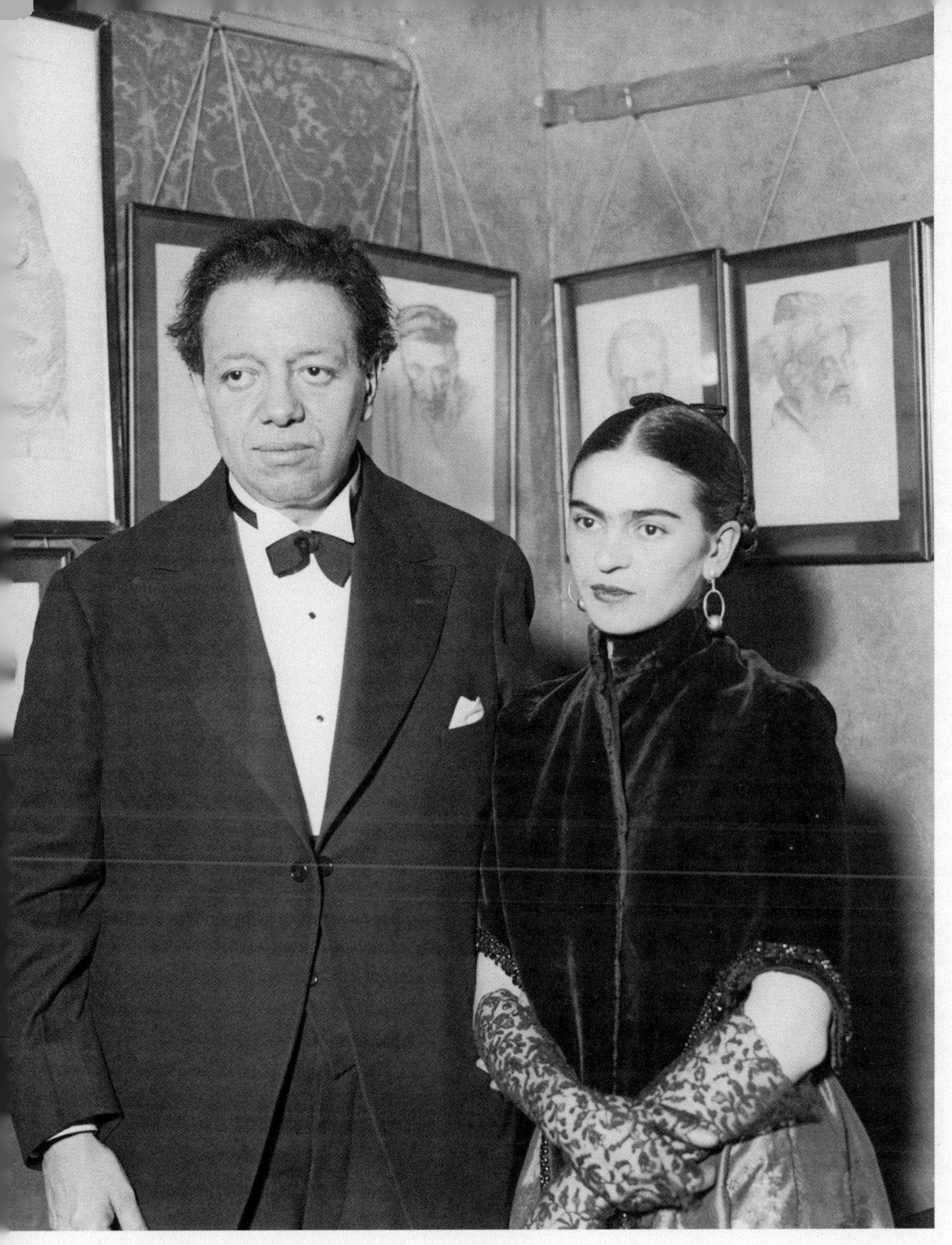

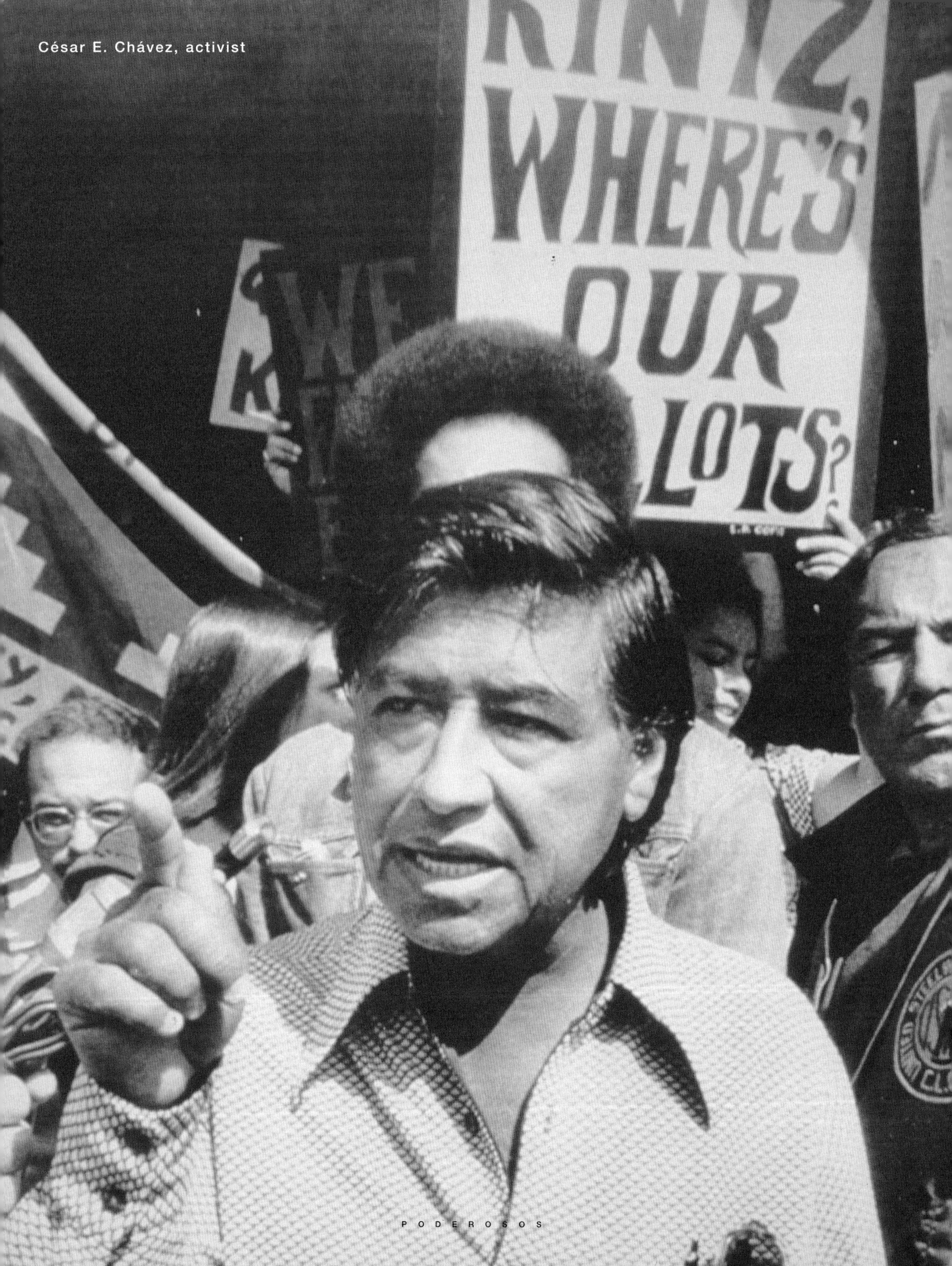

César E. Chávez, activist

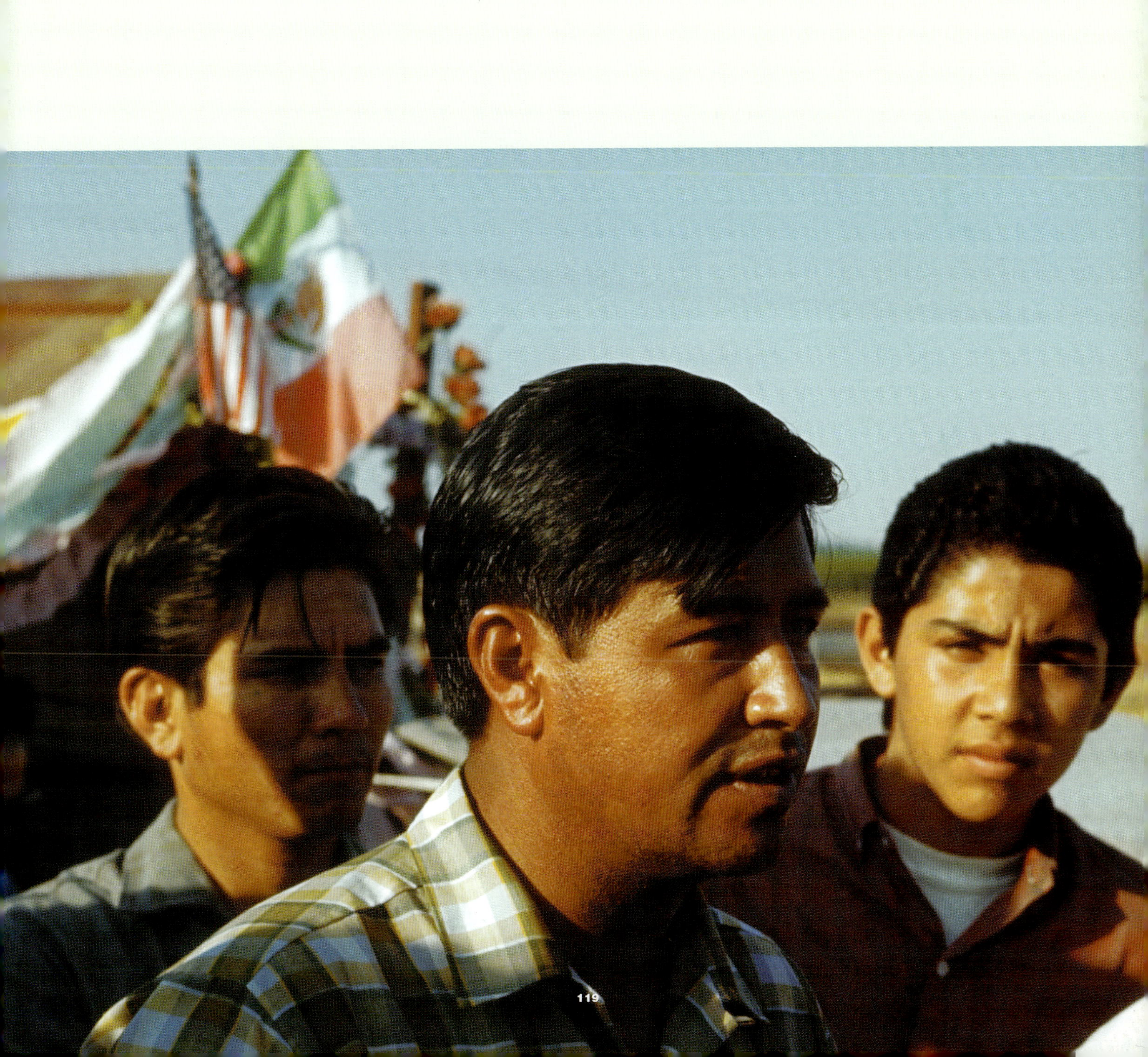

Cristobal Balenciaga, fashion designer

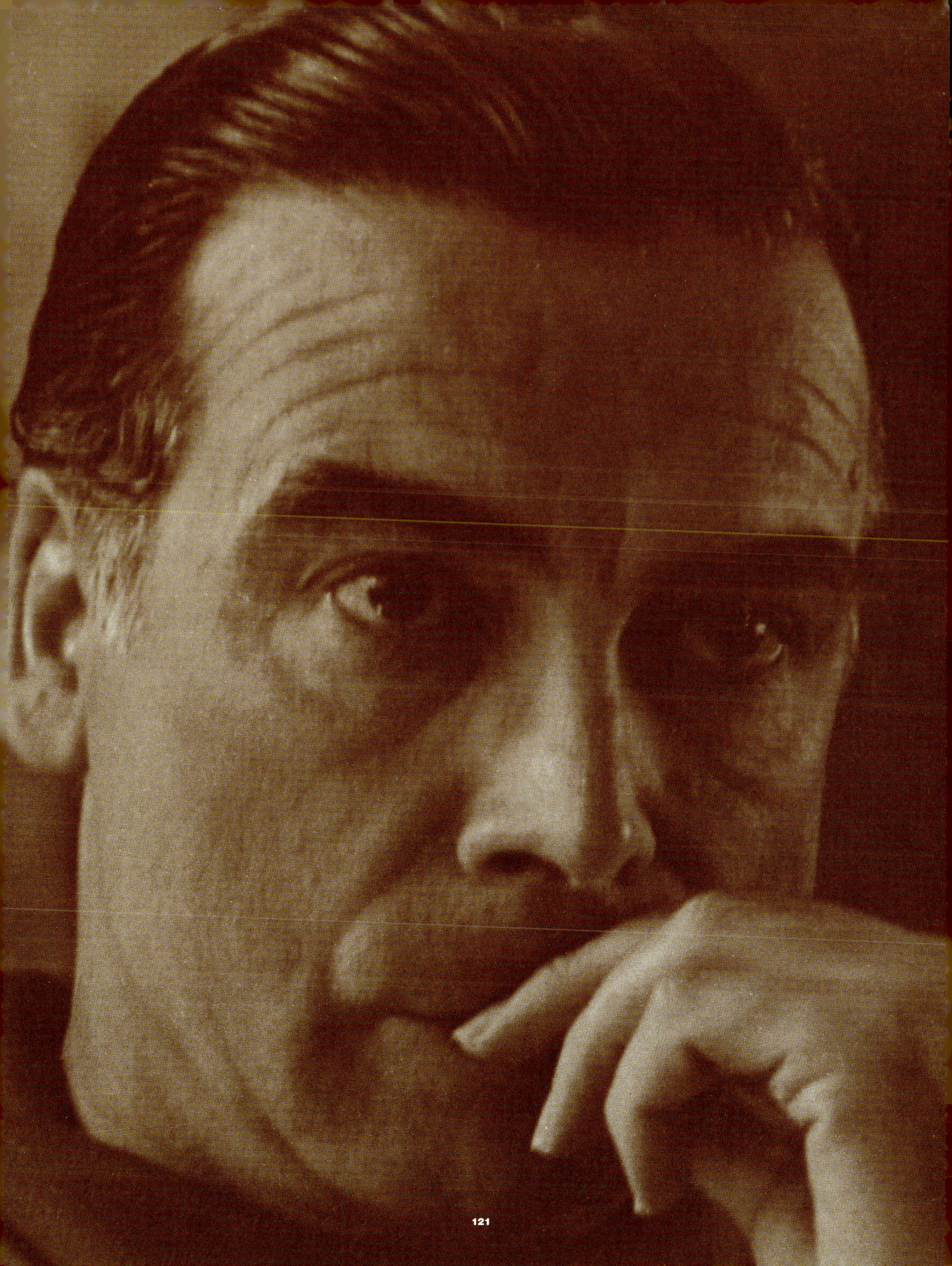

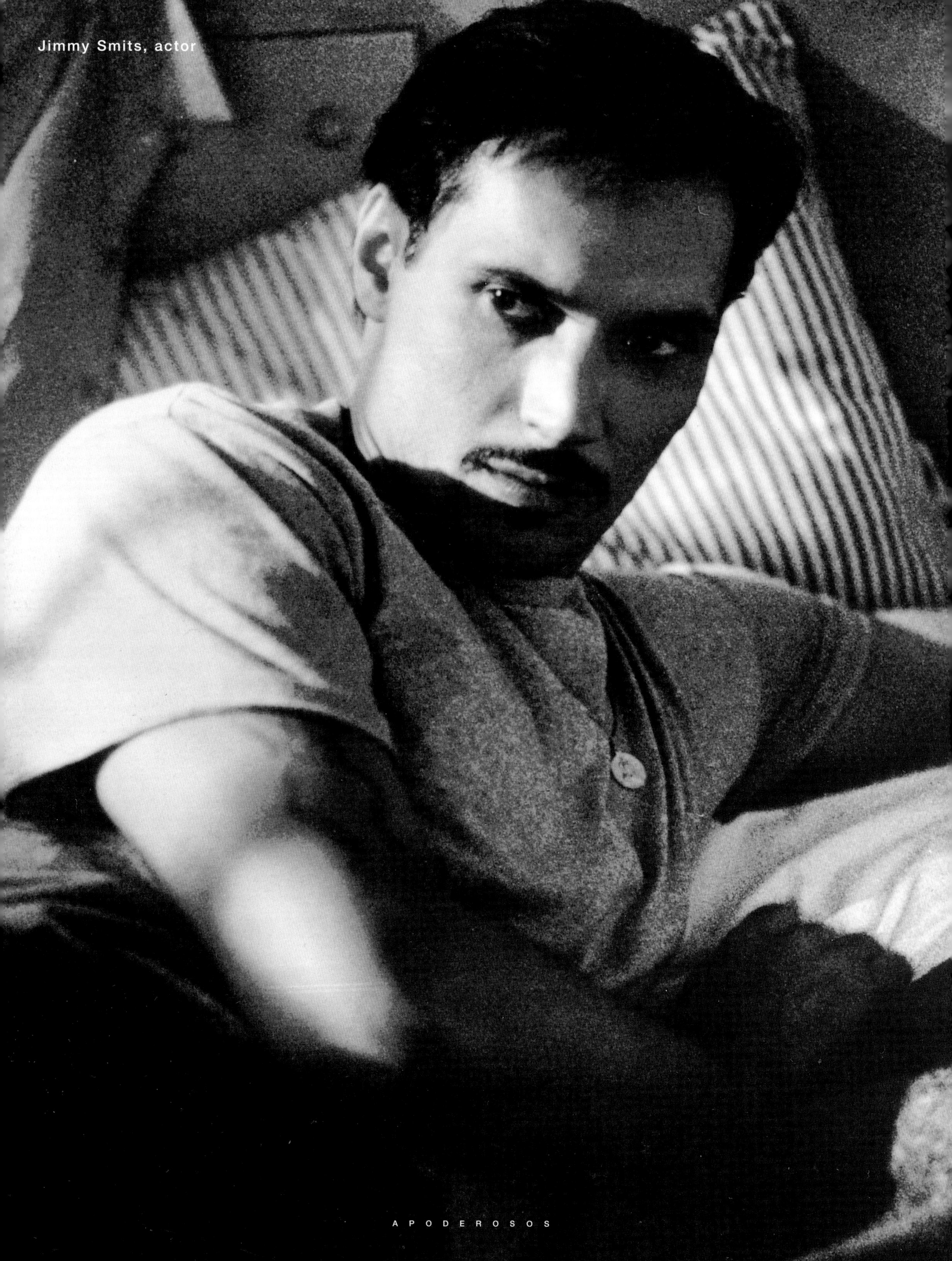

Jimmy Smits, actor

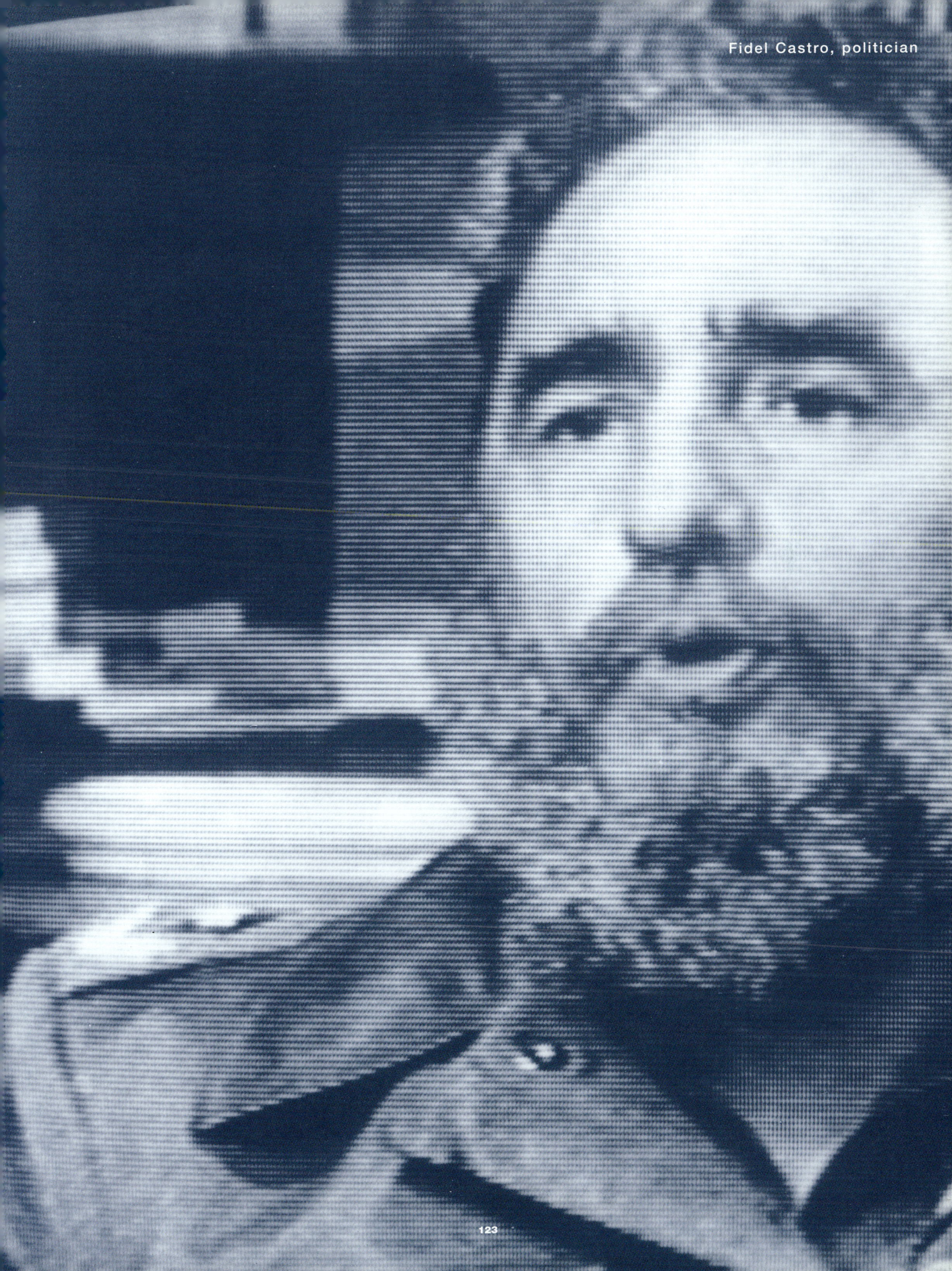

Fidel Castro, politician

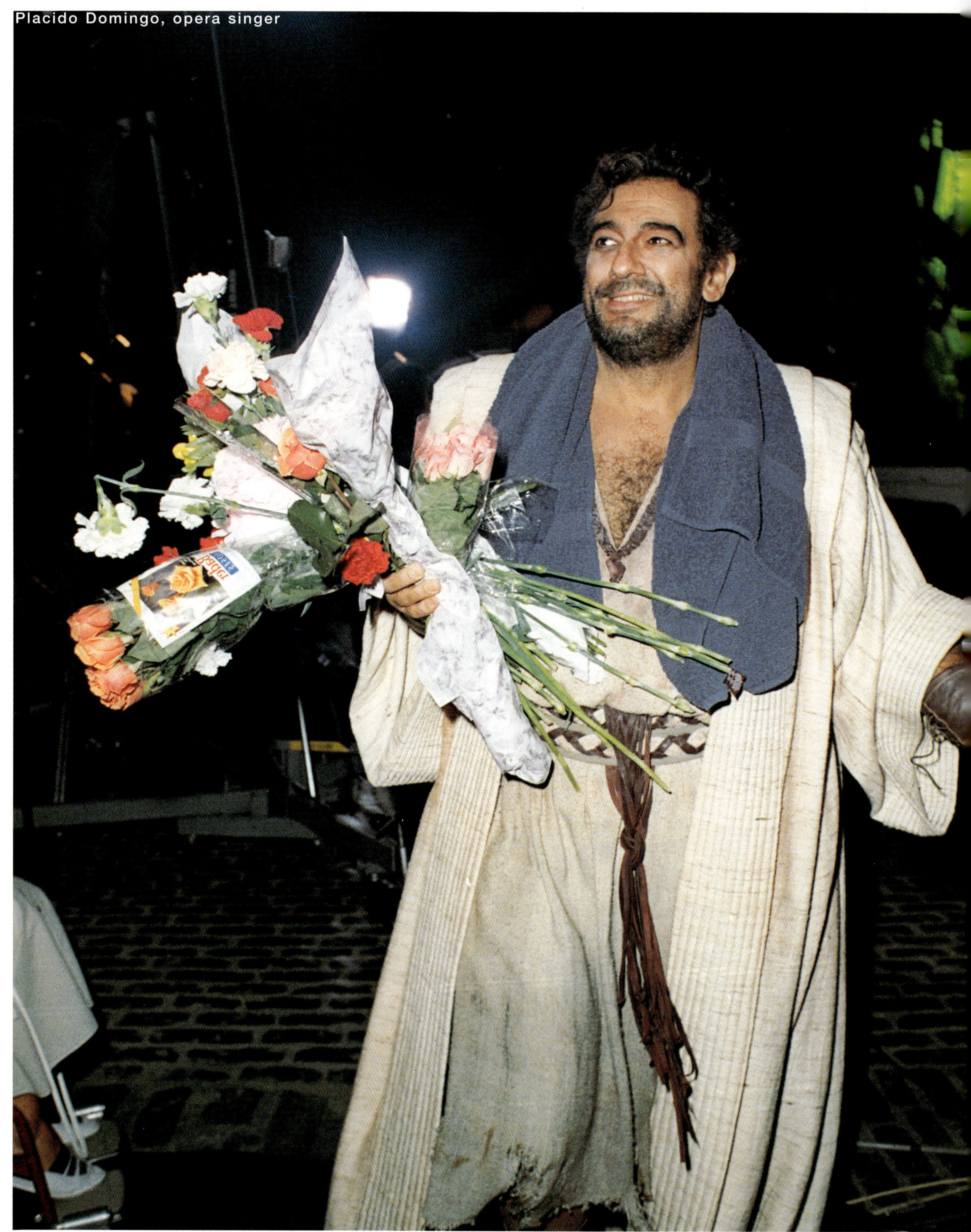

Placido Domingo, opera singer

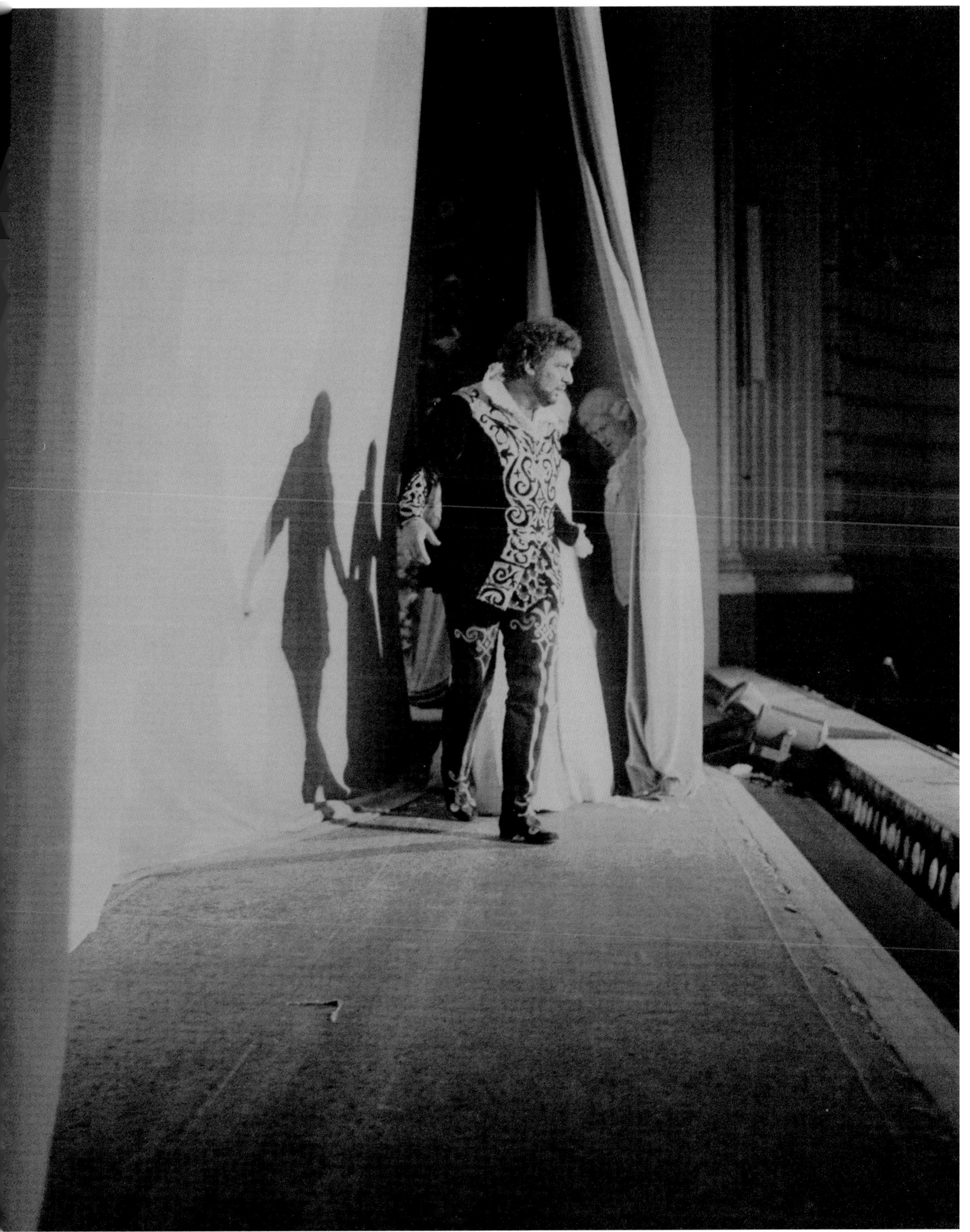

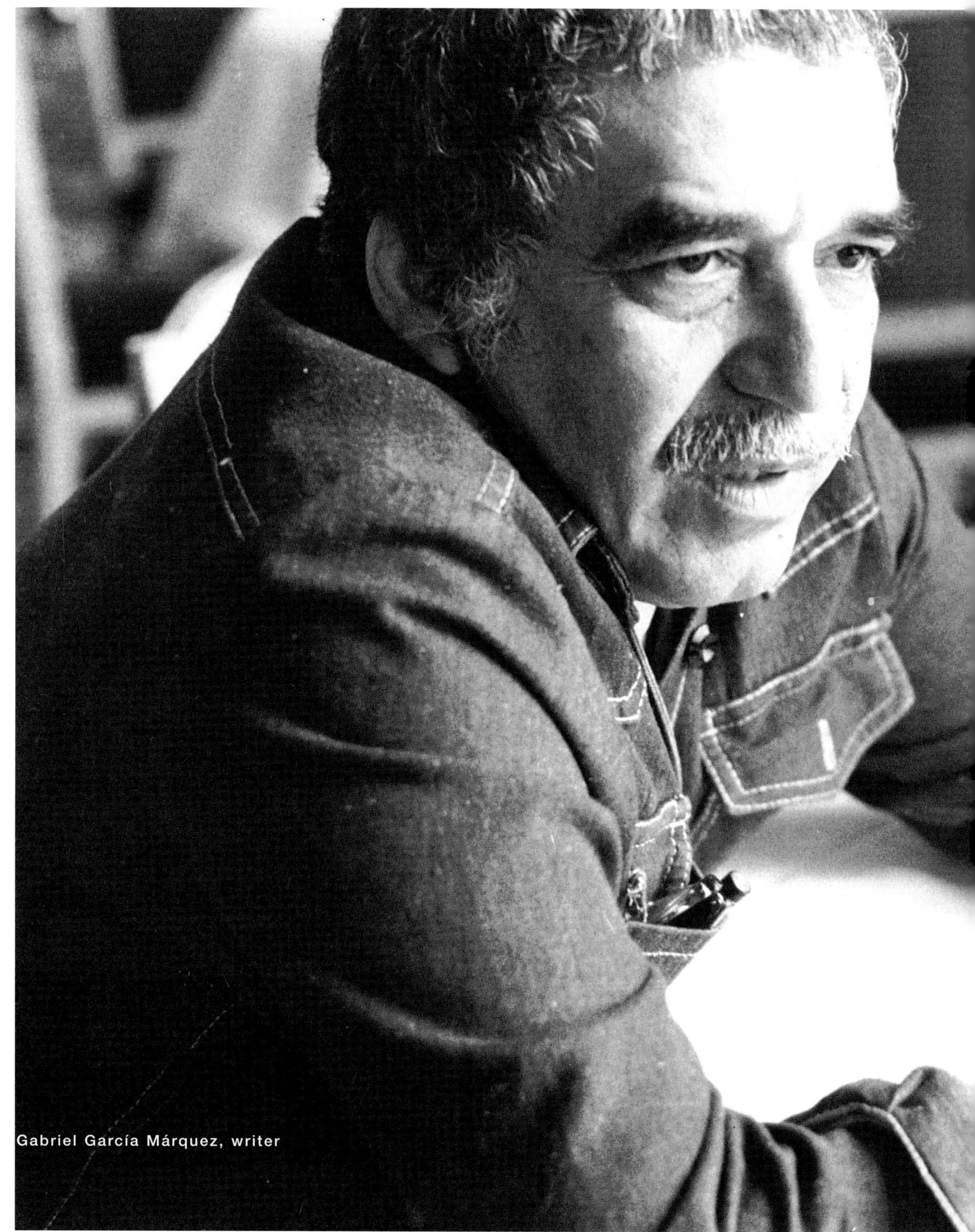
Gabriel García Márquez, writer

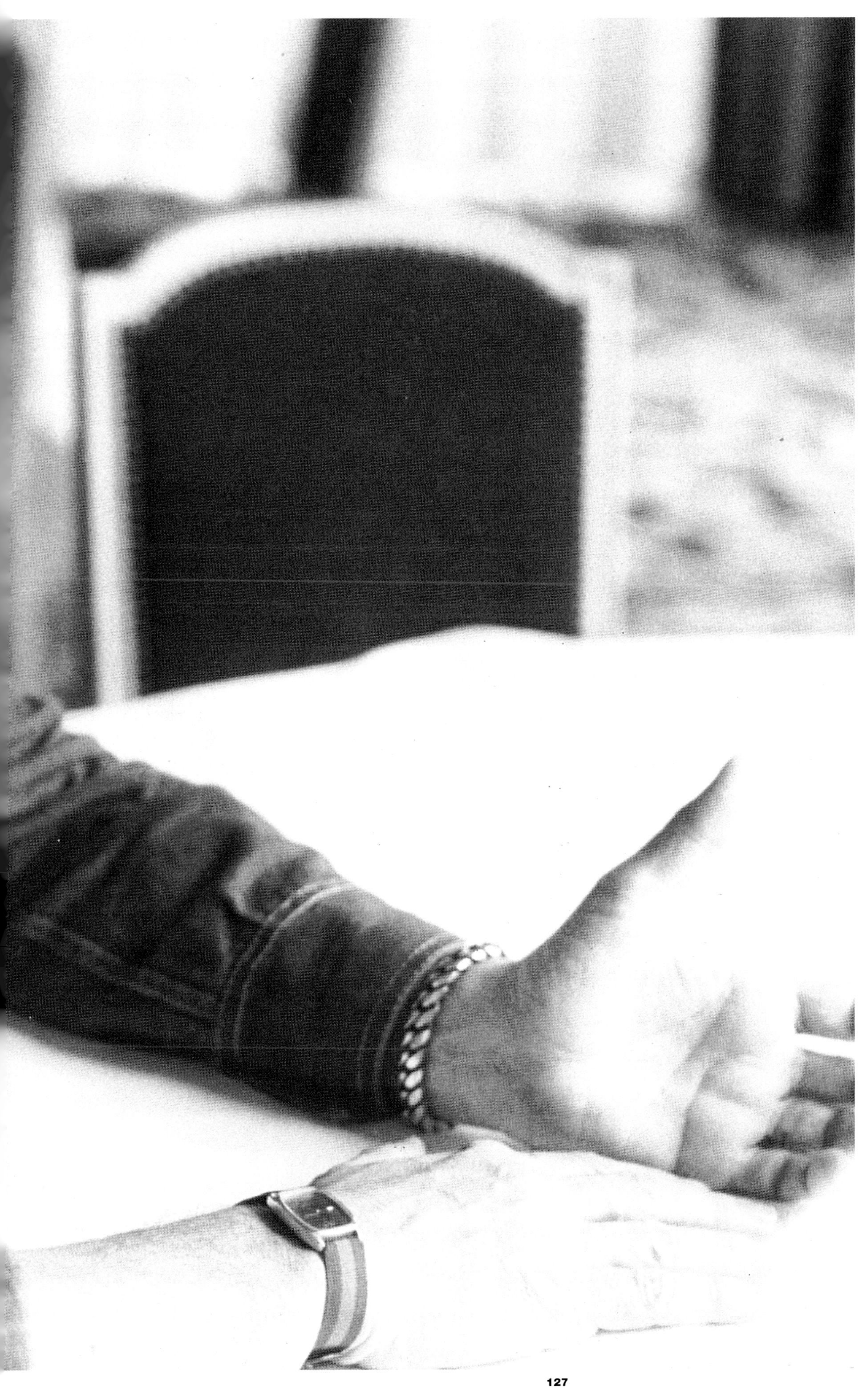

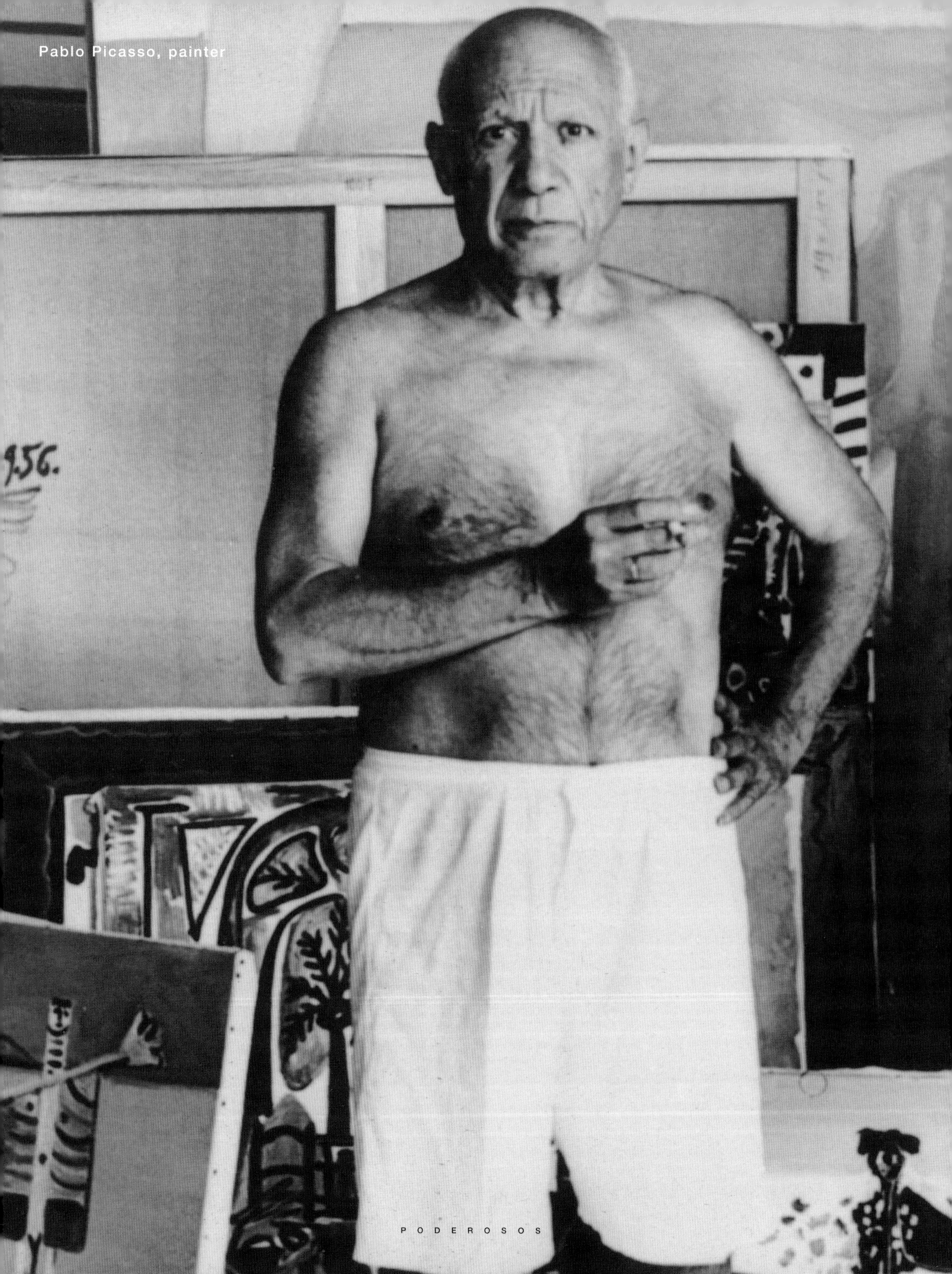
Pablo Picasso, painter

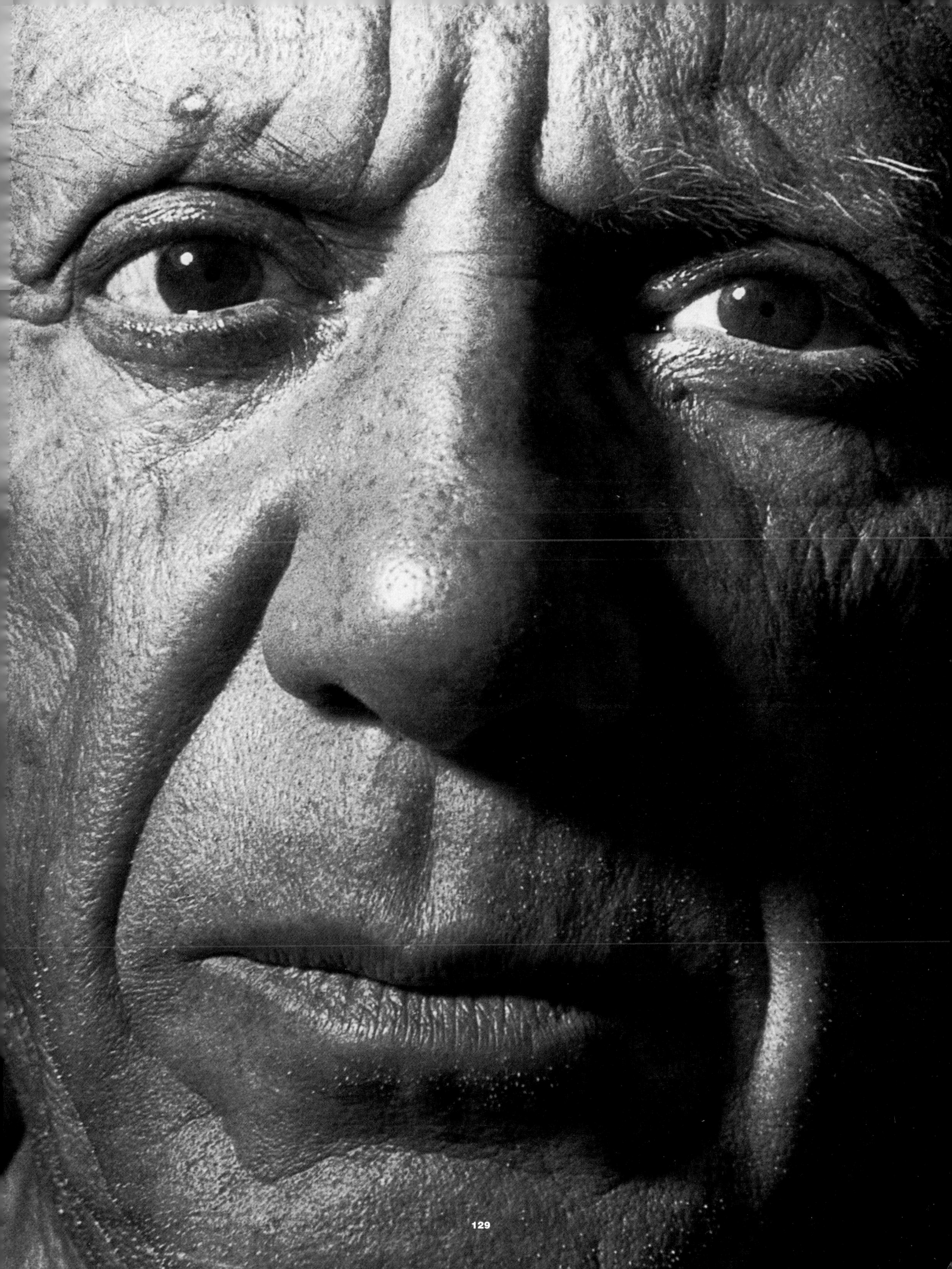

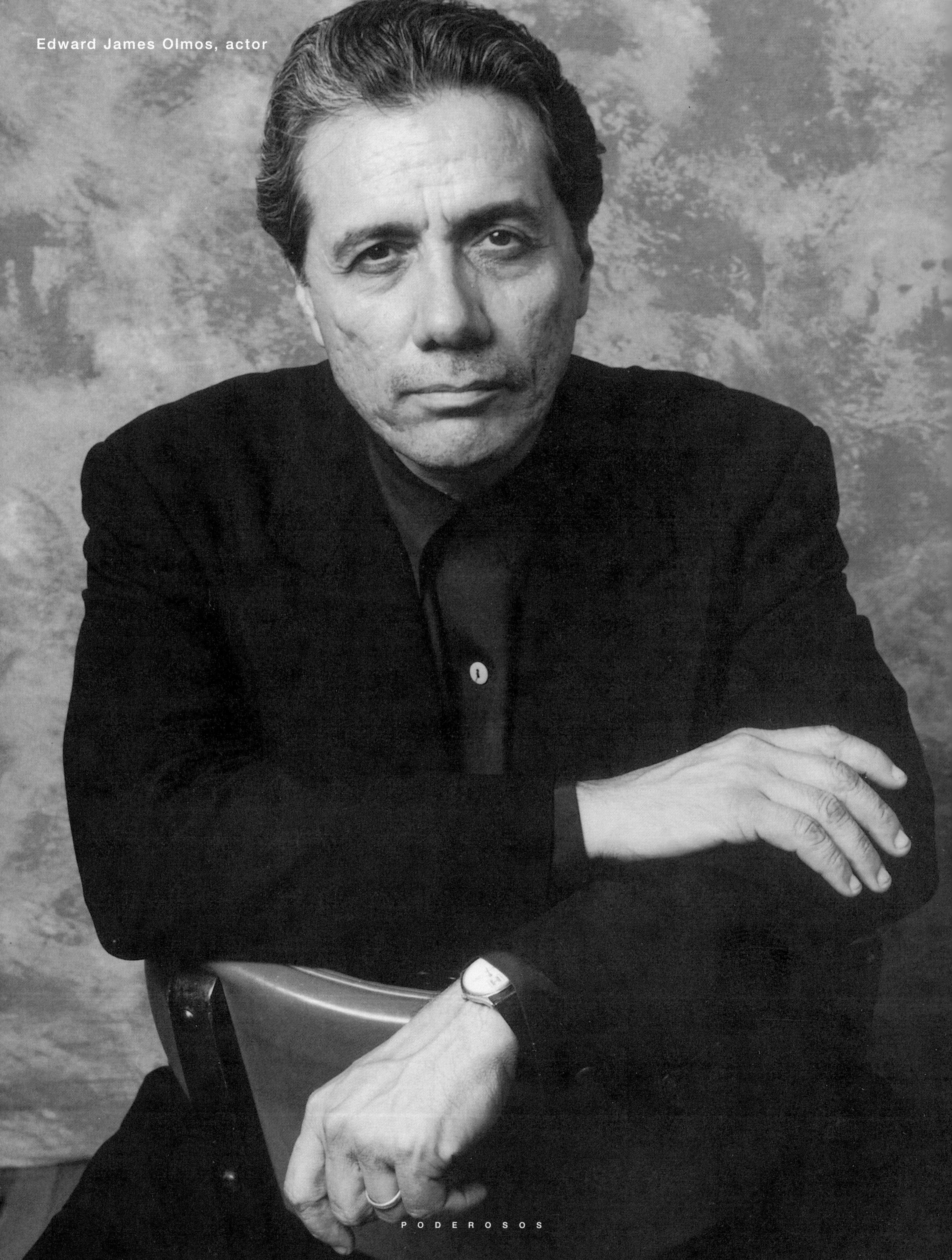
Edward James Olmos, actor

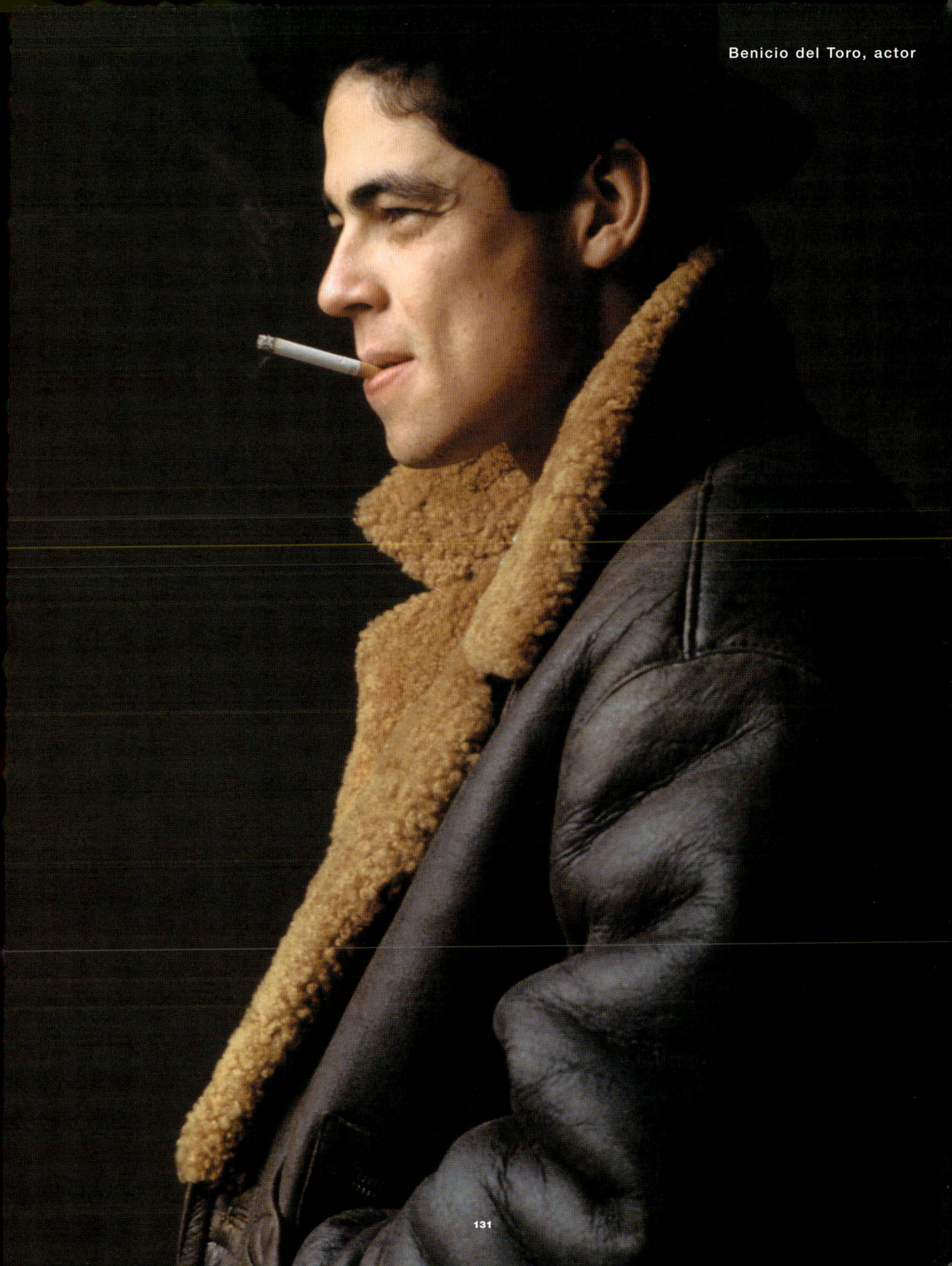

Benicio del Toro, actor

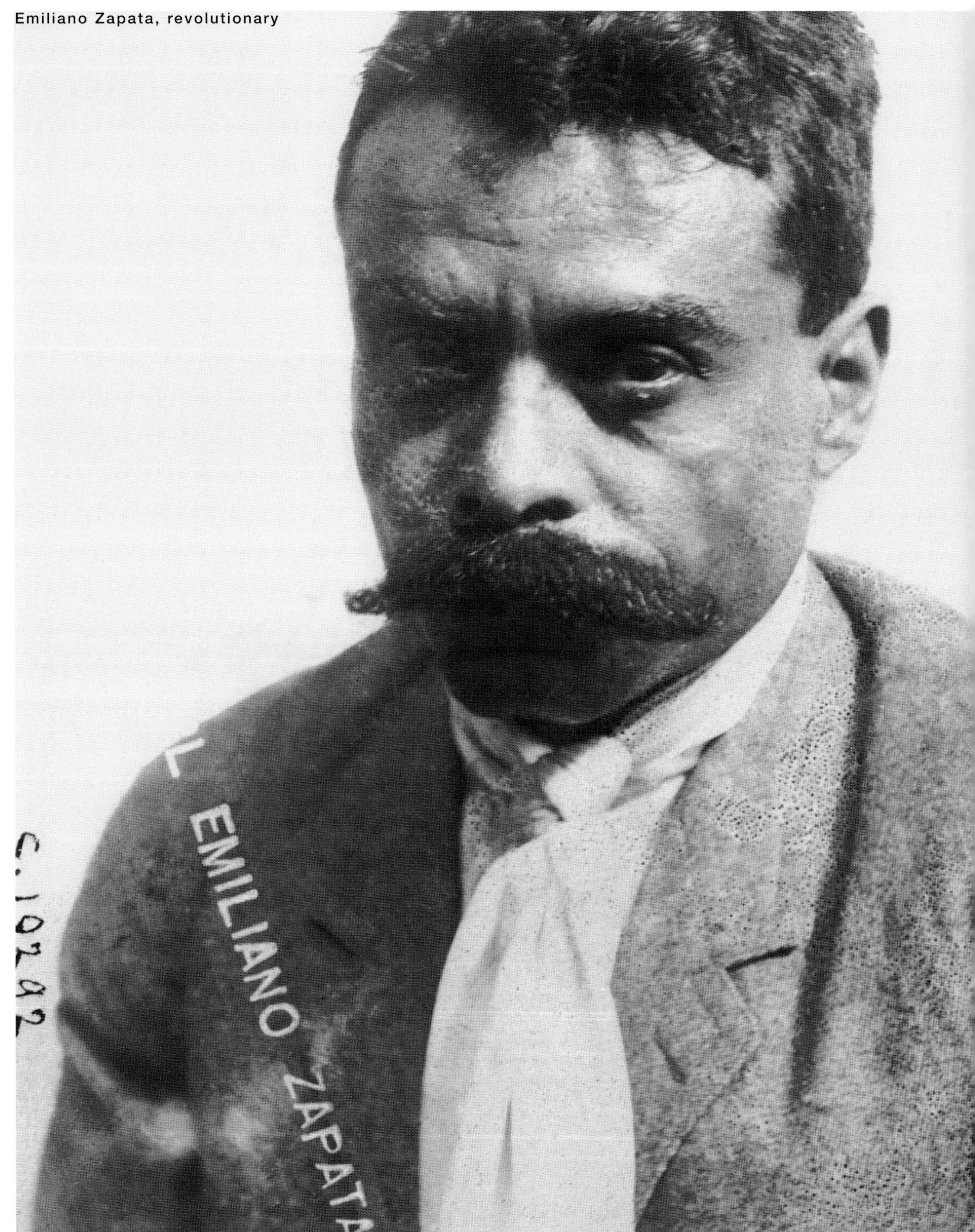

Emiliano Zapata, revolutionary

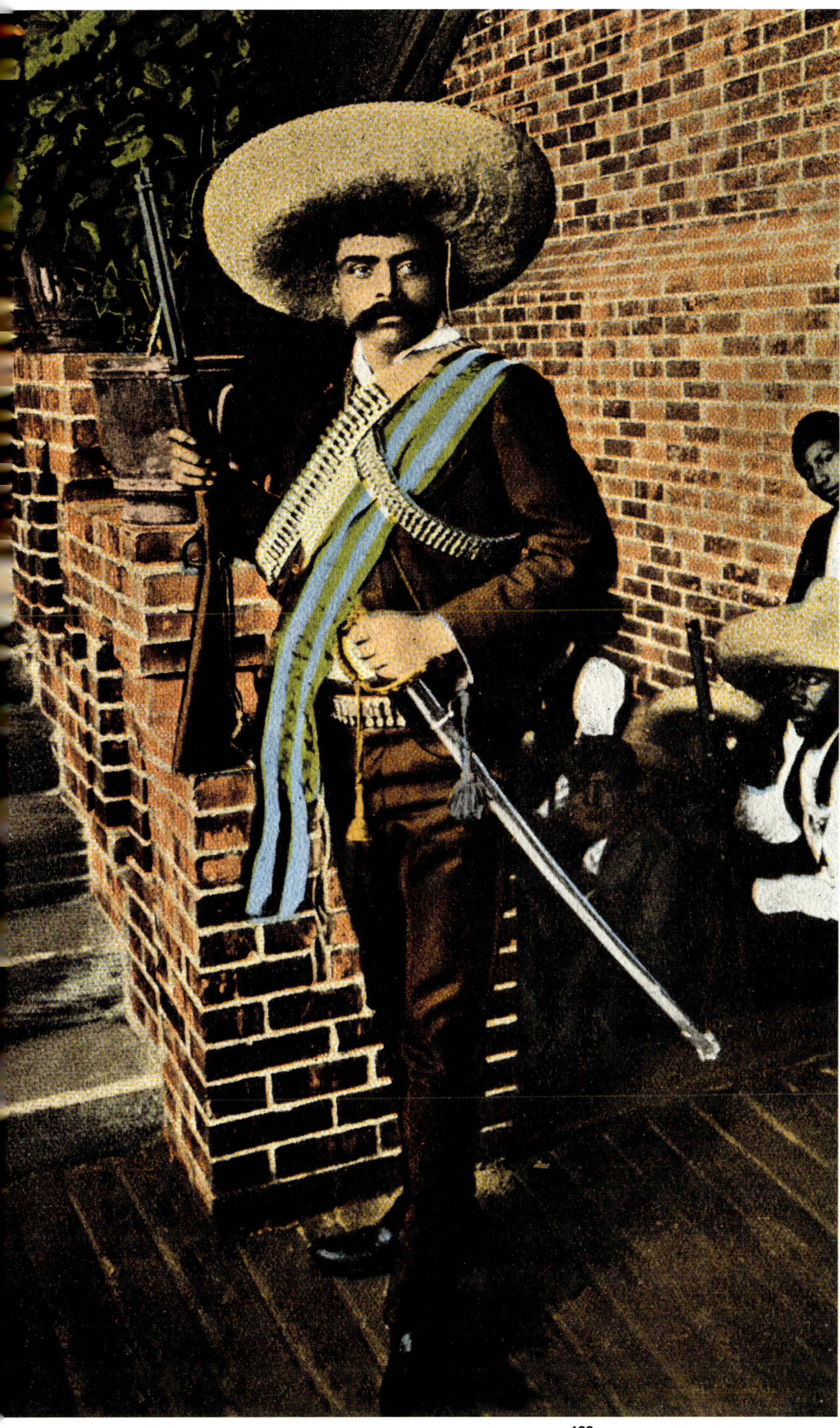

Juan Domingo Perón, politician

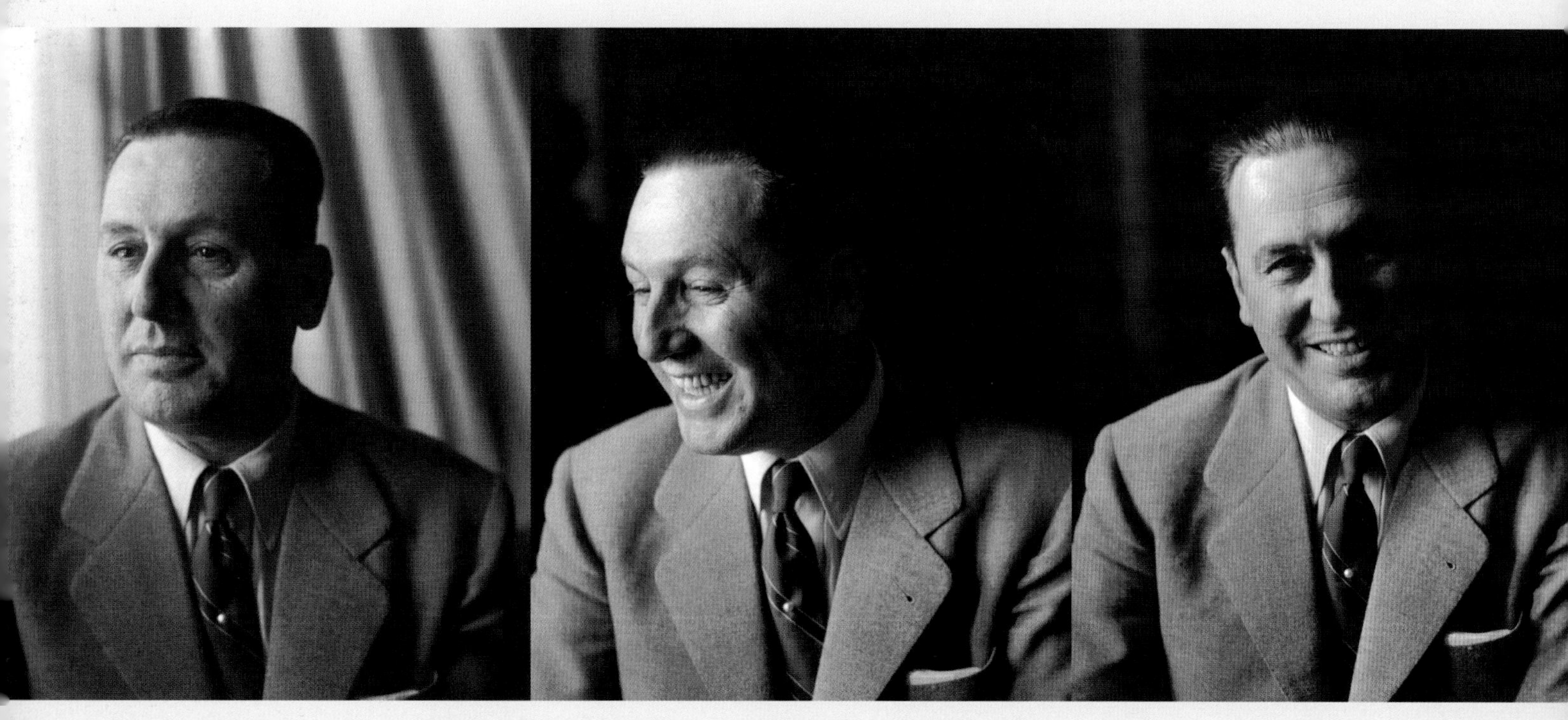

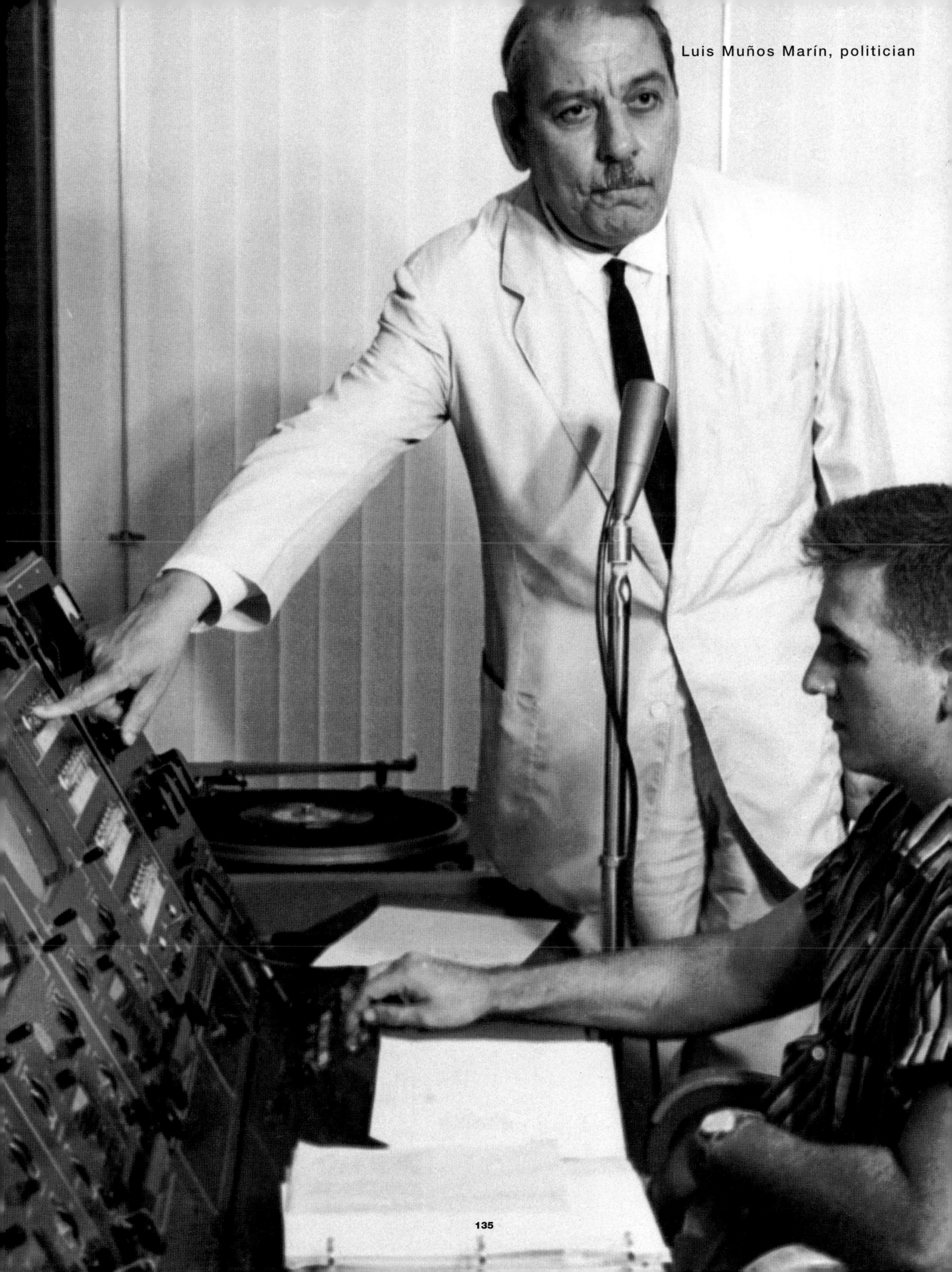

Luis Muños Marín, politician

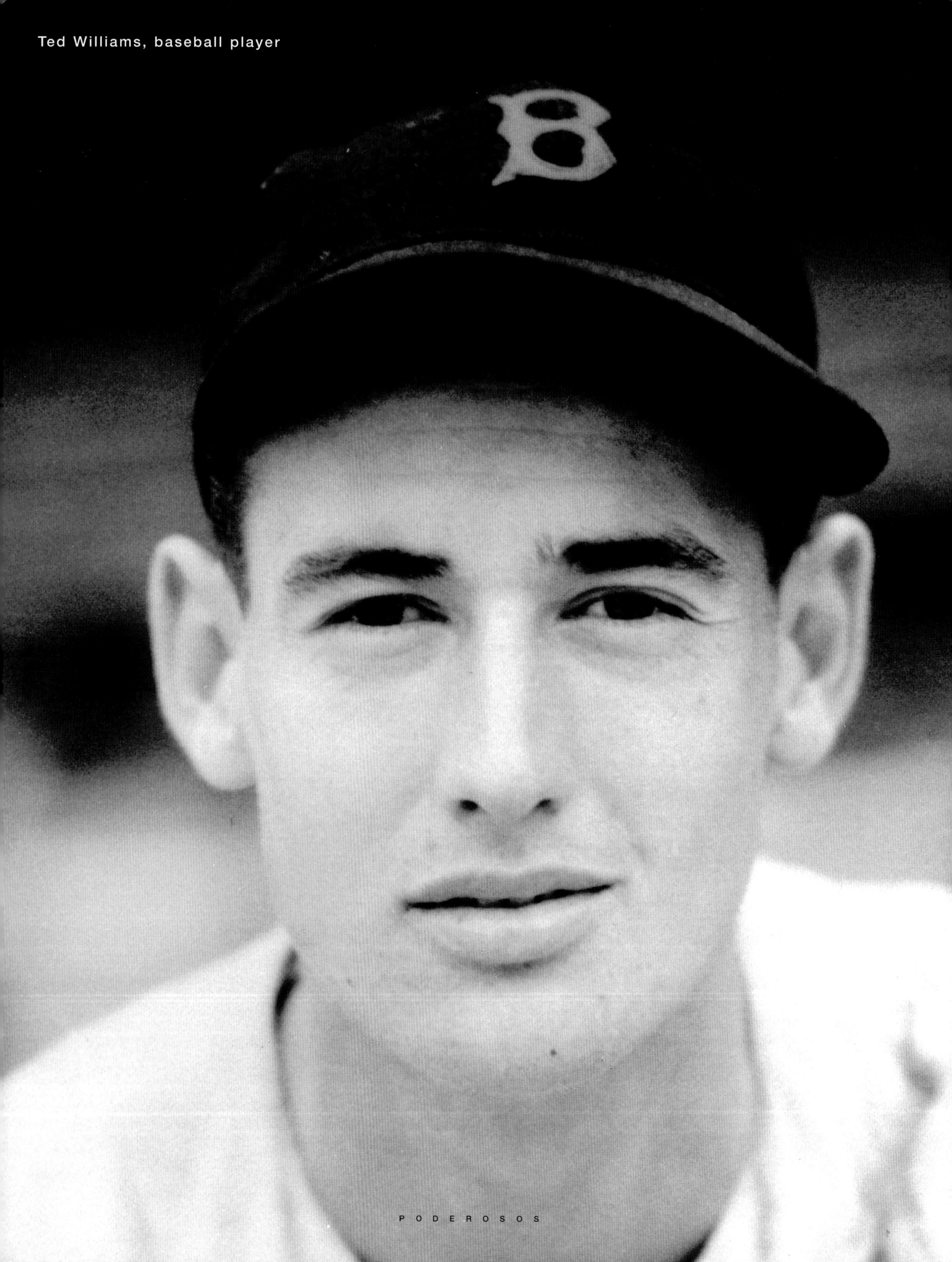

Ted Williams, baseball player

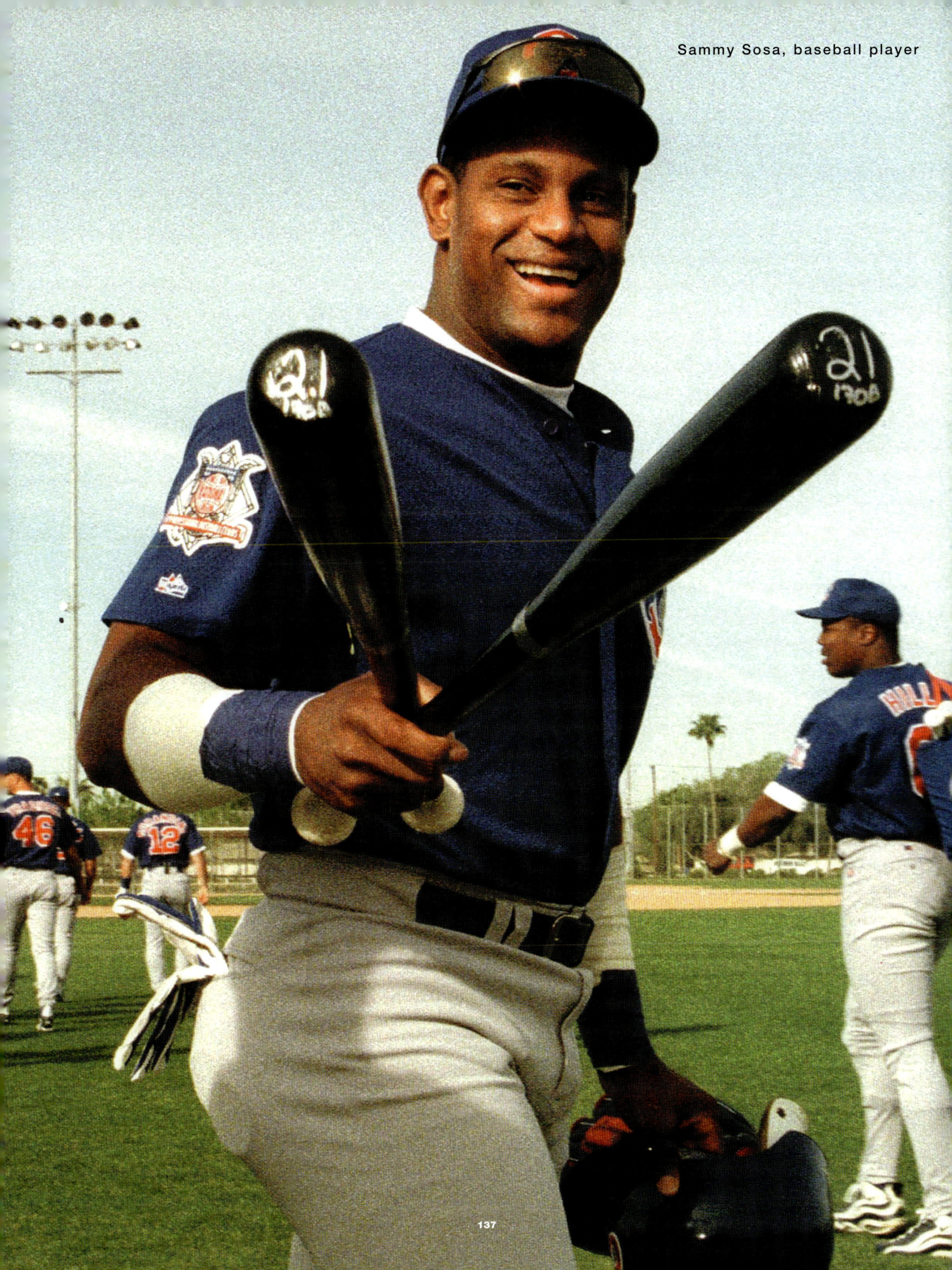

Sammy Sosa, baseball player

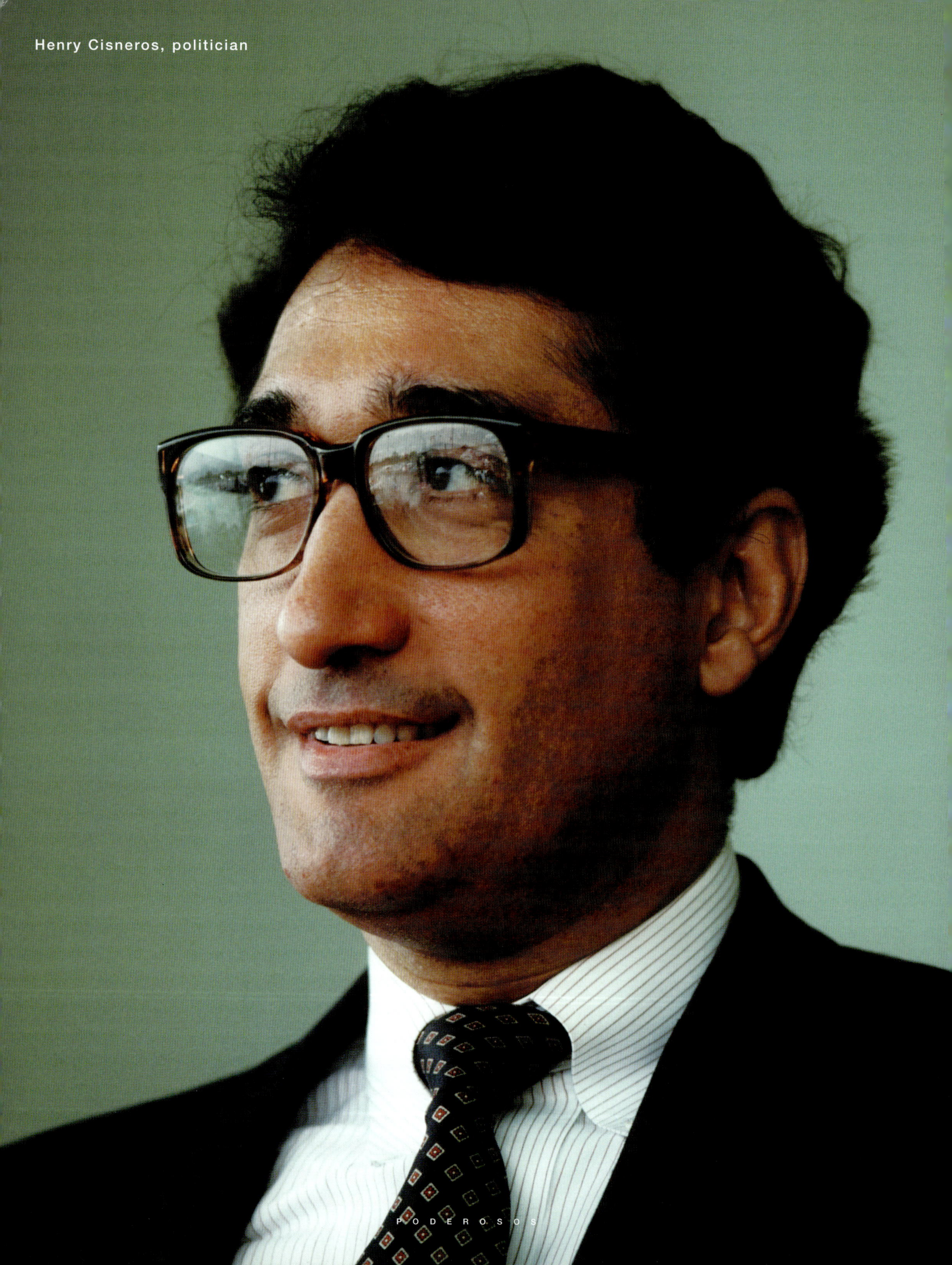
Henry Cisneros, politician

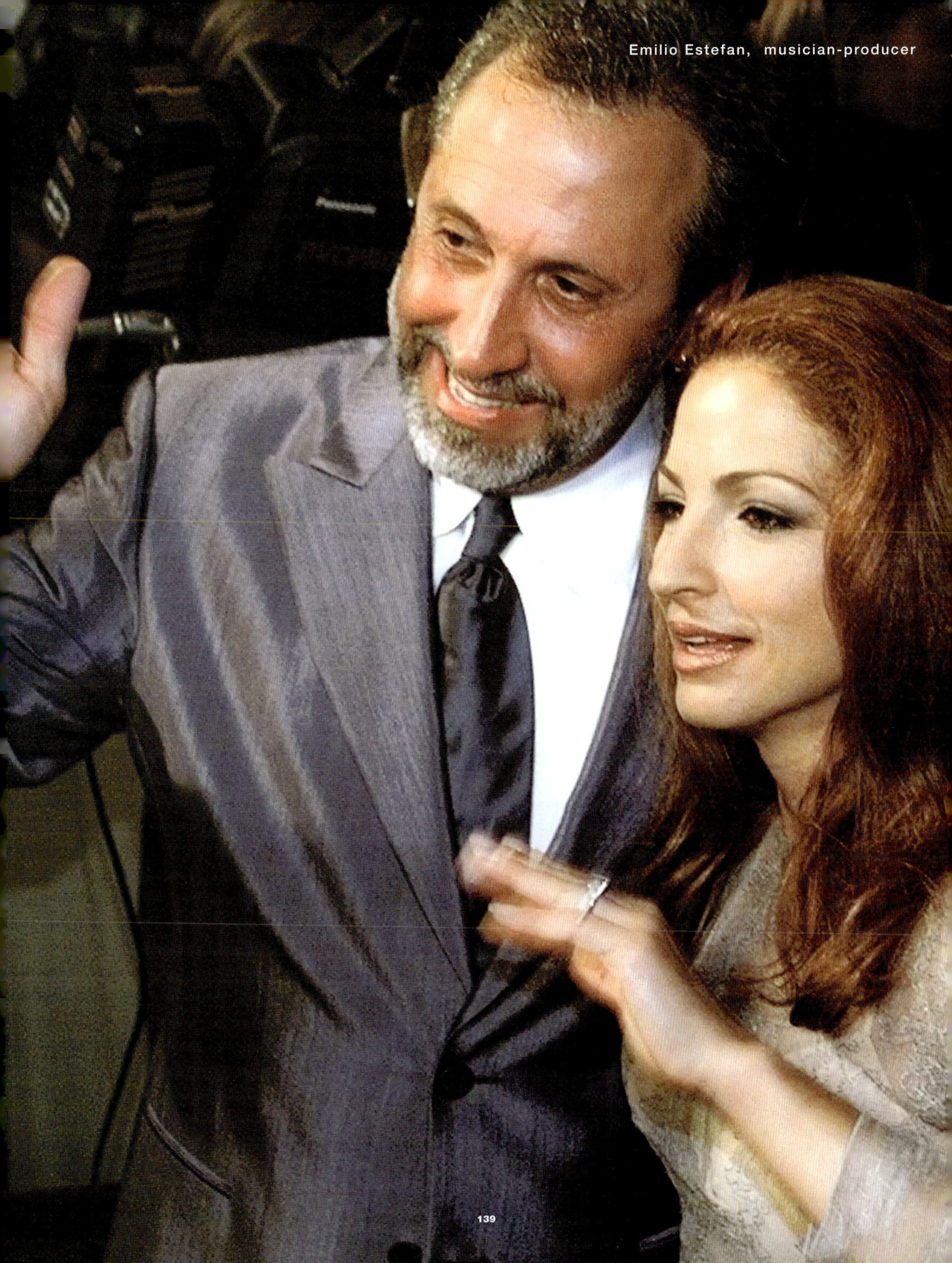
Emilio Estefan, musician-producer

PHOTO CREDITS

COVER

Antonio Banderas Photograph by Cliff Watts/Icon International

INTRODUCTION

César Romero Photofest

PEACOCKS

Salvador Dalí Archive photos

Liberto Rabal Photofest

Salvador Dalí Corbis

Salvador Dalí Archive Photos

Cantinflas Corbis

Cantinflas Corbis

Xavier Cugat Photofest

El Cordobéz Archive photo

Sammy Davis Jr. Photofest

Sammy Davis Jr. Photofest

Sammy Davis Jr. Corbis

Ricky Martin Photofest

Ricky Martin Visages 2000 Photo by Miranda Penn Turin

Pedro Almodóvar Photofest

Joaquín Cortés Corbis

Joaquín Cortés Photoraph by Jorge Represa/Globe Photo

Joaquín Cortés Corbis

Joaquín Cortés Corbis

Holly Woodlawn Photofest

Walter Mercado photograph by Walter Weissman/Globe

JOVENES

Freddie Prinze Photofest

Nicholas Gonzalez Photograph by Milan Ryba/Globe Photos

Charlie Sheen Corbis

Ritchie Valens Photograph by Dick Miller/Globe Photos

Mario Lopez Photograph by Mike Ruiz/Visages

Cheyanne Photograph by Carlos Baez

Freddie Prinze Jr. Photograph by Murray Close/Photofest

Freddie Prinze Photofest

Jon Seda Photograph by Alexis Rodriguez -Duarte

Enrique Iglesias Photograph by Alec Michael

Carlos Vives Corbis

Emilio Estevez Corbis

Cristian de la Fuente Photograph by Paul Skipper/Archive Photos

Alejandro Fernández Corbis

Diego Serrano Photograph by Mike Ruiz/Visages

Alejandro Sanz Corbis

Julio Iglesias Jr. Photograph by Mike Ruiz/Visages

Beto Courtesy Diana Baron

ROMÁNTICOS

Andy García Photograph by Jack Rowand/Photofest

Antonio Banderas Photograph by Cliff Watts/Icon

Antonio Banderas Photograph by Cliff Watts/Icon

César Romero Photograph by Gene Korman/Photofest

César Romero Photograph by Freulich/Photofest

Oscar De La Renta Photograph by Slim Aarons/Archive photos

Ruben Toledo Photograph by Alexis Rodriguez-Duarte

Ruben Toledo Photograph by Alexis Rodriguez-Duarte

Marc Anthony Corbis

Marc Anthony Globe phoyograph by Mark Allan

John Secada Corbis

Tito Puente Corbis

Rudolph Valentino Photofest

Rudolph Valentino Corbis

Oscar de la Hoya Photograph by K/Visages

Oscar de la Hoya Corbis

Esai Morales Photograph by Rita Rivera

Ruben Blades Photofest

Fernando Lamas Photofest

Gilbert Roland Photofest

Andy García Photograph by Jack Rowand/Photofest

Andy García Photofest

Benjamin Bratt Photofest

Benjamin Bratt Photograph by Ron Batzdorff

José Ferrer Photofest

José Carreras Corbis

Ricardo Montalban Photofest

Ricardo Montalban Photofest

Ricardo Montalban Photofest

Desí Arnáz Corbis

Desí Arnáz Corbis

Desí Arnáz Corbis

ROCKEROS

Enrique Iglesias Corbis

Dave Navarro Corbis

Dave Navarro Corbis

Trini Lopez Corbis

Pelé Globe Photos

Pelé Corbis

Pelé Corbis

Jean-Michel Basquiat Photofest

Fidel Castro Photofest

Ché Guevara Photofest

Cypress Hill Corbis

Enrique Iglesias Corbis

Javier Bardem Photofest

Big Pun Corbis

Scott Gomez Corbis

Zach de la Rocha Corbis

Zach de la Rocha Corbis

Milton Nascimento Corbis

Carlos Santana Corbis

Juan García Esquivel personal

Zoot suits Corbis

Zoot suits Corbis

Benicio del Toro Photograph by Alison Dyer/Visages

Benicio del Toro Photograph by K/Visages

PODEROSOS

Pablo Picasso Photograph by Horst Tappe/Archive photos

Diego Rivera Corbis

Diego Rivera & Frida Kahlo Corbis

César Chávez Archive Photo

César Chávez Corbis

Cristobal Balenciaga Corbis

Jimmy Smits Photofest

Fidel Castro Photofest

Placido Domingo Photograph by Dave Bennett/Globe photos

Placido Domingo Corbis

Gabriel García-Marquéz Archive Photos

Pablo Picasso Photograph by A Villers/Photofest

Pablo Picasso Corbis

Edward J.Olmos Photograph by Rita Rivera

Benicio del Toro Corbis

Emiliano Zapata Corbis

Emiliano Zapata Corbis

Juan Domingo Perón Corbis

Juan domingo Perón Corbis

Juan Domingo Perón Corbis

Luis Muñoz Marín Corbis

Ted Williams Corbis

Sammy Sosa Corbis

Henry Cisneros Corbis

Emilio & Gloria Estefan Corbis

Bullfighters Corbis

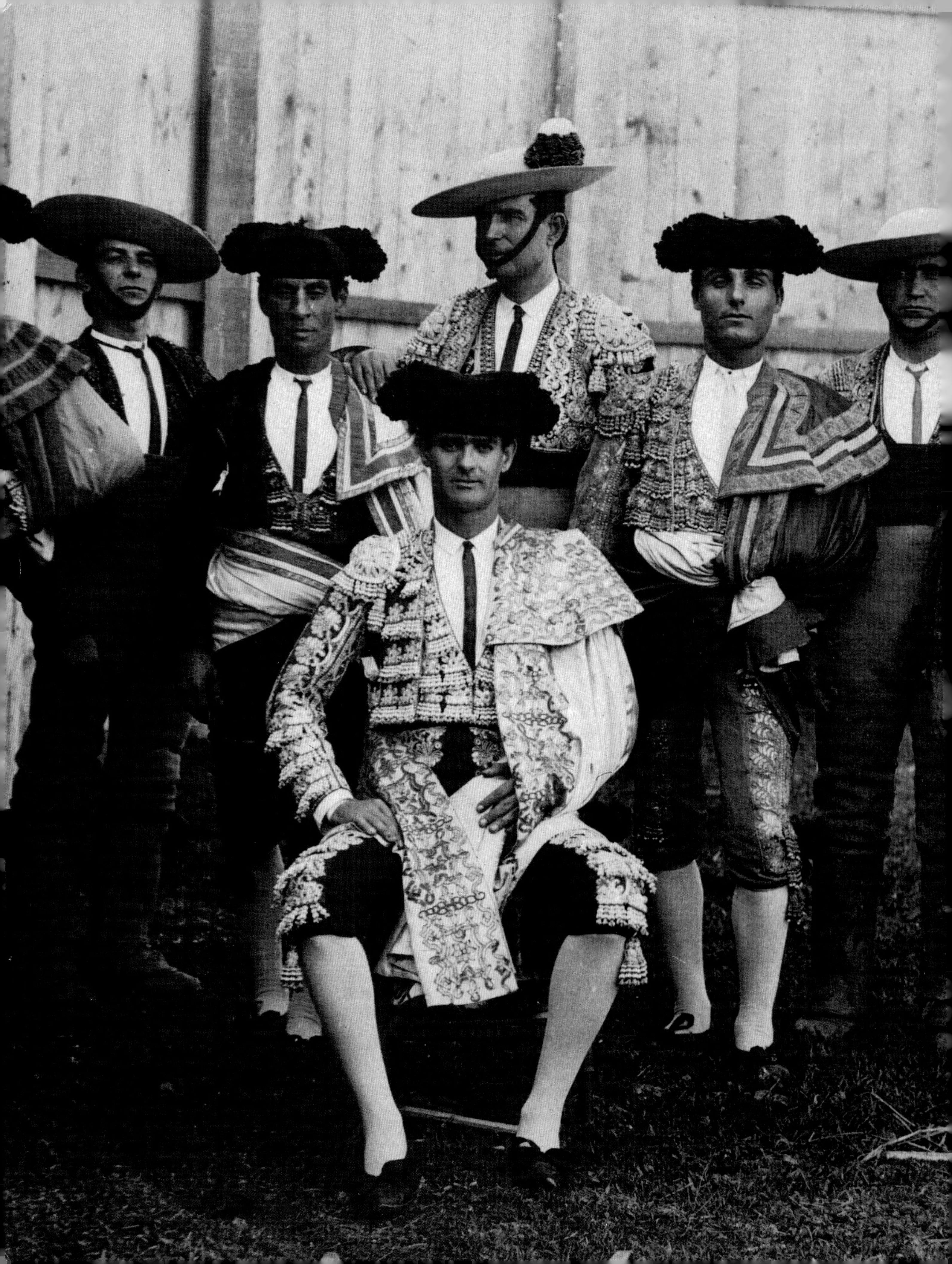